# NAIRN IN DARKNESS AND LIGHT

David Thomson was born in India of Scottish parents in 1914. Much of his childhood was spent in the country, in Derbyshire, and at Nairn in Scotland wher his grandparents lived. After leaving Oxford University, he took a job at Woodbrook in Ireland, and stayed there for almost ten years. His marvellously evocative book, *Woodbrook*, grew out of that time. Later he joined the BBC, where he wrote and produced many distinguished programmes, including *The Irish Storyteller* series, *The Great Hunger* and a number of programmes on animal folklore. During his secondment to UNESCO he worked in France, Liberia and Turkey. His book *In Camden Town*, a study of the place where he lived for the last thirty two years of his life, was published in 1983.

The author of *The People of the Sea* and co-author of *The Leaping Hare*, David Thomson also wrote several novels and children's books. *Nairn in Darkness and Light* won the McVitie's Prize for the Scottish Writer of the Year in 1987, and the NCR Book Award for Non Fiction in 1988. He died in 1988.

*Also in Arena by David Thomson*
Woodbrook

David Thomson

# NAIRN IN DARKNESS AND LIGHT

A R E N A

An Arena Book
Published by Arrow Books Limited
62–65 Chandos Place, London WC2N 4NW

An imprint of Century Hutchinson Limited

London   Melbourne   Sydney   Auckland
Johannesburg and agencies throughout
the world

First published by Hutchinson 1987
Arena edition 1988

Set in Palatino by Deltatype Ltd, Ellesmere Port
Printed and bound in Great Britain by
The Guernsey Press Co Ltd
Guernsey, C.I.

ISBN 0 09 959990 2

# ACKNOWLEDGMENTS

I am not a historian. I am an amateur of the subject, in the old sense of loving it. And so the historical passages in this book are derived from the work of professionals, to whom I am grateful, especially, among my contemporaries, to
George Ewart Evans: *Horse Power and Magic*
William Ferguson: *Scotland from 1689 to the Present*
Ian Grimble: *Scottish Clans and Tartans* – an excellent genealogical and historical work.
John Prebble: *Culloden* and *The Highland Clearances*, two detailed, vivid books which bring the past into the present.
George S. Pryde: *Scotland from 1603 to the present day*
T. C. Smout: *A History of the Scottish People 1560–1830*
   Among the many Nairnshire people who helped me in their douce and friendly way are Alistair Bain, editor, the *Nairnshire Telegraph*, Jean and Mary Bochel, Brodie of Brodie, Kenny Cameron, Lena Hay, Helen and Irene Macdonald, of Newlands of Delnies, Dr John Macdonald, Constance Macgregor, Gina Macleod, Ninie MacKintosh of Tradespark, Michie's grandchildren – Joey, Hector and Peter, Hugh Wilson, John A. Scott, Royal Marine Hotel, the management, The Newton Hotel.
   And then there are my sisters, named in the book, and my Finlay cousins Gardyne and Rosalind, whose memories helped me. Martina Mayne, who knows everyone on this list, and incidentally a lot about old Nairn, helped me too.

To Martina

and in memory of
Hugh Wilson, seaman, scholar, historian
of the Fishertown of Nairn

**North-West Scotland**

Cape Wrath

Thurso

Wick

Ullapool

Dornoch Firth

Moray Firth

Fraserburgh

Gair Loch

Loch Torridon

Sound of Raasay

Gairloch

Invergordon

Nigg

Cromarty

Elgin

Buckie

Banff

Peterhead

Ben Wyvis

Nairn

Forres

Shieldaig

Dingwall

*R. Lossie*

*R. Deveron*

Applecross

Inverness

*R. Nairn*

*R. Findhorn*

*R. Spey*

Aberdeen

Monadhliath Mountains

*R. Don*

*Loch Ness*

Caledonian Canal

Fort Augustus

Av16moree

Cairngorm Mountains

*R. Dee*

Achnacarry

*Loch Oich*

*R. Oich*

Ben Macdui

*Loch Lochy*

*R. Lochy*

*Loch Eil*

Lochy

Fort William

Ben Nevis

**GRAMPIAN MOUNTAINS**

Brechin

Montrose

Ballachulish

*R. Tay*

Dundee

Arbroath

*Loch Linnhe*

Perth

Firth of Tay

Firth of Lorne

Inveraray

*R. Forth*

Stirling

Firth of Forth

Leith

Glasgow

Edinburgh

0          30 miles

*R. Clyde*

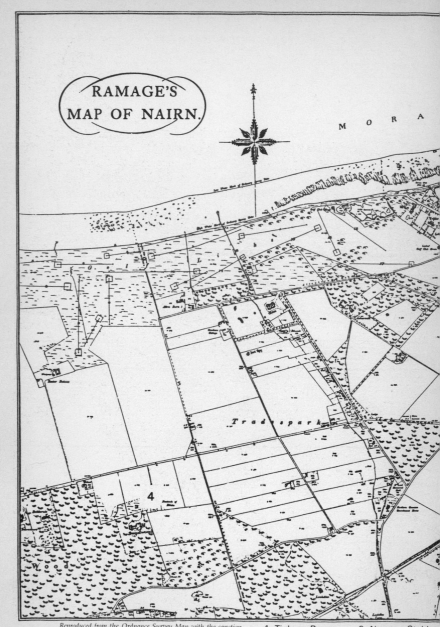

RAMAGE'S MAP OF NAIRN.

M O R A

*Tradespark*

4

1 Tigh na Rosan    2 Newton Stables

FIRTH

The Links

NAIRN

3 Fishertown    4 Sandwood Croft and Byre    5 Jubilee Suspension Bridge

This map was produced circa 1920

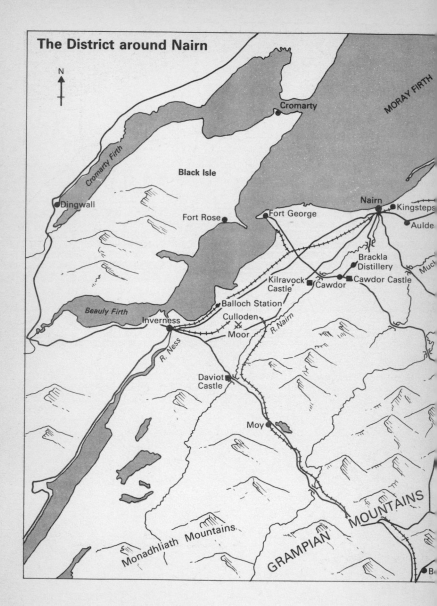

# The District around Nairn

N

Cromarty

Cromarty Firth

Black Isle

Dingwall

Fort Rose

Fort George

MORAY FIRTH

Nairn

Kingsteps

Aulde

Brackla
Distillery

Much

Kilravock
Castle

Cawdor Castle

Cawdor

Balloch Station

Beauly Firth

Inverness

Culloden
Moor

R. Nairn

R. Ness

Daviot
Castle

Moy

Monadhliath Mountains

GRAMPIAN MOUNTAINS

B

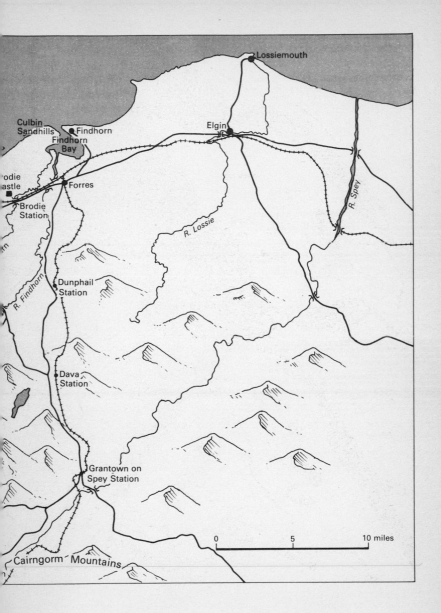

*Newton*
*Nairn*
*Nairnshire*
*By Moray Firth*
*Scotland*
*Europe*
*The World*
*The Universe*
*Add Infinitum*

*Dear Kolya, Zar of Russia Esq.*

*Pity you left by the afternoon train and not this morning's because it was funny at prayers and there wasn't anyone I could look at. I was kneeling beside Uncle Tom and you would have been beside me and he was muttering his usual cross things all through the beginning and if they hear they take no notice but today they did, because when Uncle Robert got to the Lord's Prayer Uncle T. said, 'No Popery' quite out loud, and some of the new maids giggled. Cathy and Gina, I guess, and Uncle Robert stopped and Mrs Waddell marched the maids out of the dining room but it should of been Uncle Tom who was marched out.*

*Johnstone and that English butler stayed as if nothing had happened, and Macdonald and the beastly head-gardener and all the men, I think, but I didn't dare look round enough and everyone except Uncle Tom was foamented. Then when prayers were over the men went out as usual but coughing and it was only the older maids that Mrs Waddell allowed to* come back and serve the breakfast and all breakfast no one said anything except 'Pass the marmalade, please, David,' and little mewls from Granny asking Uncle Robert what time he'd like Knowles and Cummings to come with the car and what about Culloden Moor for a change. I hope it's Culloden.

I held Uncle Tom's hand after breakfast right across the lawn and he said, 'Silent as the Grave, was it not, David,' and I said, 'What', and he said, 'They'll all be in it soon and that Lady Tin-Opener will be the First to Go.' It made me laugh because you know who he ment, because her nose and mouth could open tins, the Lord Justice Clerk's wife and they had taken away your chair and put me next to her. But Uncle Tom said, 'You must not laugh by the graveside.' He does it on perpose and it's funny but I wish he wouldn't. At prayers it's horrible as well.

How's the Auld Reekie? Reekie, I guess. Your train was reekie when we saw you off, Joan's white dress had smuts. Granny says she shouldn't of run up the platform to look at the engine. Daddy says it's the bad coal. There was good coal before the war. I bet it was hellish going home so long before the term starts. The dogs are all right,

Your aff$^{te}$ cousin and Obeed$^{te}$ subject

David

PS: Johnstone will post this. It's his afternoon off.
PPS: I'll send you a Post Lorder for the spondulicks you lent me. Two pocket-money days from now cross my heart.

Whether Kolya was really my cousin I shall never know, because there was

An old woman who lived in a shoe
She had so many children she didn't know what to do
And the children had children not few
And their children had children and uncles and aunts
Who branched like the ivy, the rose and the vine
And spread all entangled with those climbing plants

Till nobody knew which was which, who was who.
Was it uncle or cousin in laughter or tantrum
Who fired the wrath of the Great Panjandrum?

The Great Panjandrum was my name for our great-uncle
Robert, whom I feared and loved. He had seven brothers
and two sisters at his command but Tom was the rebellious
one. In my letter to Kolya I probably embellished the scene
of 'No popery!' I had just won a prize for an embellished
story which was published in a magazine called *Little Folks*.
But my sisters, Mary, Joan and Barbara, were three of the
many people at prayers that morning in the summer of
1921, when I was seven years old. They remember only a
silence as Uncle Robert's voice was suspended in mid-
prayer, not the commotion I wrote about. And then, the
crowd of ladies' maids, housemaids, tablemaids, kitchen
and scullery maids were always marched out by Mrs
Waddell before breakfast began. The butlers, valets and
under-butlers, the gardener, under-gardener and lesser
outdoor men marched after them to breakfast in the
servants' hall which, though darkly lit in the basement, was
a more homely room to us and as spacious as the dining
room in which we had breakfast after prayers. We spent
every summer holiday at Newton from babyhood until
1929 when Uncle Robert died, and the scene in that vast
dining-room was clearly stamped on us.

Twenty or thirty people waiting for prayers stood by the
walls and windows underneath huge portraits of relatives
and guests of the past, waiting for Uncle Robert. No one
dared to touch a morsel before prayers. When he was
ushered in by Gulliver, 'that English butler', he stood for a
moment near the door, glancing round the room to make
sure, I suppose, that none of us was missing, said, 'Good
morning' in a loud clear voice, walked over to the lectern
and stood before it in silence, his back to the windows, until
the servants had quietly filed into the room and assembled
near the great sideboard which stood against the inner end
wall.

My place at prayers was beside Uncle Tom; Kolly's, when
he was staying with us, was next to mine. There were

scratches on the wooden back of my chair which resembled carved lettering. I stared at them most of the time and kept on feeling the grooves. Every morning Uncle Tom would trace them with his forefinger, pretending that they stood for my name and whispering D.A.V.I.D. into my ear. (I call it whispering now, but I don't think Uncle Robert would have used that word.) Tom was repetitive, telling the same stories, making the same jokes every day; at least once a day he would touch Joan's pink healthy cheeks, saying, 'Does it come off?' and looking at his fingers as though to make sure he had not smudged some rouge away. This slight weakness in a brilliant wit deadened the rich power of his character. One of his elder brothers, Jim, another great-uncle whom we loved, was just as humorous, but everything he said was spontaneous, inspired by sudden instinct, and his jokes were original: every one of them made us laugh because we had not heard it before.

After prayers and the departure of the servants, we remained standing by the walls until Uncle Robert had reached his place at the head of the table, where he stood, his hands resting on the back of his chair, until we had reached ours. We remained standing while he said grace, a lengthy grace in Latin, perfectly enunciated. Even though I was starving by then, staring greedily at the baps and butter, I liked listening to it. Later on, after my father had gradually taught me its meaning, I understood every word and appreciated the rhythm of its phrases.

Everyone had porridge with cold milk to start with. As children we usually had eggs after that, boiled, poached or scrambled, and then lashings of buttered toast and baps with marmalade, but the grown-ups, and especially the men took a large meal of which fish, meat or a grill of sausages and bacon formed the main course. Uncle Robert ate a prodigious breakfast. I remember details of it because I used to stare at him with my mouth full, fascinated by the slow, fastidious way he chewed and by his large rather clumsy hands. After his porridge he had two boiled eggs, then Arbroath smokies, Finnan haddock or a pair of Nairn speldings, or kippers, then steak, kidneys with bacon or two mutton chops. He ate slowly. It took him at least an hour. Mother, having taught us early on not to rush scrambling and pushing each other out of the room, allowed us to leave as soon as we had finished, but she and the others had to wait till Uncle Robert rose, when the men went to sit down in the conservatory and smoked their pipes and the women to the morning room or one of the smaller drawing rooms. The men went fishing, golfing or to shoot grouse. Uncle Robert walked to the golf links, escorted by some of his brothers, every morning when the weather allowed it. On rainy days he retired to his private library near the front door, a sanctum no one entered uninvited, where he sat writing at a massive mahogany desk or reading in one of the black leather armchairs which stood beside the fire. The servants kept his fire alight, however warm the day.

At breakfast and in the conservatory and billiard room the men were usually talking and laughing. Was the wind too strong, would the grouse fly high? Was the sun too bright for fish to rise, had the rain made the golf course greens too soft and slow, the tennis court quaggy?

—— In the year of Our Lord seventeen hundred ought seven there were only three hats in Inverness.

—— How many in Nairn? said a child unheard.

—— The right of the Red Hand.

—— What, Uncle Ninian?

—— Some individuals could hang a man caught red-handed without trial.

—— The only public body to possess it was Inverness Burgh. Uncle Robert's commanding voice would silence them all for a moment.

—— The last witches to be burned in Inverness were dressed in scarlet cloaks.

—— No, no, Tom, only the gentry wore scarlet cloaks.

—— The Elgin Marbles . . .

Mary thought for years that the Elgin marbles were superior to the ones we played with and wrote to Father Christmas to ask for some.

—— The first umbrella in Inverness was raised in the year of Grace seventeen hundred and sixty-two over the head of King Crispin upon the twenty-fifth day of October, Saint

Crispin's Day, and carried through the town in the van of a long procession.

—— The birthrate's going down.

—— In the year of Our Lord eighteen hundred and eighty-six, when I was a boy, a woman sold a baby for £3 to an Inverness butcher.

Granny shrieked.

—— Not for sausages, Jessie.

—— Why then? said one of her brothers.

—— Wrong side of the blanket. It was the baby's grandmother, too poor to feed it. The butcher had no children, do you understand?

—— Oh dear.

—— The birthrate's going down.

—— Scotland is overpopulated, said Uncle Tom.

—— No Tom, said Robert firmly.

—— In August it is – the hot weather.

—— *Pas devant les petits.* Granny seemed to be quivering. Joan and Mary, who knew enough French, giggled.

—— For every grouse egg hatched ten Englishmen leave their country.

—— If you please to remember, Tom, said Uncle Robert in what he imagined to be a whisper, we have guests at the table.

One of the guests said that the Irish were coming in droves.

—— And the Welsh! Lloyd George is approaching Nairn with some of his ingrate friends.

—— All the Irish should be hanged! said Granny in a louder voice than usual. She was known to everyone as kind and gentle.

There was an awful silence until Uncle Jim spoke.

—— Even the O'Toole?

And then a roar of laughter like coal being tipped from a cart.

The O'Toole's daughter was married to Uncle Robert's son Will, and they had a daughter, about Barbara's age, who used to play and rush about with us at Newton and was one of the more memorable of our innumerable cousins. Her grandfather, an ò Tuathail, chief of that Irish clan, had altered his name to Mr Hall because, I guess, all Irish names were hated in Great Britain after the 1916 rising, but none of his friends or relations took any notice. Those who knew the history of his family regretted the change because the commonplace English surname Hall wiped out a noble and saintly tradition. He was a descendant of Saint Laurence O'Toole, the twelfth century Abbot of Glendalough and Archbishop of Dublin, whose death marked the end of the Old Irish Church which had through its missionaries converted most of Europe to Christianity. In direct line he was descended from the O'Toole chieftains who resisted the Danes, the Anglo-Normans and the Dublin English, losing and winning and losing again for generations. Castle Kevin in the O'Toole country of Glendalough had been built to keep them down, but they took it from the invaders and lived in it themselves.

The O'Toole who became Mr Hall had lovingly named his Nairn house 'Kevin', a more ancient name than the castle for it was Saint Kevin who founded the Holy City of Glendalough in the sixth century. The Nairn Kevin with its large gardens overlooking the Fifth was a lovely place for children. It was the last house in the Seabank Road, perched on the brim of a ridge that slopes steeply to the sea. It was only a short walk from Newton.

The Prime Minister, Lloyd George, was not so unpopular by reason on his nationality but had aroused fear and distrust among the gentry by his decision to discuss with de Valera a treaty giving a degree of independence to the whole of Ireland. He wished to put aside the objections of a large protestant minority who inhabited some of the counties of Ulster. Uncle Robert, as Liberal MP for the Inverness Burghs after the General Election of 1885 had – though he much admired Gladstone – spoken chillingly against Home Rule for Ireland.

Lloyd George was not approaching Nairn, but among the many newspapers delivered to Newton, the breakfast eaters must have read the *Inverness Courier* of 9 August 1921, which announced with pride that the Prime Minister 'intends to spend his autumn holiday at Flowerdale,

Gairloch, one of the residences of Sir Kenneth MacKenzie, Bart . . . amid beautiful Highland scenery on the west coast of Scotland. There is an abundance of fishing and shooting in the district. Mr Lloyd George is expected to pass the month of September in the West Highlands where his extended visit has created already a great deal of interest and gratification.' In daily papers – *The Scotsman*, *Glasgow Herald* and *The Aberdeen Journal* – they had read news that shocked most of them. The Prime Minister was willing to meet de Valera, that wicked leader of the IRA. I believe he chose the Highlands for his holiday not because of the fishing, which was just as good at home in Wales, but because of the people, their history and language which was close, as the Irish was, to his own. At Gairloch on a Sunday early in that September he went off on his own to a small Free Church where the service was conducted in Gaelic.

The Irish war of independence which had gone on for two bloody years, had been calmed by the Truce of July 11, 1921 which Lloyd George achieved. He was the only British Prime Minister wise enough to know that if you genuinely wish for peace you must meet your enemy not on the battlefield but at a conference table. He had not lost the war. The British Army supported by irregulars – that force of desperadoes nicknamed the Black and Tans, many members of which were convicts released from jail for the purpose – could have gone on with it for generations because it was a guerilla war like the one which began in the Six Counties in 1968. Granny, Uncle Robert and most of my great-uncles thought the Irish could and should be suppressed. What shocked them most was de Valera's wish to detach his country from the British Empire, to form a republic which would include its hostile Protestant minority.

It is easy in politics to turn a minority into a local majority by dividing a country by partition. Lloyd George was forced by powerful opposition to make that grave mistake in Ireland, from which the people of that country and of Great Britain are still suffering in 1986.

The Newton breakfast table was shaken again on 31

August when the newspapers announced that the Prime
Minister had reached the Highlands accompanied not only
by Mrs Lloyd George but by that dreadful Miss Stevenson:
their friend, his mistress – who could tell – and in either
case how could his wife put up with it? They came, this
ménage à trois, to stay with the Duke of Atholl at Blair
Castle in Perthshire and then advanced by motor car to the
Station Hotel of Inverness, from which the Prime Minister
went shopping for fishing rods, reels and feathery flies
which were supposed to appeal to West Highland fish. The
party then went on to Flowerdale House at Gairloch to
which Kenneth MacKenzie had invited them. The weather
was bad. The fish would not rise. But as they had been
invited to stay for several weeks, until parliament reassembled, they had hope.

The best fishing, below the fifty foot waterfall of the river
Kerry, was shared by the MacKenzies of Flowerdale and the
MacKenzies of Shieldaig and these two had made an
agreement to fish there with their guests on alternate days.
Lloyd George was 'as disappointed as a schoolboy' to hear
on the first fine day that it was Shieldaig's turn. He and his
friends had to go to the source of the river where it flows out
from Loch Bad-na-Scalaig, and where the water was
muddy from weeks of rain. No one caught anything, not
even Miss Stevenson 'who casts quite a dexterous line'.
Lloyd George left them at it flogging their hopeless flies and
went downstream alone where, unseen, he put on a worm
and landed a twenty ounce brown trout, the only catch of
the day, thereby adding to his sins in all the eyes of
Newton, where fishing with a worm was taboo. And then,
'happy as a schoolboy' he hurried through the long grass to
Miss Stevenson 'and proudly exhibited the catch on the
palms of his extended hands'. Then Mrs Lloyd George who
had spent the morning in the house arrived by motor-car
with a luncheon basket.

There was no telephone at Flowerdale and the holiday,
just as the weather began to improve, was interrupted
without warning by two despatch riders who had come
from Dublin with a letter from de Valera. They had been
told to find him at the Inverness Station Hotel, but had
come more than sixty miles over the mountains from there.

De Valera said that 'The people of Ireland, acknowledging no voluntary union with Britain . . . have by an overwhelming majority declared for independence, set up a republic, and more than once confirmed that choice . . . Canada, Australia, South Africa, New Zealand are all guaranteed against the domination of the major State.'

The letter was direct and strong, unsoftened by diplomatic verbiage. Lloyd George immediately summoned a cabinet meeting to be held in Inverness and, as Uncle Tom could have foretold, it was a convenient place because most of his cabinet ministers were in the Highlands fishing or shooting grouse and red deer. Only seven ministers left London by the 7.30 night train from Euston and leaving at such brief notice no special arrangements could be made. 'Berths were booked in one of the ordinary sleeping carriages, a narrow six foot bed, a grey blanket with coloured stripes, a clean white sheet and pillow and a spare blanket folded on the rack, such as might be booked by any undistinguished passengers. There was no special lounge where they might all foregather comfortably. Mr Shortt was on the platform thirty-five minutes before the time of departure. "I have brought two fishing rods with me," he said. Sir Alfred Mead was not looking forward to the journey: "We don't get there till 9.40 am and I want to get back as soon as I can." As the train moved out of the station Mr Austen Chamberlain was seen on the corner of a compartment attacking the contents of a dinner basket. Sir Alfred Mead was similarly occupied. Sir Arthur Griffith-Boscawen, who had no dinner basket, sat watching them. The Lord Chancellor (Viscount Birkenhead) in his sleeping berth sat on his bed smoking a cigar.'

The King was already in the Highlands of course. He was staying with The Mackintosh and Mrs Mackintosh at Moy Hall near Inverness where Lloyd George went hurriedly to consult him before the cabinet meeting. On his way there from Balmoral the King had driven through Nairn.

—— Can we go and see him?

—— You'd see nothing. The crowd!

—— The bank! Mr Lamb will let us watch from his upstairs windows.

—— Mr Hay! He's got the best view in the High Street.

You ask him, Daddy – the room above the shop where his tailors and ironing women work.

My father laughed.

—— You'd see nothing but the roof of his car.

—— If it's fine he'll have the hood down.

\*

*Saturday. Newton, Nairn.*

*Dear Kol,*

*Here's your honourible bill. $6^d + 8^d = 1/2$.*

*Hope you weren't stony. I had $H2^o$ all this time, no minerals, to save up. I was going to write a letter with it but what's the good if you don't get one back. There's lots of DREADFUL things to tell you.*

*Your aff$^{te}$ cousin, David.*

*PS: You're lucky to be in The Stink. It's raining cats and dogs here. The Sun is lost in the mists of antiquity – D.*

It often rained at Nairn for days and days but I think most people's memory of childhood summers lives in blue skies, white clouds, the dust of the roads, the earthquake cracks in sun-baked pathways, the blue and white sea, green leaves and grass, hot pebbles and the yellowy whites of the sea-sand. Mine certainly does. I remember the rainy days and nights too, the splash of gutters, the pang-ping drips on the tin roofs of the lean-to sheds by the kitchen gate, the flurry of wind and water on the glass of the conservatory; the battering of slates, the smell of newly wet dust, earth and grass, patter on leaves of sycamore and beech, rustle of almost ripe oat fields, crash on the turnip leaves, the sting of the rain on my sunburnt back as I ran down the beach to swim in the sea – all that so-called bad weather which we complained of and were bored by at the time has also distilled itself into something beautiful, and the happiness of these memories, of brilliant days, and dark, is unique in my mind, for my most vivid recollections of the years from adolescence to old age are painfully cutting and vicious.

Our summer mornings at Newton have melted into one idyllic morning. I awoke at about six on my narrow bed in my father's dressing room which opened through a door into the wide bedroom where he and my mother slept in a four-poster bed. Probably it was a two-poster, with curtains at the pillow end and none at the foot. The bedroom and dressing room faced north-east and the early sun slanted across our windows. As I lay in bed all I saw was the sea and the dark cliffs of the Black Isle far away broken in the middle by the entrance to Cromarty Firth. As I sat up I saw the yellow oat field and the rich smooth golf links which sloped steeply down to the beach. When I jumped out of bed and ran to the window I saw the great green lawn, sheltered by pine woods on either side, sloping away to the edge of the oatfield from which it was divided by a wire fence on wooden posts. Below me was the semi-circle of dark grey stone steps which went down between balustrades from the huge front door to the gravelled circle into which Newton's front and back drives led.

At about seven o'clock I would creep out of the room to meet my sisters on the landing, tiptoeing in my bare feet past my parents' bed, hoping not to wake them; but Mother was often awake by then and pushing the bed curtain back with her bare arm, would pull me to her and kiss me. 'You'll never find your fruit today,' she sometimes whispered. 'You'll have to look in places where you've never looked before!' Knowing that breakfast was not till nine o'clock she made provision for our early mornings just before she went to bed each night, by placing biscuits, apples, black or red currants from the garden, plums from the wall or peaches and grapes from the two vast greenhouses which stood against the southern boundary of the vegetable garden; and these four little heaps of bright delicacy, one for each of us and each composed of different fruits, she hid in a new place every night. Our search behind the curtains of the staircase windows, behind the bowls and ornaments on the hall table, in the carved woodwork of the grandfather clock by the front door, on top of the brass fire extinguishers which hung from the walls of the wide and long passages on the ground floor, was exciting and difficult. Each of us took possession of the first heap found and began at once to eat while the others went on searching. My sisters, who had good eyesight, gave me hints in riddle language if they saw me in despair, and often we would share or swap our treasures. Mary or Joan, the two elder ones, would lift up our little sister Barbara to enable her to find her portion in high places. There were small doors in the wooden panelling giving access to pipes and bellwires. Barbara thought they had been made to help the mice to come out for crumbs and get back in safety to their dark nests.

Running through the long corridor that leads from the front door to the back of the house, we would turn to the right into a narrower and darker one, laid with the same thick Indian carpet, red with gold and black patterns on it, until we came to the double doorway that led to a stone stairway, similarly curved but smaller than the one at the front of the house. Running swiftly across the gravel path on to the back lawn, we came to a lily pond and fountain in the middle made of white stone. I cannot remember the fountain playing. It had probably broken down from neglect during the four years of the war, those first four years of my life. Our bare feet left a lovely tread on the dew, as on ice but transparent, and looking back on them we could see how we had separated clusters of dewdrops, some silvery, some crystal clear, some with the colours of the rainbow shining in them. We went deep into the woods and gathered fir cones, birds' feathers and sticks when we found strangely shaped ones. We climbed trees, then went into the orchard and ate apples which were sour and unripe in August, with white pips.

As soon as we guessed it was near feeding time we walked back towards the house and round it, through the stable yard and under an archway between low buildings to the hen yard to watch the henwife feed the geese, ducks and hens. She lived in one of those low buildings over-looking this yard and emerged from the darkness of her doorway like a fat mole, hunched, covered from head to thigh by a heavy grey shawl with a long black dress beneath it, under which as she hobbled along you could see bits of her black boots stained with poultry muck and ashes from her fire. When she was in a good mood she would allow us to scatter some of the grain or fill troughs with mash, but we feared and hated her, partly because of her hostility towards us, and the vicious bad temper with which she treated any servant from the house who was sent to give her instructions, but mostly because she was ostentatiously cruel. We often watched her killing poultry, my sisters by chance when they happened to be passing the hen yard at those times, I, occasionally and in secret, by design; for the sight and sounds aroused an emotional tension in me which was at once repellent and attractive. I would think about it in bed with sorrow and compassion for the bird and yet I would long for the day when I would be old enough to kill one with my own hands. The henwife would catch a bird roughly, handle it harshly before it was dead, then kill it slowly by wringing its neck in the old-fashioned way, instead of dislocating the neck with one pull which causes instant death. I believe she relished the agonies of her victims.

The little we could see of her face beneath the shawl was cruel: tiny black eyes that gleamed and were rounded like hatpin heads, lips as thin as razors and blue, a revolting button of a nose which looked as though someone had cut its tip off with a pair of curved scissors. Her moustache was thick and short, her beard wispy: both grey. She killed prime chickens, capons, old hens for boiling, ducks, geese, guinea-fowl, as the cook, Mrs Waddell, ordered them. Mrs Waddell needed much meat, fish and fowl to feed us, our many uncles and aunts, the numerous household servants and all those guests whom Uncle Robert invited to spend the summer vacation at Newton.

Only the royal cock lived on throughout my boyhood. I have never seen so large a cock in all my life. We all admired him, watched him as he moved about, brought friends to the henyard to see him. My father, who had excellent and gentle manners, especially when he was in the company of women, appointed this cock as one of my early mentors by calling my attention to the courtesy he showed towards his hens. Whenever I threw some breadcrumbs to him, or a worm that I had found, he stood over the tit-bits without touching them, clucking loudly in his deep voice to call the hens. They came and ate ravenously, quarrelling with each other. He would not deign to pick a morsel from the ground until some time after they had begun to eat.

'Isn't he douce,' my father said. 'And look how upright he stands. Those claws and straight legs!'

The cock trod hens fiercely. It took him only three seconds or five to serve each one.

When we got back to the house we went straight to the dining room to look whether the breakfast table had been laid, hoping that some toast or a few of the baps had been put out, that we might help ourselves. The baker with his pony and cart had delivered hot baps and loaves by that time, but these were kept in the pantry until breakfast was served. Only Elsa who was indulgent of us put a few out on a plate whenever it was her turn to lay the table.

The tablecloth had usually been spread out before we came in. It was in one piece, starched and beautiful – a clean one was provided for every meal – long and wide enough to touch one's knees as one sat down at table. I preferred to see it before china and silver had been set upon it. Granny had inherited many old damask ones, each with a different watery pattern woven into it, of leaves, grass, fruits or flowers. Granny told me that the flax had been grown in the flax-growing land near the great river Tay, that her oldest ones, some of which had frayed but had been neatly patched, were spun and woven in the eighteenth century in cottages by men and women skilled in that craft. Those made in the later years of the nineteenth century came from one or other of the manufactures at Dundee whose work was famous all over Europe.

I loved to see the tablecloth spotless before anything was placed on it. It was like a frozen lake covered with snow in the early morning. At least that is what it made me think of because, although I did it myself, – we used to slide stones over icy ponds to see whose would go furthest, just as we played ducks and drakes with flat stones on the sea – I was always sorry to see sticks and stones thrown on to a snowy lake.

Morning prayers were supposed to be at nine o'clock but even with the help of Johnstone who went up to his bedroom every morning, Uncle Robert was slow to get into his clothes of which he wore layer over layer during hot weather or cool. Everyone was impatient. The servants waiting in their basement quarters were not allowed to eat before prayers. No one could smoke and we grew fidgety and greedy, our mouths watering like dogs held back on leashes from their food, for the table had by then been loaded with oatcakes, silver toast racks, little heaps of floury baps in china dishes, rows of marmalade pots, each furnished with a curved silver spoon, and glass butter bowls. You could sometimes steal a bit of butter and put it into your mouth without being seen because it was all in small pats, firm enough to pick up between finger and thumb.

The butter was sculpted by Johnstone before each meal into shapes which changed from day to day: balls the shape and size of marbles, but grooved; oblongs with blunt ends; thinner ones with pointed ends; pyramids and convoluted pats like seashells which were the most difficult to make. Sometimes he allowed us to go into the butler's pantry to watch him and try to learn. He used a pair of large ribbed wooden butter pats and gave us smaller ones. Once he congratulated me on my attempt but as I passed the open door of the pantry a few minutes later I saw him rolling up my sculpture into a slab.

*

The stables which formed part of the rectangle of low buildings out of which that archway to the henyard led, had long been disused but somebody swept them now and then, dusted the curved metal hay racks, wiped mangers and woodwork and shone the brass tethering rings so brightly that whenever we pushed a door open and looked into the dusky twilight we were welcomed by a small round gleam of light. Uncle Robert had parted with all his horses soon after the beginning of the war but we soon refilled his stables with horses of our own, and our dog Kuti, who was not allowed in the house at night, slept on a bed of straw in one of the mangers which she seemed to prefer to anywhere else.

Our horses were made of tangie, that large species of seaweed, plentiful on Nairn's beaches, which has long brown leaves like the fingers of a giant's hand and a thick rhubarb-like stalk. We dragged these home after swimming. On the way home we called them dragons but they turned into horses as soon as we entered the stable yard. They were stiff and dry by then, coated with dust from the roads. We sluiced them under the stable yard tap until they were soft and shiny again.

There was also a large garage, a converted coach house, in which we played and which had in the middle of its floor an oily pit in which men used to stand as they repaired the underneath parts of Uncle Robert's car, a big Daimler, I believe, which he also disposed of in 1914, the year of my birth. He employed a chauffeur to drive it, who lived with his family in one of the stable yard cottages. I once jumped into this pit and climbed out drenched in oil mixed with sticky débris and dirt which had accumulated over the years. My sand shoes and bare legs were wet with oil, my pants and shirt smeared with it and when we went back to the house for lunch I made indelible stains on the hall carpet. Mother was very cross, made me take off my shoes, go upstairs to have a bath and change all my clothes.

There was a large whitewashed laundry in the basement where linen, curtains and everybody's underwear were washed, but Mother used to take ours once a week to a washerwoman who lived in one of the lanes which twist out of Nairn High Street and slope towards the riverbank. Hers led directly to Jubilee Bridge, a graceful metal network footbridge with a wooden floor, which wore out some years ago probably because we, like all Nairn children, used to bounce on it and make it swing. It has been replaced by a straight concrete one which does not look so nice.

The washerwoman was short and fat, her house tiny, her wash-house roomy and furnished with ironing boards, a wide wooden shelf on hinges which she could raise when she wanted to work on it or let down against the wall. There was a giant copper in the middle of this room heated from below by a red glowing wood fire. A long-handled wooden club stood in it which she used for pounding clothes. You entered by a wicket gate which was usually propped up by a stake because one of its hinges had collapsed, and walked a few yards along an earthy path between a narrow bed of marigolds and pansies below her windowsill and a flourishing vegetable patch, flourishing because Michie who lived nearby gave her plenty of horse dung, and the soil, being near to the riverbank was moist and black. She seldom stopped talking and laughing. My mother laughed, too, at her incessant gossip about neighbours and some of the grander people of Nairn of whose love affairs, marriages, illnesses and deaths she knew every detail. Because of this, our weekly attendance at her house took longer than our mother cared for and just as she was saying 'Goodbye' the washerwifie would say 'Wait. I maun bring out a bit jammy piece to the bairns. It is lang syne they took their breakfast.' She went into the house and came back with a piece of bannock for each of us, spread thickly with jam or sometimes with white crowdie.

There were scandals in our huge family too. I cannot remember details but like all children, inquisitive and quick to eavesdrop, I interpreted hushed voices in my own way. Aunt this who looked sedate was a scarlet woman, Uncle that, so long in India, a spendthrift and a rake. Our great-uncle Alick was the one my mother asked us not to stare at. He had a little knob fixed into his throat and whenever he wanted to speak he pressed it. I think it hurt him. He tried not to use it and instead, when the message was not urgent, passed a note down the table. He always had beside his plate a little writing pad and pencil. He and Granny, whom my mother called Aunt Jessie, were the only ones who stayed at Newton all the year round.

Her brothers, our great-uncles, were of different shapes and sizes. Most of them were sturdy and admired by me, especially Uncle Ninian, the youngest, a tall, lean, and melancholy man. Robert and all his brothers had been educated at Edinburgh Academy. Four of them, Ninian while he was still at school, had played rugger for Scotland, with Uncle Gardyne as a reserve, which made four Finlays and one extra in the International Fifteen and which stirred my ambition, for when I was seven years old I wanted to be a dustman, a Field Marshal and play rugger for Scotland in my spare time.

These old uncles entertained us with games, rhymes and jingles and I liked Ninian's funny ones about illness:

> If it were not for my gouty toe
> Up I'd get and off I'd go.
>
> Send for the doctor, Charlie dear,
> Tell him I'm feeling awfully queer.
> Tell him I've got the old attack
> Thingummy up and down my back.

My father said as a joke that he learned those from their father who had been a doctor.

Uncle Robert, so far as I can remember, was always dressed in black – black knickerbockers for golf, black trousers in the evening, black frock coat or short coat to fit the time of day, black tie and white starched butterfly collar, white hair, stern face whiter than the faces of his brothers. His wife Biba, a daughter of Cosmo Innes, had died before I was born and it was the custom for widowers and widows to wear mourning for the rest of their lives. Women changed from black to purple after some years. Both men and women used black bordered envelopes for their letters. His younger brothers appeared at breakfast in tweed clothes of different herring-bone patterns and light grey or fawn colours, in breeches or narrow trousers and jackets with bulging pockets and leather buttons. In the evening at whisky time, just before we went to bed, they put on dark and formal clothes. Some of the guests wore kilts. I thought the butlers grander than any of them.

Jim was the only fat and untidy uncle. He had several ample chins and his clothes which he never bothered about were ancient, the cuffs frayed, sleeves out at elbow until someone remembered to patch them and the whole of the front of his grey tweed suit was usually spotted with gravy and soup. He could not see his feet nor the lower part of his belly and when he leant back, sunk deep in one of the billiard room chairs he would lose things and say to whichever of us who was there, 'Can you see my spectacles? I had them at the bookshelf just now. I put my pipe down somewhere – try the grate. My pen? I was writing to my W S before lunch.' We would search the whole room, then suddenly hear him cry, 'Have you looked on the ledge?' The ledge was the crease, or rather one of three or four creases which stretched like deep capacious furrows across his waistcoat and tucked into one of them we often found pen, spectacles and pipe. The pipe burned holes in it. His sense of smell was weak.

—— What's your W S, Uncle Jim?

—— My legal eagle.

I thought he meant Uncle Robert who looked like a white-headed eagle, but my father said it was a Writer to the Signet which in England means a solicitor.

Children have a sense of smell almost as fine as that of wild animals and I remember the Newton women more by smell than by their clothes, especially the younger ones. I could tell without looking up from my book which of them was walking into the room but although I was even then very short-sighted, I could recognise some at a distance from their clothes, the maids only by height and width because they were in uniform, but the kitchen and scullery maids, who wore blue not black, were few and easily distinguished, especially Gina, who was pretty and slim and not much older than my sister Mary. Judy, the young widow of my father's only brother, Bill, was pretty too and she put on rouge and lipstick and wore narrow short skirts, not even long enough to hide her knees. Grown-ups disapproved of her – she had a Glasgow accent as well as the bright, tight clothes – but I now believe Uncle Tom loved her because when, a few years later, he became bedridden and a bit forgetful he called his day nurse, who looked a bit like her, 'Judy' all the time. I could see Granny from a distance too, walking on the lawn in her wide-bottomed purple dress which trailed behind her over the grass, her slightly puffed sleeves, and straw hat widely brimmed with a bouquet of flowers made out of cloth on top. She would lift her skirt with her left hand when she reached the gravel, raise her veil, spring her lorgnettes and stare through them to see which of her guests or brothers was sitting in the basket chairs outside the conservatory.

*

*Dear Kol,*

*I got it it's no good. Can't you say anything? So short. Only as everybody else gets letters except me I better answer in the hopes you'll answer answers and even if you don't diserve it I'll put in dreadful things like I promised because I said last if you wrote I would. I don't call it writing, that crumply scrap of paper, more like those little messages Daddy sticks on the hall table to say where he's gone. There's some people never kept promises. When I'm 10 like you I'll write letters with bits of Latin in.*

*Here goes*

*DREADFUL THING no.1*

*It's about bears so look out.*

In the middle of breakfast ages ago Uncle Tom suddenly said: Did anyone see two young bears crossing the lawn this morning. And everybody laughed the stupid way they have, only he really had seen them out of his window when he was getting into his clothes. You've been in his bedroom that funny day when he asked us and had lots of bulls-eyes on the mantelpiece in that silver cup thing that's got his name on for winning at golf when he lived in America.

Really he was just pretending because the bears were really dogs – one great bit mongrelly woolly one and a fairly big thick one with floppy ears that sounded, like what Uncle Tom said, like a hound, Basset or Harrier or something – the thick hevyish sorts who have shortish legs and smooth long tails. In a bit there was a frightful camoufletty in the henyard of cackling squawking etc. I heard it, so did Joan, Mary and Barbara but we thought it was just the witch catching a goose to kill and anyway we wouldn't of wanted to go and look at that.

Only next minute Uncle Tom said he met MacDonald when he was taking his before-breakfast dander and MacDonald said a whole pack of stray dogs had got into the henyard and shortened all the hens and it looked like Culloden after the battle. When Uncle T. said that we all rushed out without finishing anything up and I bet Uncle R. went red in the face but Mummy wasn't a bit cross afterwards. Then on that path near the garage we saw a

*bloody white hen and all its guts were hanging out. Stink.
Kuti sniffed it a lot and kept on walking round it. We thought
she was going to eat the sticking out bits only she never even
licked it. All the geese were ok because of the old gander, the
one that bit your legs, but there wasn't much else alive only
the Emperer perching on top of the witch's roof and flapping
his wings and crowing and a bunch of hens, hudling by the
wall. Nairn's crammed with trippers and mostly disgusting
Glasgow keelies on our beach, so we stick to the golf course bit
just below the club house – too shallow and rocky and it takes
years to get deep enough at low tide to swim.*
    *DISTASTER No.2*
    *I'm not telling it. If you want it send a proper letter. I hate
you, love from David.*

Joan was angered by the result of the massacre. One of the
dogs belonged to Major Clarke of Achareidh whose land
adjoined Newton. He apologised and came to see Uncle
Robert and Granny with a present of game he had shot and
was forgiven with friendly jokes. The other belonged to a
fisherman to whose house they sent a policeman telling
him to impose a fine on the spot, not to bring him to court
which would have brought hordes of journalists and
headlines like 'Viscount Finlay of Nairn, ex-Lord Chancellor sues Nairn Fisherman.' The fisherman had to pay up.

                              *

Kolya – Nikolai Ivanovich Bersyenev – was born at Kiev
where his father conducted a medical practice which
necessitated long journeys to patients who lived in isolated
houses in the vast surrounding countryside. His family
occupied a huge old dwelling built entirely of wood in
which several rooms to the left of the main door as you
entered served as surgeries, waiting rooms and offices.
Kolya's father, Ivan Yakovlevich, had qualified at the
School of Medicine in Moscow but, adventurous and
ambitious as he had been since early childhood, he then
took a ship from St Petersburg to Leith and went to
Edinburgh University for a post-graduate course. There he
met Catrìona Ferguson who was also studying medicine

but in the end failed all her exams. He fell in love with her, they got married and went back to Kiev together.

Catrìona parted with her husband in some sad way I never heard about and returned to Edinburgh with Kolya.

Kolya was the only one of his names which Scottish people could pronounce and most people called him Kolly.

Catrìona was a friend of my mother's. They had known each other all their lives, played tennis together most afternoons at Nairn. Mother loved her and always kept in touch with her. I liked Kolya but was a bit afraid of him; he did so many things I could not do. He used to pocket bars of chocolate, pencils and rubbers, all sorts of little things from the shops. People said he was mad, a delinquent, but he conquered most of them by his natural charm and good looks. I suppose they had never seen anyone like him, thick black hair, slanting eyes, full dusky cheeks and a huge sudden smile that came on like a horse yawning. Granma, my mother's mother who lived in a house called Tigh-na-Rosan near the sea, wanted him to be sent to Borstal. Of all the little bits of damage he did in her house, taking a beautiful ormolu clock to pieces, thumping out tunes on the piano until one of the strings snapped – the worst happened when he climbed up to the top of her roof with me and, holding on to the chimney stack with his hands, began to dance the Highland Fling. It smashed slates. The roof leaked when it next rained and water got in, bringing down part of a ceiling and wrecking a Persian walnut escritoire whose lid was inlaid with the finest peccary, engraved with gilt lines at the edges and delicate ornamental patterns on each corner.

I saw Kolya nearly every summer until I was seventeen. We went everywhere on our bicycles, travelling miles into the country, up the Findhorn and Spey Valleys, high up among the Cairn Gorm mountains and sometimes walking over rocks and bogs to the heights of Monadhliadh.

I guess that my 'Disaster No.2' must have been a horrible accident which happened to our younger dog Pidgy at Sandwood Farm, two miles from Newton. One afternoon at hay time when Mary and Joan were playing there, with Pidgy out of sight searching for field-mice in the long grass of the meadow, one of his hind legs was cut off by the blades of the horse drawn mowing machine. These shining, sharp pointed, saw-like blades are attached to a steel bar. They work like scissors and are invisible beneath the grass as the horses walk slowly round and round the field. Old Duncan MacDonald, who was driving, wanted to go into his house for a shotgun and shoot the screaming dog but Joan and Mary, who were both greeting, pleaded with him not to, so Bob, his son, ran to catch the pony which was grazing on the paddock next to the house, yoked it into the milk-float while Joan and Mary climbed on, nursing Pidgy with a bundle of oily rags to try to staunch the blood. Old Duncan drove the float much faster than was safe, trotting swiftly down the steep bumpy track which led from the steading into the main road and all the way to the veterinary surgeon's house at Nairn. The vet also wanted to send Pidgy out of his misery by putting him to death by an overdose of chloroform, but my sisters persuaded him to operate instead and he lived the rest of his life hopping about with agility on three legs.

Sandwood farm, which was really a croft in Delnies, had been renamed Sandwood by old Duncan because his letters got mixed up with Wester Delnies. The croft was at the edge of an ancient wood known as Newlands of Delnies. Several gentlemen had cleared patches of it and given English names to the houses they built. Sandwood House was one. Its woods made the western boundary of the MacDonalds' croft.

My mother's youngest sister Edith, very pretty, very 'modern', married to a Lloyds underwriter called Buke Dick-Cleland – Buchanan I suppose – hired this big newish house for summer holidays and that was how we came to know the croft. Her children, our first cousins, John, Patsy and Donald, took us there to see the animals.

We called old Duncan MacDonald 'the Farmer' to distinguish him from his son Duncan who also lived and worked on the croft. They were both distinguished men in appearance, manners and intelligence. Our parents liked them. We were fascinated by them at first sight, especially by old Duncan who had only one eye that worked. When he looked at me with his good eye I would be looking at the bad one. Both were blue, but the blue of the bad one was pale and crumpled. It had no pupil. After I had got to know him well, I asked him what had happened to that eye and all he would say was,

—— I caught a cold in it, and it just ran away.

He was more than sixty years old by then and we thought of him as an old man, but physically he was much more agile than any of our Newton great-uncles. He leapt gates with one hand on the top bar. He ran up ladders instead of stepping up. He sometimes rode twenty miles on his bicycle to visit friends.

His liveliness showed in his face too, and that was another thing that attracted children to him. He had a round expressive face fringed by a grey beard, neatly trimmed and rounded. It was weatherbeaten but his fair skin went red, not brown, in sun and wind, and when he was amused by anything we said it crinkled up with little darting furrows by his eyes. He wore an old, faded bonnet with a crumpled peak, and when occasionally he lifted it to wipe the sweat off his head, we saw he was bald.

Old Duncan had been even more creative than Uncle Robert's father, Dr William Finlay. He had thirteen children, seven girls and six boys, five of whom were living with him in his little croft house when we first went there. He was born in 1862, his wife Isabella in 1867, and all the children had been born on their croft at Auldearn, poor land two miles to the east of Nairn where, when the family grew too large for one cottage, they had to take a second one nearby. There was a good deal of poverty in Nairn in spite of its prosperous appearance.

*Most exelent Excelency Kolya, Grand Duke of Auld Reekie and High Admiral of the Trans-Siberian railway — here goes. But only because it's Sunday and we're not allowed to play in case the great panjam sees us breaking his Sabbath to bits and your one wasn't awful this go. There's some not bad stuff in it only I don't see why going to have tea in Princes Street with the anteek aunt Thing was so boring. I got sick on merangs and eclairs when Mummy took me to Mackies.*

    DREADFUL THING No. 3

    *I was going out with Uncle T. to down the Green Walk. He'd seen a huge clump of foxgloves in a thicket and wanted me to pick some for him to give Judy. It was her birthday I think. Daddy says he's not in good form lately and misses golf and sits in the front outside the conservertrie, rattling* The Scotsman *and having whisky and soda and masses of those black charcoal biscuits, Dr Wilson said for his tummy. He's got a walking-stick nowadays even in the house and has gloves on except when he's eating and was a bit slow in the passage out of breakfast but I never dreamt there was anything the matter only it was funny how he holds on to the bannister going down the front step pushing on his stick with the other hand and on the bottom step he caught his toes in that iron contraption you're supposed to scrape the muck on your boots off, and Kol – it was ghastliest because I didn't know what to do and he was all crumpled up on the gravel and made no sound at all as if he was dead. He was all stretched out like that huge capercailie Cluny shot when he took us in the forrest at the back of Cawdor Castle. You came and Joan.*

    *Well, in the end when I'd stroked his face a bit I just stood there yelling for Gulliver who'd been in the hall but he'd gone somewhere and it was years till anybody came. Then Johnstone and him heard me and came rushing down the steps and lifted Uncle Tom up, only he's terribly heavy and it hurt a lot and he was groaning awfully because it turned out his hip was bust. Everybody came rushing, even Uncle Robert and Mrs Waddle and lots of the maids so they blocked up the passage like at a motorcar accident when all the starers won't let the doctor get at the wounded bloke lying on the ground. Gulliver and Johnstone put him on the hall sofa. Granny rushed to the linen press for blankets. Mummy telephoned to Dr Wilson and he came fairly quick on his bike. They got a proper bed down and stuck it in the littlest drawing-room – only no one lights the fire there in the mornings and it's pretty cold in there and nasty I think because it's always darkish looking out on the north, but there was that silver thing with Bluebell Matches in, on the mantelpeace and Daddy got it going with one match. He's clever at everything don't you think? I think the army makes you clever because there's plenty of fierce Afghan savages with simitars to kill you. In the Indian army I mean.*

*Kol, it's awful. He's still lying there only a lot better. Granny says he was very brave when they put splints on and he makes jokes when we go – me and Barbara and Mary and Joan go and sit on the chair beside his bed often, one at a time of us, I mean, and I've been reading out loud to him –* Red Gauntlet *which he was in the middle of when it happened. It's quite exciting, only sentences a mile long and full of huge words I can't say, only Uncle Tom helps me out with them. He knows what they are when I get to one, without looking. Only it's a bit annoying not knowing what happened at the beginning.*

*Another thing happened but a nice thing this time. A tiny aeroplane landed in the field where they have the cattle show just across the Inverness road opposite the front gate lodge. There's a man who drives it all covered with helmets and straps like a horse's harness. We were out on the lawn when it came. It made a noise like the Elgin bus and circled round Newton quite low. Joan thought it belonged to the navy and was going to cross the Firth to Invergordon. But in a second it disappeared behind the house, so we ran all the way down the avenue and there it was in the field. You can have flips on it for 6$^d$ a go, pretty dear and only 5 mins. He only takes one person at a time – no room – and only goes over the harbour and a bit out to sea, then in a circle back over Newton and lands in the field. It makes a hell of a row. He gets very low over Newton because he's got to get down gradually and we are so near his aerodrome. And the other day when I was watching he aimed straight at the narrow top part of the tower and I could swear he'd break the flagstaff and his propeller would get tangled up in the flag. Then he'd of crashed through the billiard-room roof and smashed up the slate of the billiard table, which I nearly did once, banging the poker on it because they wouldn't let us have their grand cues and Uncle Alick smacked me. Uncle Robert's fuming and Mary says he's written to the Provost to put the man in prison or something. I guess Granny wouldn't mind if he*

*was hanged at Aberdeen. You see he does it nearly all day
with all those people waiting in the field for him to get back.
He's a millionare I bet – one bloke at each go forking out 6ᵈ.
I've just counted 3¾ᵈ, my total assets till Friday.*

*School next week. You too. Prison again. Revolt of the
plebs. Cut the throats of all the senators.Rush the Capitol
with testudos. But the way South's going to be nice because
we're starting off early on Thurs. and staying the weekend
with the Macpherson and Co. at Cluny Castle. They've got
hundreds of ponies and you can ride high up in the
mountains and you can go on Loch Laggan with no grown-
ups fussing. There's three boats in the boat-house, nice ones.
Then it's special and grand on the train. You have to
telephone to the station master at Inverness and say you've
got to get out at Newtonmore – that tiny station remember
where the train usually rushes through without slowing
down a bit. But when he answers the phone, the Station
Master rushes out up to the top end of the platform to the
engine just as the engine-driver's shutting off the steam
safety-valve and shouts at him that a whole lot of important
people want to get out at Newtonmore. But you have to get
all your valises and portmanteaus and the dogs near the door
as soon as the train leaves Kingussie and hurl them out on the
platform at Newtonmore because the engine hates getting
held up and only stops a second. Write to*

*Your affct. cous. David*

I have been told by several people that Uncle Tom
fell and broke his leg inside the house and that I was
not at Newton when it happened.

*

We did not always live in Scotland. From about 1919 for a
few years after our father had come home from France we
followed him from little job to little job, each of which he
obtained with difficulty, staying in boarding or hired
houses in various counties. I loved new places and remember saying to my mother in Derbyshire where we lived
at one time, 'Why can't we go somewhere else? We've been

here for two Christmasses.'

I had been carried to Nairn from India in the autumn of 1914 as a baby, nine months old, with Mary and Joan, who could walk by then. My mother brought us to her mother's house Tigh-na-Rosan. There was nowhere else for her to go and I have heard she had a horrible voyage with us on a troopship bound for France, worried too about my father because she did not know where he was; so close was the secrecy after 4 August when the war began that women were not told where their men had been sent to. She was one of many with young children who were confined to the ship for three weeks in Bombay harbour because of a rumour that one of the sailors had bubonic plague. The quarantine rules were strict, the children bored and restless; she was ill and their quarters on board unbearably hot.

My father had lived in India since 1897 when he joined the Indian Army at the age of twenty-three. He had been gazetted to the British Army after Sandhurst but soon found that he could not afford to remain in it. Pay was small and officers needed a private income to live like well-off gentlemen; if they could not manage that, their life in the mess and throughout their regiment would be one of misery and humiliation, for although fellow officers might sympathise with them, private soldiers would despise them. Officers had to buy their own uniforms, battle and dress uniforms; dress, of which more than one was needed – a plain one for ordinary and evening dinner in the mess, and at least two grand ornate ones for state occasions. Equipment also cost a lot, including, as it did, two expensive swords, one for the field and one for ceremonial occasions. The Indian Army which was usually short of officers provided everything free. And in India, infantry officers were mounted. That appealed to my father. The polo in India was better too.

When he left the country, he was in love with his first cousin, Miss Annie Wilhelmina Finlay, a striking girl aged fifteen. 'Is this Miss Finlay?' asked a visitor to Newton taking a framed photograph from the drawing room mantelpiece. 'Oh no. We are a good-looking family,' our great-aunt Jane Grace told her. And that was certainly true of Annie and her sisters. She, who became our mother, had lovely hair; fair but not yellow, more russet than red, and fine in texture. I remember it by touch and sight better than any other of her features and everyone except Granma, her mother, admired it. Granma did not like the curls. Her bluish eyes, too, I remember without the aid of photographs especially when they melted with sadness.

When Annie became engaged to my father during one of his spells of home leave all the Finlays and her mother's family, which was also huge, turned against her. The Episcopal Church of Scotland had only recently altered its rules to allow marriage between cousins. Her mother said she was getting married 'from pure laziness'. In fact she was overworked and unhappy. She had been engaged at Trinity, Edinburgh, to a young Doctor Taylor who was her father's assistant in his practice there. When he jilted her she went to be trained as a hospital nurse and was sent to London where she could not understand a word the patients said. Cockney was to her like a foreign language she had never heard before and that brought her into trouble with sisters and matron. It only lasted six months. She told me when I was seventeen and in torment between two girls that the worst thing possible in life was to be in love with two people at the same time.

She went to India, chaperoned by Aunt May, the wife of our fat Uncle Jim, who was in the Indian Civil Service, and got married to Captain Alexander Guthrie Thomson of the 58th Vaughan's Rifles, Punjab Frontier Force, on Christmas Eve, 1907, and during the next nine years we came to life – Mary in 1909, Joan in 1912 and I in 1914. Barbara, the youngest of us, was born in England during the war. Our father was a doctor's son too, of John Thomson of Brechin where he and his brother Bill were born. Dr Thomson had married Miss Jessie Bannatyne Finlay whose uncles and aunts had spread all entangled with climbing plants.

We all went to school at Miss Squair's, each of us starting as soon as we were old enough for any school at all. She was one of an old Nairn family, some of whom had been teachers before her and their house near Tigh-na-Rosan was distinguished from the others by memories of the sudden death from lung congestion of Alexander Squair, a much loved teacher at the Church Street School. He was only twenty-three. His death in April 1886 caused grief throughout Nairn. His coffin was followed to the graveyard by a procession longer than any laird's pupils, fellow teachers, members of the Free Church Guild, and thousands of others walked behind it. The High Street was lined on both sides by mourners.

His father, Robert Squair, lived on in the house and some years after his death our Miss Squair, left alone there, turned the front room into a school.

There were six forms in her school arranged literally as forms, long benches that is to say, which is a good arrangement because the taller children could see Miss Squair at her table facing us over the heads of the younger ones. Barbara and I sat on the first form near her, Joan and Mary on other forms behind us. Barbara remembers being frightened, not so much of Miss Squair as of the other children. I remember only Miss Squair's little finger which was bent and very near to my spectacles when she pointed to mistakes on my slate.

We learned to read and write there and she was good at teaching us spelling by repetitive rhymes. I loved the slates we wrote on, which were like blank photographs in wooden frames. Each had a damp sponge attached to it by a string for rubbing out mistakes. For the geography lessons we had maps marking different countries in bright colours and our task was to count those patches and dots marked in red, places which were part of the British Empire. Discipline was strict in that small room; none of us, not even Kolya, dared to play about – but lessons were not boring. Her way of teaching Scottish history made it like a story book and we liked the poetry she made us learn by heart: 'Young Lochinvar', 'Love flows like the Solway', 'A fair little girl sat under a tree/ Sewing as long as her eyes could see'.

—— Fair does not mean fair like Jo-an. It means pretty, said Miss Squair.

We learned to recite '*Maître Corbeau sur un arbre perché*' and '*La cigale et la fourmi*' in some sort of French.

Miss Squair could read French, but she had taught herself the language with the help of a book of phonetic symbols and our French lesson books had those symbols in them which we had to learn along with every French word. The symbol for the double 'l' in, for instance, 'fille' looks very much like a 'j'. She taught us all to say 'la feedge' and when we moved on to other schools we could not believe we were wrong.

Everyone, I suppose, has a peculiar memory of one day in early school days. Mary remembers the long walk back to Newton up that frightening avenue darkened by trees which she did daily from school, always looking over her shoulder for The O'Toole, who often gave her a lift on the step of his tricycle, but on one day, which she remembers with horror, he caught her up, said he was in a hurry and would turn back if she would carry a hare he had just shot to the house. She took it from him by the hind legs, in the usual way, but found it was not quite dead. We were all used to handling dead animals and birds but this hare which came to life in her hand was pitiable and frightening. When she told me about it I thought of 'The Judgement of Solomon', a picture Uncle Robert had on the wall outside his study, of Solomon on his throne and below him two women and a soldier. The soldier held a baby in one hand by the ankle, head down, and in the other a sword raised, ready to slice it in two.

My own most fearful memory is of being woken early one morning by the noise of a cloudburst. It was as unreasonable as fear of thunder – it is thunder not lightning that dogs and children fear – and if we had been sleeping in the house as usual I would have been aroused by curiosity, not fear. But we had been sleeping for weeks in a tent on the sheltered little lawn outside the dining room windows and near the plum wall, and this was because we had to be isolated from Barbara who was very ill with scarlet fever, a deadly fever in those days. We were told that the door of the bedroom in which she lay was draped with a sheet soaked in carbolic. We could smell it from the bottom of the front stairs. There was a strained and gloomy feeling in the house. Our cousin, Patsy Dick-Cleland's sister, had died of scarlet fever not long before at the age of six and it may be that my worry about Barbara strengthened the clap of the cloudburst.

Of course we loved sleeping in the tent. The rabbits came so close to it in the early morning that we could hear them cropping the grass. It was more like Henry the Fifth's pavilion at Agincourt than a tent, it had been an appurtenance of the great marquee which Uncle Robert had used before the war for garden parties attended by four or five hundred guests. It was square and spacious with vertical sides held up by four wooden poles topped by ornate knobs, gold and blue, which protruded through the roof, which sloped from a ridge like the roof of a small house. On sunny mornings it glowed pale green and flickering shadows from trees moved on it. We woke up in a magic palace under the sea. But on the morning of the cloudburst the green canvas was black and the deluge clapping on it made a noise I had never heard before. I cried out. I was in tears. Joan held me, tried to comfort me, saying, 'It's only the rain.'

We put on our clothes and made the beds and waited hoping for a moment of less powerful rain. Mary, pretending to be a priestess and Miss Squair all in one, put on a funny voice and said:

Repeat after me,

> Rain, rain go to Spain
> Fair weather come again
> Rain, rain, go away
> And home to us another day.

Then with our shoes and socks in one hand, because the lawn was inches deep in water, we ran round the house, up the steps to the front hall where we had to dive through a crowd of men who were arguing with our mother, 'I'll go!' 'Let me go.' 'You'll catch a chill, Annie.' 'Dares't thou Cassius now, leap in with me into this angry flood?' Mother was the only one with a waterproof on. She was holding ours in her arms.

We usually found many people in the hall when we came

in for breakfast, tapping the barometer or looking out through the glass doors at their other barometer, the Black Isle, seven miles away. The Black Isle was invisible that morning and the people excited and chattering as though they were at a party, some laughing, some huddled close with quiet gloomy voices as though the end of the world was near.

——  Two thousand were drowned in the Nairn Valley alone.

——  The Findhorn had more.

——  A mighty fortress is our God . . . Someone was singing a psalm, in a joking way, I suppose . . . A bulwark never failing/Our helper He amid the flood of mortal ills prevailing.

——  What shall we do then?

——  Play billiards?

——  All day?

——  The thirsty earth soaks up the rain/And drinks and gapes for drink again.

——  It's not soaking it up.

Throughout breakfast and after it they were looking through the windows and talking about deluge.

——  It is one hundred years this Lammas since the Great Flood.

——  Ninety-two years, Tom.

——  In some parts of India it happens every year.

——  Is it going to happen here then, Uncle Jim?

——  Did you not see the rainbow yesterday David, a full one right across the firth?

——  God's promise.

>       ——  My heart leaps up when I behold
>       A rainbow in the sky
>       So was it when my life began
>       So it is now I am a man
>       So be it when I shall grow old
>       Or let me die!

——  The good rain, said Uncle Robert, looking down at me smiling, with his hands on my shoulders – the good rain

like a bad preacher does not know when to leave off.
Emerson was a writer not only wise but witty and if the
weather continues to preclude recreation out of doors
please come to my study at eleven o'clock. I shall show you
books that may be of interest to you, and read to you
something from Emerson's Journals.
—— Must I go? I asked my father when Uncle Robert had
left the room.
—— Go. You'll like it and it's an honour. The Lord
Advocate's the only other man to be invited to his study in
the mornings.

*

We were not supposed to go into Uncle Robert's study, nor
into his private lavatory which adjoined it in a dark corner
hidden by the front staircase, but of course the temptation
had been as irresistible as that of Bluebeard's wife and
sometimes when I knew he was out I crept into both
forbidden rooms. At first I found the lavatory more
interesting than the study because it had an extra-ordinary
urinal in it made of white porcelain and shaped like a heart.
It was fixed to the wall too high for me to reach and until I
noticed the smell of it I thought it was meant to wash your
hands in, but there was a proper basin with taps and
flowers on it and in one corner a WC which was also
covered with flowery patterns. This room was not much
larger than a railway train lavatory and had a narrow
window looking out on to the side lawn.

The study was a large almost square room with beautiful
windows looking over the front lawn across the Firth to the
Black Isle. It had a fireplace, smaller than the one in the
billiard room, but except for that the lower parts of the four
walls were furnished with varnished wooden cupboards
about three feet tall. When I opened a cupboard door I saw
nothing but documents tied up in red tape. From the top of
these cupboards to the ceiling there were bookshelves. The
room smelt of leather bindings and ink. I used to take out
some books and read parts of them in terror of Gulliver who
might come in at any moment to mend the fire.

There was near the wall opposite the fireplace a massive

desk which had on its red leathern top a pen-tray, two inkwells, one for black and one for red, a long ivory paperknife, an ebony-handled blotting roller and a special separate inkwell made from the hoof of his favourite old horse which had died before the war. It had silver mountings and its base was a silver horseshoe – shod after death. The place where the pastern and fetlock had been had a silver lid which when you raised it showed the inkwell inside. On the front of the hoof there was a curved plate engraved with the name and dates of the horse, a memorial plaque set into part of its body. There were shapely white goose quills and a penknife for sharpening them, but I think Uncle Robert had taken to steel nibbed pens by then, as he had changed from sand to blotting paper.

I was very nervous when I tapped on the door of his study that rainy morning and heard his voice say 'Come in!' But he quickly made me easy. He asked what books I liked reading and I said George Macdonald's, especially *At the Back of the North Wind* and Rider Haggard's, especially *King Solomon's Mines*.

—— From the North Pole to the Equator, said Uncle Robert. He was standing with his back to the fire with his thumbs in his black waistcoat pockets from which dangled watch chain and key chain like Michie's.

We sat down. He read bits from Emerson and then, without books, recited verses from Robert Burns which I liked better and something from Ovid in Latin which he translated for me. It was about a flood. At the window he said,

—— The rain has ceased. If it is fine after luncheon, let us drive to Dulsie Bridge – the Findhorn will be in spate today and the waterfall magnificent.

Almost every afternoon the stately, ancient Daimler with its stately ancient chauffeur came from Knowles and Cummings' garage and with a crunch of gravel drew up at the front door. Johnstone was always there to meet it with a picnic hamper and a folding armchair for Uncle Robert to sit on at tea time on the moors. These and some rugs he put into the boot before the party assembled with us on the front steps. The car held a lot of people, six or seven in the

back, two on pull-down seats like those of a taxi and
children on laps or on the floor; two men or women beside
the chauffeur in front who were separated by a thick glass
screen. There was a flower vase filled with fresh flowers by
Knowles and Cummings every day, numerous contrap-
tions and hooks for putting things in or hanging things on
and a speaking-tube which came out like a trumpet beside
the chauffeur's ear. In this battered vehicle of fading blue
we explored the country, sometimes visiting Uncle
Robert's friends at Brodie Castle, Cawdor Castle, Kilravock, Geddes, Daviot House, Lochloy, but more often
climbing slowly into the mountains to one of his chosen
picnic places beside a loch or river or on the wide moor.

The Highland roads were narrow old military roads built
in the eighteenth century, just wide enough for a farm cart
or ordinary car. The Daimler was too broad for them and
had difficulty at corners but the passing places, which still
exist, enabled us to get along at about ten miles an hour
without a hold-up, for any driver seeing our magnificence
would hide in a passing place until we had sailed by. These
little roads have not changed since then, except that they
are no longer dusty or muddy, the old Macadam having
been smoothed over with tar.

Uncle Robert used to chant:

'If you had seen these roads before they were made,
You would lift up your hands and bless General Wade.'

No one in Wade's lifetime blessed him. Even his own
soldiers who did most of the road building between 1724
and the early 1730s hated working in that cold desert of
mountains and the native Highlanders did not want any
road at all. The roads from Perth to Fort William and
Inverness were intended by the English to suppress the
natives after the Jacobite Rising of 1715, to speed up the
movement of troops, but that was not the reason for their
unpopularity. The old ways through the mountains and
bogs had been made by wild horses and cattle, creatures
which like sheep go about in herds and choose the safest
route. Barefooted men with unshod horses kept to these

tracks and the brogues which some men and women wore
were made of thin leather all in one piece. The military
covered the old ways with broken stone and sharp gravel.
There was no wheeled traffic until the Hanoverian armies
came with their cannon and baggage trains. 'Why do the
people not have their horses shod?' said one army officer.
But there was no blacksmith nearer than the coastal towns,
and of course no money. Instead, the people, horses and
black cattle made new paths where they could. The
chieftains and other gentlemen complained that the roads
opened an easy passage for strangers into their country and
that the bridges 'would render the ordinary people
effeminate'.

The most beautiful of all the Highland bridges I have seen
is Dulsie. Probably it was the most difficult to build and
certainly the ford over the river Findhorn, which can still be
seen fifty yards from it where the river emerges from the
Dulsie ravine, was the most dangerous. The bridge crosses
the ravine high above the river and because the cliff on one
side is lower than the other it seems to slant uphill; if you
look at it from the greensward upsteam it seems to cross
diagonally, a single arch over the water and a narrow one
embedded in the rock. It is made of the same grey stone as
the rocky cliffs and has at its apex a great keystone,
wonderful to look at, hanging above the black pool far
below where salmon lie at spawning time before they leap
the falls. The deep water of this salmon pool appears to be
still with clusters of foam floating on it, some brown, some
white, but in the middle where the stream runs fast the
clusters sail like boats till they go out of sight under the
bridge. The great waterfall upstream flows swaying like a
muslin curtain in a breeze; below it the rocks curve and hide
the water which reappears at another bend in a succession
of smaller waterfalls. Glisters and shadows, whisper of
waters, the roar of the white cascade. There are old, gnarled
weeping birches hanging over it from the rocks and above
them dark pine trees. For me as a child it was an enchanted
place. It is still enchanted now when I am old. Burns wrote
of it on his way from Aviemore to Nairn in 1787: 'Come
through mist and darkness to Dulsie to lie [to sleep at

Dulsie House], Findhorn river, rocky banks.'

In the Gaelic language where the letter 't' is soft it is called *Tulla sidh*, the hillock of the fairies. The people said that the building of the bridge had driven the fairies away. That was one good thing. The other was that it led to nowhere, for the road on the north side of it which was planned to join General Wade's road near Nairn and link the south with Fort George, was not made for several years. The old horse path remained. The bridge itself was completed between 1755 and 1757 by an Irish engineer, William Caulfield, who had been Wade's Baggage Master and Inspector of Roads. Wade died in 1748, so on the road to Dulsie Uncle Robert praised the wrong man.

I was on one of the tipseats as we drove towards the bridge and when we bumped over one of the deeper potholes, a worm-eaten window frame spattered dust in Uncle Robert's face.

—— This car has seen better days, he said.

—— Yes, said Granny, glancing at Uncle Tom, who was in front beside the chauffeur, but he still enjoys himself.

Uncle Robert had taken these afternoon drives with brothers, sisters, friends and children since long before the war when he had his own car, and he knew the country and its history well, from the shores of Loch Ness to Loch-an-Eilean, near Aviemore, from Grantown-on-Spey to the monastery of Pluscarden near Elgin, from Lochindorb to the Culbin Sands. We learned a lot from him without knowing we were learning anything and much of it was mysterious.

We ran or climbed trees while the older people sat and talked. Our parents always came with us on the Culbin Sands which were said to be dangerous and Culbin was the most mysterious and exciting place of all, for underneath the sand dunes where we walked and had our picnics there is a buried village.

—— Take care, said Father, the wind shifts the sand and turns things up. You might trip over the church steeple.

From 1921 until 1928, when he was eighty-six years old, Uncle Robert was judge of the Permanent Court of International Justice at the Hague. On his vacations he often

brought us presents from Holland which he gave us
without ceremony. It may have been his age or the blustery
weather which caused a frightening prelude to one presen-
tation. I was under the beech tree on the swing within sight
of his study windows when Gulliver came down the front
steps like a lord all in black and beckoned to me to stop
swinging.

—— His Lordship wishes to see you in his study.

He escorted me there. I was shivering and thinking of all
the things I had done wrong, but it was not a Sunday. We
were allowed to swing on the swing on weekdays. Gulliver
knocked on the door and opened it when an answer came,
put on his grand voice and said:

—— Master David, your Lordship.

Our lordship was sitting at his desk half hidden by a large
Dutch boat with sails, full rigging and a wide curved prow.
I gazed at it. I did not speak until he picked it up and put it
into my hands. He showed me how to furl the sails and
move the side boards which it had instead of a keel. Mary,
Joan and Barbara were sent for later and were given Dutch
dolls, each of them different, and beautiful in a different
way.

As he grew older he sent servants to fetch children to him
more and more. Rosalind, alone in her bedroom one
evening when her parents were out, heard a knock at her
door. It was the butler. She was reading a book.

—— His Lordship wishes to read to Miss Rosalind in the
billiard room.

—— Why must I?

—— Well . . . Grandpapa is lonely tonight.

She went and sat on his lap while he read from *Tales of a
Grandfather*. She wanted to get back to her own book.

*

King James VI, exchanging pleasantries with foreign
envoys at Holyrood Palace, boasted that he had in his
kingdom a town whose only street was so long that the
people living at one end of it could not understand the
language spoken by the people who lived at the other end.

He was speaking of Nairn. He could have added to Gaelic and Lowland Scots a dialect incomprehensible to strangers – a way of speaking more Scandinavian than Scots which outlived Gaelic and is still spoken in the Fishertown.

Dr Johnson, approaching Nairn from Forres with his companion, Boswell, in 1773, wrote: 'We had now a prelude to the Highlands. We began to leave fertility and culture behind us . . . and came to Nairn, a royal burgh, which, if once it flourished, is now in a state of miserable decay . . . At Nairn we may fix the verge of the Highlands, for here I first saw peat fires, and first heard the Erse language.'

He says little about food but from Boswell's account of their journey together, it seems he did not like what public inns near Nairn prepared for him. 'We breakfasted at Cullen. They set down dried haddocks, broiled along with our tea. I ate one; but Dr Johnson was disgusted by the sight of them, so they were removed. Cullen has a comfortable appearance, though but a very small town, and the houses mostly poor buildings.'

On 27 August: 'We came to Nairn to breakfast. Though a county town and a royal burgh, it is a miserable place. Over the room where we sat, a girl was spinning wool with a great wheel and singing an Erse song: "I'll warrant you, (said Dr Johnson) one of the songs of Ossian." '

Nearly forty years later, in 1810, Walter Thom, a Scottish traveller, was shocked by the squalor of Nairnshire, particularly by the dilapidated state of the dwellings of the common people neglected as they were by the landlords who owned them. He too preferred Moray. The clothes and manners of people there, their habitations, land and roads delighted him and at Forres in particular the girls were neatly and cleanly dressed. He and his companion found a good inn at Forres, and excellent dinner and a civil landlady, who told them that the road to Nairn was so bad that she did not think they could reach it that night, but after thanking her they went on. 'When we had ascended the hill, we had another peep at the fairest of Moray; but soon found ourselves on a bleak heath [Macbeth's blasted heath near Auldearn, I think] and entering the county of

Nairn . . . and now we had bid adieu to sweet Moray. Oh! Thy pretty girls, thy fertile fields, and thy delightful prospects will ever be dear to our remembrance! If Samuel Johnson had had eyes to have seen thy beauties, thou wouldst have saved Scotland all his sarcasms . . . We left Nairn early on Sunday morning and soon found ourselves in a poor miserable country. Everything but the road was bad [the military road to Fort George]. The few spots of green we saw were just such as might be expected in such an uncultivated country. The dress and language of the people were altogether different from what we had seen, and the hovels in which they lived were worse than pigstyes. These dwellings had neither window nor chimney, and the smoke issued out from the roof and through the walls, so that, at first we thought these houses were on fire.'

The census of 1811, the year in which Thom's Journal was published, gives the population of Nairn as 2,215. In Dr Johnson's time it was, according to Dr Webster's report 1,698. By 1861 it had risen to 4,486 and by 1881 to 5,386. That rapid rise in population was made by an influx of respectable people.

It was not until the eighteen-sixties that Nairn became a respectable and popular holiday town and like many such transformations this came about by chance. In the eighteen-fifties Mrs Grizel Grant, relict of Major John Grant of Achindoune, died and left her house to her daughters Jane and Eliza, who bequeathed it to a wealthy physician who had a flourishing practice in Rome. The rude Gaelic name Achindoune (field of the dwelling place) had been changed according to the Anglified fashion of the time to Larkfield, and Dr John Grigor, when he retired, came to live there. He valued the health giving climate of Nairn and advised wealthy patients to come and stay there; new houses and hotels were built for them; a fifteen mile railway from Inverness to Nairn had been opened in 1855 and travelling from the south was not so long and tiresome as it had been. He also, so say the holiday brochures, persuaded the Gulf Stream which had till then got no further than the Atlantic coast to find its way to Nairn. This Gulf Stream,

which eels swim in on their way from the Sargasso Sea to
Europe, had never had any trouble in warming up Gairloch
on the Atlantic coast but to please the hotel and boarding-
house keepers of Dr Grigor's time, it kindly found its way
round Cape Wrath and John o'Groats into the Moray Firth
where, missing out all the other seaside towns, it began to
warm up Nairn.

The first of the large and comfortable hotels which is now
called the Royal Marine was opened on the 1st of June 1861
under the name 'Nairn Marine Hotel and Family Board-
ing-House'. We knew it well as children because friends of
our parents who spent their summer holidays in it sometimes asked us to tea there. It was built near the sea
between the links and the beach where our bathing coach
was, and its turrets and bow windows overlook the
harbour and the firth. The announcement of its first
opening still hangs in the hall, and is addressed to the
'Nobility, Gentry, Tourists and Public Generally' and after
boasting, truthfully, of its 'capacious rooms which command views which cannot be excelled' it says that 'Post
horses with convenient conveyances, under the charge of
careful drivers, may be had. An omnibus will be in waiting
on the arrival and departure of the Trains and Steam Boats.'

In the eighteen-seventies William McGonagall was able
to write:

All ye tourists who wish to be away
From the crowded city for a brief holiday;
The town of Nairn is worth a visit, I do confess,
And it's only about fifteen miles from Inverness.
And in the summer season it's a very popular bathing place.
And the visitors from London and Edinburgh find solace,
As they walk along the yellow sand inhaling fresh air;
Besides, there's every accommodation for ladies and gentle-
    men there.
Then there's a large number of bathing coaches there . . .
Besides there's a golf course for those that such a game
    seeks,
Which would prove a great attraction to the Knights of clubs
    and cleeks . . .
And as the visitors to Nairn walk along the yellow sand

They can see, right across the Moray Firth, the Black Island
   so grand . . .
And in conclusion I will say for good bathing Nairn is best
And besides its pleasant scenery is of historical interest.
And the climate gives health to many visitors while there.
Therefore I would recommend Nairn for balmy pure air.

Dr Grigor brought permanent prosperity to the 'Up-
town' and 'West End' of Nairn and by his philanthropy he improved during his lifetime the condition of
the poor. When he died in 1886, he left bequests for free
scholarships at Nairn Academy, for university bursaries in
medicine, money for a Nairn museum and for the Nairn
Literary Institute.

The people commissioned a costly bronze statue of him
which no one who knew Nairn in my boyhood will ever
forget. It was put up on a wide granite pedestal in the
middle of Leopold Street where that joins the High Street,
leaving only a narrow pass on either side of it for carts and
motorcars. When cars became common in the nineteen
twenties it was disfigured by signs 'instructing the motorists how to find their way. Surely everything is not to be
subservient to motorists!' The roadsigns were removed.
Then the statue was removed and placed in the gardens of
Viewfield House near Tigh-na-Rosan.

During the reign of King Edward VII Uncle Robert
travelled to Nairn from London by the night express from
Euston, first class, accompanied by forty servants, who
went second or third class according to rank. His chauffeur
started off for Nairn a day earlier in the Daimler and arrived
at Newton before him. Uncle Robert with his entourage
had to change at Perth early in the morning, with some
commotion, on to a Highland line train which took them via
Dava Moor and Forres to Nairn. This train was long and
heavy. It needed two engines in front and a shunter to push
it from the back over the steep mountain passes. It had,
behind its eleven passenger coaches, three private family
saloons, two trucks for private carriages, five luggage vans,
one meat van, one travelling post office, thirteen horse
boxes and one guards van. The grouse and red deer
shooters brought their horses and carriages with them.

In the nineteen-twenties, while we lived in London, part of the train from Euston went all the way to Nairn. We started from Euston at 7.30 pm and reached Nairn about midday next day. Second class had been abolished by then so we went third and our journey was one of the most enjoyable things I can remember. Father made stretchers for Barbara and me, the smallest of us, out of canvas and bamboo sticks cut to the width of the carriage, their ends resting across from seat to seat. He and my mother slept on the seats, their feet against our stretchers and Mary and Joan were on the two luggage racks which in those days were wide and made of baggy soft net. We hired pillows and blankets from the platform trolley.

The start of our excitement was the arrival of the little bus which Father ordered from the railway company. It was made of brown varnished wood with big windows and a luggage rack on the roof. The driver and one porter who rode with him went upstairs when they arrived and carried down our trunks, then went back for the valises and suitcases, bicycles, pram, push-carts, which were in the hall. Our parents carried the smaller things like golf clubs, hat boxes and fishing rods, and we looked after the animals – two dogs on leads, thirteen guinea pigs and two tortoises in baskets. Then the bus carried us all to the bustle of porters and passengers at Euston.

—— Thirteen pieces, my father used to say at Euston, or eleven or fifteen, whatever it was, remember that David, thirteen pieces; and at every long stop such as Crewe or Perth he took me down the platform to the guard's van to count them. The notion that some might have been stolen was thrilling. As soon as the train moved out of Euston my mother would gasp and say she had left the gas-fire on, the kettle boiling, the iron on the gas ring.

From Perth to Nairn, in the morning daylight, we learned the names of the stations by heart, and I have never forgotten them. They became like a poem in my head: Dunkeld, Dalguise, Ballinluig, Pitlochry, where the train goes through the pass of Killiecrankie to Blair Atholl, Struan, Dalnaspidal the highest place where a board said SUMMIT in large letters, and going faster downhill,

Dalwhinnie, Newtonmore, Kingusssie, Kincraig, Alvie, Aviemore. At Kingussie a piper in grand Highland dress got on and walked up and down the corridors playing his bagpipes. Our parents hated the noise, which shatters one's ears when the instrument is played in a narrow space, but they gave us pennies to give him and we followed him up and down the train until Aviemore where the main part of it, with him on board, went on to Inverness and our part, with only one engine forked right to Boat-of-Garten, Broom-hill, Grantown-on-Spey, Dava Moor, where you could not see the country because of the barricades made of old railway sleepers against snowdrifts, Dumphail, Forres, Brodie, Auldearn, Nairn. After Perth this great long train from London became a local train, stopping at every station and people travelled in our carriage for short distances. We each strived to be the first to call out the names of the stations and Barbara once made some strangers laugh by shouting, 'There's another station called Gentlemen.' At Forres we heard the first seagulls and at Nairn the cushie doos said 'Take two coos, Taffy, take two coos Taffy. Take!' to the thief who had planned to steal only one. At Newton the cock said 'The whisky is dear' which sounds more like a cock-crow in Gaelic – *Tha an t-uisqe-beatha daor*!

At Nairn we were received by Michie who had been my hero ever since I could remember and was my close friend for many years. He was my Rob Roy, gallant, fierce, generous. Perhaps I was more intimate with the Mac-Donalds of Sandwood, but Michie was unique. There were gipsy like things about him which would appeal to any child – red neckerchief, blue or yellow waistcoat with silver watch chain looping from the pockets, black jacket, narrow trousers and soft leather boots. His grey tweed bonnet seemed to my short sight, when I first saw it, to be covered with birds' feathers, bright blue, red, brown, green like a mallard, white like a ptarmigan. These were the fishing flies which he used every day on the river Nairn and sometimes on the Findhorn and which he made himself, choosing feathers from birds hanging up at the poulterers. They were fixed by their hooks all over his bonnet which was frayed in places where the barb got stuck and he had to tear it out. He had a moustache more bushy than my father's and, like my father, walked and stood very upright in rather a military way. When he stood still he held his thumbs in his waistcoat pockets. He usually wore a white shirt with no collar or tie but a bright brass collar-stud which gleamed beneath the neckerchief.

Michie was said to have second sight, but rumour travels faster than trains in Scotland, so it may have been some tip-off from a *Nairnshire Telegraph* reporter that told him exactly which morning to expect us every summer. During the summer holidays there would be ten or twelve cabs, some horse drawn, some motor, drawn up in an orderly rank outside the station. The convention was the London one of taking the cab at the head of the rank, or the first of the taxis if that was what you preferred. But Michie had adopted Parisian ways. However far back his cab stood in the rank, it was ours. We could not escape it. My mother preferred motor cabs. We always clamoured for a horse drawn one. But if it had to be horse drawn she would have chosen one with a strong well fed horse, for we inside and our 'thirteen pieces' on the roof made a heavy load. Michie's horse was as thin as himself – you could count its ribs or hang your coat on its hip bones – but as Father said, they would both grow thinner still if no one employed them.

It was Michie, not my father, who saw to that, for in spite of his lack of flesh he was a powerful man, tall, long legged and broad. He was always in the guard's van before the train had stopped, had seized and shouldered one of our heavier trunks before any of us had got out of the train, run across the line with it behind the stationary train and, climbing on to the 'Down' platform, fled out into the station yard like a looter pursued. Then climbing on to the driver's step he would heave the trunk on to the roof rack – a job for which most cab drivers would have asked the help of a porter. But Michie in that goldrush had to stake his claim in secret and alone. Having secured us, trapped us, by taking possession of one trunk he would cross the line again at his own easy pace, and jealously watching the guard and porter putting the rest of the things on to the platform, interrupt my father who was counting them as they came out with 'Ye are welcome back to Nairn, Colonel. Tis a braw day isn't it? But I doubt we may get a bit rain afore night.' Then he would see my mother, raise his bonnet and apologising for his bad manners in speaking to Father first, say 'Now, Mrs Colonel, isn't that grand to see ye! And ye look a thousand times better than ye did last summer. Ye are stouter. I'd say ye look to be a fine stout woman, Ma'am!'

My mother hated this, because she did not properly understand what country people meant by 'stout', which in Scottish usage, or at least Nairnshire usage, stood for half a dozen of its obsolete English meanings: healthy, robust, full of heart and courage, vigorous, unyielding in adversity. It meant physical strength as well of course. Men admired big women with plenty of flesh on them, able to work like men on land or beach, sexy too, and able to bear and rear large families, carrying on with the farm work at the same time.

Mother was very fond of Michie, far closer to him than Father who liked him too but was frequently irritated by his 'Highland' good manners which mean making promises and not keeping them – a custom derived from the belief that it is rude to say no. Mother had always been grateful to him for the way he had looked after me since I was small, going with me to the harbour to watch the herring boats, up the river which was dangerous in places, across the main road; if she knew I was out with Michie she never worried when I was late for dinner. This mutual respect between him and my parents added a little to his meagre income.

He came to Newton frequently at breakfast time, carrying a large freshly caught salmon, a hare he had just shot, or a pair of grouse. Any other man would have taken such things to the kitchen quarters and tried to sell them to Mrs Waddell. Not so Michie. He knew the hour at which my father usually set out for golf and without knocking would stand waiting unobtrusively near the front door. If he saw me on the lawn, he would cry, 'Davy! Come to me one minute!' And when I came

—— Go into the house and look for your father. Michie

will be waiting on you. I have something bonny to show him.

My father always bought the salmon or whatever it was, but resentfully. He didn't want it. There was always plenty of fish and game in the house, caught or shot by the guests, and then he hated having to go and search for a servant who would take it to the kitchen. If he rang the front door bell Gulliver would come with his manicured fingers and black suit, drawing back from the very smell of Michie's offering. And then there was the price, the worst part of it, which Father also called 'Highland'.

—— Now what shall I give you for it, Michie?

—— Give me, Colonel?

In this way – this Highland way – Father thought Michie always gained more than the value of what he had to sell but the truth was that Michie seldom sold his catch for money. He would go into the poulterers or fishmongers and lay it on the slab. Some days later the shopkeeper would send him a bottle of whisky or a new fishing reel. He would willingly have given his catch to us, just as he always gave game, trout and salmon to poor families. But because my father expected to pay something, he accepted money.

Our holidays were enriched as we grew older, by our friendship with 'the Farmer' and his family at Sandwood. He gave us responsibilities, such as folding the sheep, taking horses to the smiddy, accompanying him on the milk round until we learned to put the right can or bottle on the right doorstep, without instruction. His West End customers were usually asleep, but in the Fishertown we grew to know some people and some of the 'witches' we had seen in the woods became real and kindly people. When the circus and fair came to the links he took us to them. At the Highland Games we left the grandstand where our parents sat and sought him out in the crowd. He was very fond of graveyards, where peering at headstones with his one eye, he would tell us stories about the people buried at Nairn, Auldearn, Geddes, Cawdor, Petty. He told us how corpses rose up and spoke as they were being lowered into the grave, how robbers would come at night and cut the fingers off a dead woman's hand to get the rings, but what shocked him more was an incident that had happened in Geddes kirk yard when he was a young man in 1885. A funeral had been arranged on a Monday; two labourers started to dig the grave on the day before – the Sabbath Day – Six days shalt thou labour – and then when the Monday came there was no one to finish the grave, because the labourers and even the sextons were working on the roads. It was, I now know, during the great depression of the eighteen-eighties.

One day the Farmer even took us as far as Inverness where instead of seeing the sights of the town – castle, docks, the Old Kirk – we went beyond it and spent the whole day in Tomnahurich cemetery, the rounded hill above the left bank of the River Ness. But it was an adventure because instead of going on our bicycles we rode to Inverness on his milk float which he furnished with cushions and a fisherman's chaff mattress, and all the way he told us thrilling stories or made us laugh.

He liked reading and speaking about the devout works of Spurgeon the Calvinist and knew most of the prophecies of the Brahan Seer by heart. Spurgeon is dull matter for a child but his vivid sense of humour drew thousands of people to listen to his sermons, so many that a new church was built to hold them, and perhaps the Farmer possessed a similar gift. When he quoted sentences from Spurgeon he made us laugh.

He quoted the Brahan Seer in Gaelic, a language I loved the sound of, but only knew a few words, and then translated the sayings for us:

> The day will come when policemen will be so numerous in every town that a man will meet one at the corner of every street.

> There shall be a hand with two thumbs at I-Stiana, in the Black Isle, a man with two navels at Dunean, and soldiers shall come from Carr a Chlarsair on a chariot without horse or bridle and the raven shall drink his three fulls of the blood of the Gael from the Stone of Fionn.

We passed the site of an old mill at Milburn near Culloden Moor on our way to Inverness. The Brahan Seer, passing it about a hundred years before the Battle of Culloden, told the people of the village that their mill wheel would one time be turned for three days by water red with the blood of men.

Tomnahurich was well-known in places as far away as Nairn and Cromarty for its legends and because some of the powerful families miles from it had burial grounds in it. *Tom* is in Gaelic a rounded hillock or knoll and *hurich* is a corruption of the word for fairies – *Sithichean* – so that the name means Hill of the Fairies. The Farmer said that Saint Columba on his first visit to the North of Scotland preached Christianity from the top of the hill and drove the fairies, who had till then roamed the countryside night and day, underground. When he left they came out, but only at night, making mischief as far north as Wick, and at dawn came home to the caverns underneath the hill. The seer foretold that the hill would be under lock and key and the fairies imprisoned in it. It was turned into a cemetery with railings and gates that were usually kept locked two hundred years after his death. He said too that ships with unfurled sails would pass and repass Tomnahurich. The Brahan Seer died in the seventeenth century. The Caledonian Canal was opened to shipping in 1823. Andrew Lang and others doubted the truth of some of his prophecies because the dates of their publication may have been later than the dates of fullfilment. But the gift of second sight is possessed by some people, as I learned later in life by making friends with a few in the Highlands, Western Isles and Ireland, who had it.

No one knows what education is while it is going on but I am sure that our minds and our knowledge of life were enriched by friendship with Michie and old Duncan MacDonald, 'the Farmer', not only by what they told us but from the people they talked with on the riverside or road; for instance the gangrels, as people who walk or gang about were called, wild-looking men and women who lived in shacks, tents or bothies outside Nairn and outside the society of Nairn, of whom we were afraid. We would cross the road to escape an encounter with any of them, but when we met them with the Farmer they lost their spectral countenance. As I grew older, I got to know two of them well: English Fred and Johnnie Morgan. Others, whom I remember by sight or hearsay are described in Charles Sellar's *A Glimpse of Old Nairn*. There were Long Tom, who always had a roll of oilcloth under his arm and went about with his wife Lady MacIntosh, who made crochet as she walked about the country and sold it. Their end was tragic. When he was found dead near the Beauly Firth she was put against her will into the Nairn poorhouse. She said 'I would rather die a cadger's donkey's death at some dykeside than end my days in a poorhouse.' She died in it soon afterwards. Melodeon Nellie, who sang Gaelic songs all over the town to her melodeon, was approached by the Bailie who said kindly, 'Would you not be better off in a home?' 'Ach,' she said, 'It's a puir hen canna scratch for itsel'.'

Happie Lachie in a bowler hat with lots of grey hair and whiskers sang his own songs:

> Happy Lachie never tell a lie
> Lachie go to heaven when he die
> Ah, fellow men, I wonder when
> I'll pay your goodness back.

There was a bird man who bred and sold canaries and caught and sold wild birds, a horse dealer who lived with dozens of horses on the carse beyond the Dunbar golf links, and a lonely old woman in tatters to whom Granma sent coal and food.

English Fred did not seem English to me; some people called him London Fred or Irish Fred, but it seems he was the son of a Welsh minister who left his parents and wandered about. He had come to Nairn with a travelling circus and stayed there when it left to work as a dairyman, but when I knew him he was doing any job he could find, usually for food not money. He had long flexible fingers, even in old age, a broad pleasant face and thick white hair which came in a fringe on his forehead. He wore a thick waistcoat which came almost down to his knees and over it a long top coat. His trousers were wide and black or dark brown with faint stripes on them. He always had a brightly coloured neckerchief and he wore his bonnet sideways with the peak over his right ear. In 1926 when I was fourteen his dead body was found in a shed in the nursery gardens of Lodgehill Road.

I cannot remember how we first came to speak to Johnnie Morgan. It was probably by way of our mother for he was such a gruff, bad-tempered man, skinny as a devil and covered with black hair, that we would have run away from him if he said anything to us. Everyone in Nairn knew him by sight, or if not by sight by smell, for he collected pig food from hotels and houses in the town driving a pony and cart which you could smell a mile away. He often came to Tigh-na-Rosan where left over food was kept for him in a special bin away from the ordinary ash buckets. He had a beautiful blond Highland pony, a fat mild-tempered garron, and he never said anything when we stroked it, brushed its mane and gave it lumps of sugar. Mother persuaded him to let us ride this pony on the carse of Kingsteps, a lonely flat place across the river towards the Culbin Sands where he lived with his pigs. You could smell your way to the corrugated iron hut he lived in all alone. His pigsties, much larger than his own dwelling, were roofed with corrugated iron as well. It was lonely and mysterious. There were tumuli nearby, said at the Newton breakfast table to be prehistoric graves, and the only place where other men were to be seen was a stone quarry. The quarrymen seemed wild and uncanny to me – at one time I wished to be one of them when I grew up – and the great-uncles stirred me one day when I was about ten by speaking of a stone club which one of the men had unearthed that day and of a doubled up skeleton found in one of those ancient mounds we often rode round. One of these was called the Fairy Hill

I guess that my sisters pretended to believe that the fishwives gathering fir cones in the Newton and Achareidh woods were witches; it was a game of ours to hide in the bushes creeping as near to them as we dared without being seen and probably Joan and Mary tried to add to the thrill by frightening me. I certainly did believe they were witches when I was young. For one thing they were dressed like the witches in story books and for another the faces of some of them when they stood, upright or bent, to walk to the next tree were grotesque. Each wore a mutch, a tight fitting brimless, woollen cap and a shawl, grey or black, either over it or gathered round the neck, and the mutch, when the shawl was worn gathered and the hair pinned up in a bun, made the woman look bald. Their wide thick skirts touched the ground. And as can be seen on old photographs in the Fishertown Museum of Nairn some did look mentally deficient – a condition attributed to hundreds of years of inbreeding.

There were of course many bright, intelligent and pretty fishwives but I never perceived one in those dark woods. My first sight of one such young woman was like the unveiling of a portrait which you expect to be grim but suddenly appears as a revelation of friendly beauty. I was bicycling home with the Farmer from Brackla distillery about four miles from Nairn, where he had been to order draff for the cows, when we saw her in front of us, shrouded by the customary shawl, although the afternoon was hot, with a big creel on her back and a long flat basket in the crook of her arm. When we caught up with her we slowed down to her pace and they talked. He said something that made her laugh. That was all. That was my revelation.

She was one of the few who still walked twenty or thirty miles a day to remote hill crofts loaded with the fish their father or husbands had landed at the harbour in the early morning. Before the railway came to Nairn most of the women did this. They were usually paid not in money but with butter, eggs, oatmeal or potatoes.

My book education went on even during the summer holidays when I was ten and eleven because I was supposed to get through an examination called Common Entrance, the entrance being the forbidding gates of a public school which were not common at all. I was bad at every subject except history and English which I liked. My knowledge of maths was feeble and confused. Barbara who was two years younger was good at it.

My maths tutor at Newton was Ninie MacKintosh, an undergraduate at Aberdeen University who spent her vacations at home in Nairn with her parents. She was about seventeen. I liked her but not my lessons which took place in the billiard room after breakfast while everybody else was out playing. Uncle Robert used to come in and ask Ninie what progress I was making, to which she would obligingly answer: 'He's a good boy,' upon which he would say, 'Then don't keep him too long, Ninie. The sun is shining.' She was well known at Newton because her mother had been nurse to Uncle Ninian's children. My sisters came into the billiard room, too, to ask when I would be free, but these brief distractions were trivial compared to my wandering gaze and thoughts.

The billiard room was to me the best place in the house, the least tidy and formal, where even the grown-ups did not have to behave sedately – a long wide room with a door at each end through which everybody passed, to save going round by the corridor on the other side of the courtyard. It had no windows looking down on to the courtyard. It was lit by a skylight as long as the billiard table and a wide oriel window overlooking the kitchen gates, the trees and rhododendrons, beyond which you saw the roofs of the dovecots and stables. Ninie and I sat on the window seat from which I could watch the coming and going of delivery bicycles and vans, men, boys, horses, ponies of different shapes and colours. There were two steps up to the window seat and two to the dais at the far end of the room which was furnished with small tables, a musical box, a couch and upright chairs. The window seat and dais had been built higher than the floor and the great fireplace which was surrounded by armchairs at the other end, to give people a good view of the game of billiards.

I liked billiards and liked to watch the men playing it. I liked the slow calculation, the silence of it before the sudden click of ball against ball. The men played billiards only, with very few balls – ivory, white and a red one – but in the long chest beneath the cue rack, where the balls were kept, we found dozens of others, in many colours –

intended for pyramids or snooker, and when no one was using the table it was these we took out and knocked with the cues, playing no proper game but trying to get them into pockets or make patterns. The bright colours of these balls, large clusters of red, with a few scattered ones dotted round in blue, brown, black, yellow, pink and white, on the green plain, were like towns on a map, and with one touch of the cue you could change the map. The taut green cloth which covered the slate of the table made me think of a kind of seaweed, common in Nairn, which lies flat on rocks at low tide. During my lesson the table was usually covered with a blotchy dust-sheet the colour of sea mist. But the carpet had patterns in which I saw images and the bookshelves had books with brown, black and red leather bindings.

On the day when Uncle Alick died upstairs at Newton, I had my maths lessons as usual because no one had been able to warn Ninie not to come. All the curtains on the ground floor were drawn. I thought the maids had forgotten to open them, and I pulled back the billiard room ones. No one came in during the lesson and after Ninie had gone, leaving me alone, I went on to the dais and opened the musical box, a beautiful magical instrument, which I have never seen anywhere except at Newton. The box was made of walnut or some such patterned wood as smooth as polished marble and when you opened it, it gleamed like a golden lamp because everything inside was made of brass – a long cylinder with tiny spikes on it gathered closely in places, scattered in others, a row of brass teeth against which the spikes turned to make the tune you chose, brass hinges and sliding arms which held the lid up; a curved brass handle which you raised and lowered to wind the clockwork up and a bar with an ebony knob which moved the cylinder along. On the inside of the lid there was a list of tunes written in old-fashioned curly handwriting and bordered with flowers in blue and gold. Each tune had a number corresponding with the number engraved on the bar which held the teeth. By moving the ebony knob you could get the tune you wanted.

I started it off on a Strathspey and was dancing to the

music all by myself when Granny burst into the room in a rage. There was music in the house on this tragic morning and I – she could not believe her eyes – was committing the blasphemy of dancing. She shut the musical box with a bang. When you closed the lid it stopped; there was no switch.

——— Have you no feeling for Uncle Alick?

She rushed to the window stretching out her arms, dress and black muslin scarf flying, like a mad woman, and drew the curtains. In the darkness which also cast me into gloom she seized my wrist and dragged me out. I did have a feeling for Uncle Alick. I had been alarmed and very sad when my mother told me before breakfast that he had died in the night. It was the first death I had been near to and in spite of the impossibility of understanding what he said we all liked him and admired him for the adventurous life he had led, which we knew of from his brothers and our parents. His was one of the many lives I wanted to lead then – sheep farming in Australia, gold prospecting some-where. Like many Scotsmen of any social class he could not have earned a living at home.

And now, sixty years afterwards, I know that Granny's rage in the billiard room was inspired not so much by the music as by the horror of her brother's death.

\*

We went to many schools after Miss Squair's as we moved from place to place where my father found jobs. I remember three of them; one in Buxton, Derbyshire, while my father was managing a factory at Manchester where disabled soldiers worked, one in Buckinghamshire and one in London. I did not like any of them. I hated the Bucking-hamshire one enough to rename it Dotheboys Hall when I read *Nicholas Nickleby* later. It belonged to an eccentric and sadistic couple who, in those days before private schools were subject to inspection, punished the boys not only with cricket bats and canes, pulling hair and punching faces, but by near starvation – their favourite punishment, I think, because it cut down expenditure on food. For a small offence you were deprived of jam at tea or pudding at dinner and sat at the table watching those who were not guilty eat. A boy called Ian Gordon who was a special friend of mine was locked up in an upstairs room for a week on a diet of dry bread and water because he could not learn by heart the words of the Sermon on the Mount. 'Blessed are the meek, etc.' He was meek. That was his trouble.

That school had been highly recommended to my parents by the Hall family of Nairn, son and daughter-in-law of The O'Toole, whose son Christopher was my schoolmate at Dotheboys Hall. But they lived near it at that time and he as a dayboy did not know what was going on. When at last my parents found out, they moved me to University College School in London where all the boys were dayboys. It was there that a misfortune which turned out to be good fortune happened to me – a circumstance that occurs in many people's lives. At the time it seemed to be a calamity. I was eleven years old when my eyes suddenly went wrong.

I remember every detail of that November day during my second year at University College School and of the sleepless night that followed.

On the previous afternoon at Rugby football in which I played Forward – which now seems most improbable for although I was taller than most boys of my age, my thighs and the calves of my legs stronger – perhaps from climbing the Cairn Gorms so often – my shoulders were narrow and my eyes, without spectacles which of course I could not wear at games, so weak that the ball was invisible to me most of the time and the other players blurred like white ghosts, someone on my own side kicked me on the temple just at the side of my right eye. It did not hurt much until I was on the bus on my way home and I went on playing until we won the game.

We had geography next morning, which I liked, and each of us had a section of the ordnance survey map before him on his desk. They are beautiful maps, as everybody knows, delightfully precise and well printed. Almost every country house and even spring wells are marked, woods made of little dots, common land green and the sea in shades of blue, pale or deep according to depth. The geography master asked us to find a town, a small one in Wales which I had never heard of, with a long name which he wrote on the blackboard and which we laughed at in the dinner break, inventing our own versions of it, most of them obscene.

When I looked at the squares for large towns and the round black dots for smaller ones, each was immediately covered by a shapeless green patch. Only by glancing to the side of it, by shifting the patch to one side, could I make out the mark.

After dinner we had rifle practice in the range in the basement of the school. This, although I was the very worst of the OTC cadets, scarcely able to see the targets, small cardboard squares with rings printed on them and a bullseye in the middle, was my favourite sport at school. Is it a sport? It was conducted by a fierce pot-bellied Sergeant Major dressed up in a grand uniform. I loved the rifle range, the smell of gunpowder, our miniature bore rifles and tiny bullets in copper cartridge cases. I loved lying at the dark end face down on a sandbag and aiming at one of the squares, each of which had a light above it. My bullets normally fell into the pit beyond, but occasionally I succeeded in piercing some part of the square.

During this rifle practice, the last in my life, which took place on what turned out to be my last day at UCS, the target before me was obscured by protozoa, the simplest of all animals which has no sexual life, is fluid, acellular, metamorphic and reproduces itself by splitting into parts. Protozoa were for me the best part of biology lessons. I liked the names these creatures had been given, their extraordinary shapes, which were vividly illustrated in our book, and I had learned a good deal about all four classes.

The simplest of all these simple animals is the amoeba which is to be found on the mud at the bottom of fresh water pools. People with good sight can just see it with the naked eye as a tiny white speck. We saw our living specimens under microscopes; none remained the same shape for more than a moment, they were composed of protoplasm, a jelly-like material with an external ectoplasm and an inner more opaque endoplasm in which was a round colourless body called the nucleus. I remember how the diagrams and drawings of protozoa in our book were colourless. Some of those which began to inhabit my eyes that day were colourless too, resembling cobwebs or shifting hairs, but most which came and went, taking me by surprise and giving me some pleasure each time, were green, red or mauve, sometimes containing yellowish blobs that moved about as their fluid bodies slid across my eyes. From that day for about six weeks, after which I regained normal vision (my normal), everything I looked directly at was hidden by amoebae, but as soon as I stopped staring, straining, the coloured shapes flowed to one side and I could catch sight, from the corner of my eye, of whatever object it was that interested me. Looking at houses from the top of the open bus on my way home, I saw similar translucent screens; they appeared in the white bread and butter at tea. I told my sisters what funny things I had been seeing all day and Mother, who did not sit down to tea with us in those days, but wandered in and out with little things for us from the kitchen where she was preparing vegetables for dinner, overheard me, stood still with a plate of biscuits in her hand and an expression on her face which frightened me, and said,

——— You've been seeing coloured spots before your eyes?

——— Only today, Mummy. I described them again.

I know now that during that tea time with only the children at the table and she working hard in the kitchen next door, an anxiety about me which was to last all her life settled in her mind.

She had suffered many cruel adversities during the war, the death in infancy of our baby sister Lily, her own severe illness at the time, the drowning in a torpedoed civilian ship of Bill, my father's younger brother, the almost mortal wounding of my father whose mutilated living body had been sent home to her from a field hospital in France. My older sisters remember how she nursed him as he lay for weeks in a darkened room and how they had to creep about on tiptoe. And soon I was to be in a darkened room.

Instead of going to school next day I went with her by bus to Dr Burnford's house in Wimpole Street or Devonshire

Place; I forget. He was a famous specialist and I suppose an expensive one to consult, but he treated poor people without any payment and according to the tradition then existent, no daughter or son of a doctor had to pay. He had, my mother told me, saved her life in the wartime. He was a close friend of hers and I was not afraid of him. I had often been taken to see him. But sometimes his jokes and satirical teasing embarrassed me. I could not understand them and answered solemnly.

There was about his mouth and eyes a satirical look, not unkindly. His sense of humour was something like my mother's which must have been one reason for her fondness for him, that deep affection which amounted, I now believe, to love. When I was small his blackness frightened me. His hair was blacker than Granma's sable muff, his chin and the shaven parts of his cheeks were blue, his forehead, neck and the whole of his face dusky with here and there a ruddy glow beneath the skin. He was handsome, intelligent, unmistakably Jewish. Mother told me he had changed his name from Bernstein, not only because so many English people hated Jews, but because in 1914 they had been taught to hate Germans as well. I knew his face in detail because every time I came to see him he peered into my eyes through a small spyglass torch and sat on a stool very close about a foot away from me. He did this again on that foggy November day. Then he went over to the window and spoke to my mother so quietly that I could not distinguish a word. Then she came to me, saying, 'Where's your cap? We are going to Mr Maclehose.' His house in Harley Street was at the most five minutes walk away, but Dr Burnford would not let us walk. We got in beside him in the front seat of his long car and he drove us there, which was for me by far the best part of that peculiar day.

Mr Maclehose had been my oculist since I was three years old. He was cadaverous not only in the face but all over. His fingers were like wax candles, except when they moved. He was tall and always dressed like a funeral mute. He treated me as though I was an adult. The only thing about him that I ever feared was the way he fingered my eyelids and eyes; to this day I am like a nervous twisting cat if

anybody tries to relieve me of a speck of dust from my eye.
Mr Maclehose asked my mother to wait in an adjoining
room, furnished with out of date copies of *The Field* and
*Punch*, and took me into his black closet whose only lamp
shone on a letter board for testing sight. During the longest
examination he had ever made of me he had to inflict
several distresses, new to me and only one old one which
he rarely used and which I dreaded more than any. For this
he took something shaped like an orange-stick and rolled
back my eyelids on it, as one might roll a map on to a pole.

When my turn came to sit in the ante-chamber my
mother went away with Mr Maclehose and stayed away so
long that I thought they had gone out together for coffee. I
was in a bad mood when she returned. But in the hall she
asked a tonsured cipher to find a taxi for us, which put me
in a good mood again; it was a surprise and I worked it out
quickly as twice as long a ride as from our house to Euston.
We never took taxis unless we were going somewhere with
trunks.

The cipher stepped on to the pavement, leaving the front
door open behind him, and within two seconds he was
holding a taxi door open for us. As I waited for my mother
to get in, I saw her give him a coin, which annoyed me –
why should anyone get paid for waving his hand in the
street? – but I did not say so; I could not say anything to
Mother, she was distraught, and in the taxi she said
nothing to me, and only now and then made her usual
taxi-going remarks, 'I knew he'd miss that turning. This
really is a long way round. Robin says they do it on
purpose. I'll tell him, I think,' (leaning forward) and (sitting
back), 'Oh, well, I suppose we'll just have to let him
manage.'

We went into the drawing room where Mrs Lunnon had
lit the fire; we could hear her upstairs cleaning the
bedrooms. We were alone together – my father at work, the
others at school.

Mother asked how much Mr Maclehose had told me and
I said, 'Nothing. Except, your eyes will get better if you do
what you're told. If you rest for a while.'

—— Can you pretend to be ill, do you think? my mother
said.

——— Old Kendal will soon find out. (Guy Kendal was the headmaster.) This made her smile and say,

——— I mean pretend to yourself. You see David – your eyes – Oh, how did it happen? She stopped. She took a handkerchief out of her purse. I said,

——— Oh, Mummy, don't. It's only spots. Lots of people see spots and they go away. Look at Daddy's General in the Piffers.

——— That was too much whisky and soda. Liver spots. You don't drink much whisky and soda, do you David? She laughed, then moving to a chair beside me and holding my hand, she described the cure that Maclehose had recommended, without telling me how long it was likely to take.

I was to go to bed that very afternoon and lie there in a darkened room -- for at least six weeks, but that she did not say. I was to give up reading and writing entirely – until I had stopped growing at about the age of twenty-one, but she did not tell me for how long this, the most difficult part of the cure, would last.

Gradually, during those six weeks in bed, during which she and Father read aloud to me and a young man came daily from the Blind School in Great Portland Street to teach me Braille, I learned the rest of my cure. I could see that it was difficult for my mother to tell me the parts of it most distressing to a boy, but she had to tell me before she allowed me to get dressed and walk about the house again, because any one mistaken action might have revived the Protozoa in my eyes.

I was never to exert myself, lift weighty objects, carry suitcases, never to play games, not even cricket, keep upright all the time – if I dropped something and wished to pick it up I must curtsey, feeling for it with my hand, not looking down at the floor. Diving was strictly forbidden. Running was forbidden at first, but would probably be permitted after a few years had elapsed.

Mr Maclehose did not consider the kick on my head to be the cause of the haemorrhage behind my eyes. It may have hastened it, he said. But certain bloodvessels were very weak and, kick or no kick, would have soon begun to leak.

*

While I lay in my darkened room all through those long boring six weeks my parents made a wise decision which was to benefit me for the rest of my life. They decided to send me to live in Nairn, to find private tutors for me there. It is true that good tutors would have been more easy to find in London, but they had perceived, foreseen, the doom that would have beset me there, living at home as before, meeting my old schoolfriends daily on the streets but no longer going to school. How could I have explained it to them? What could I have said when one asked me to play tennis with him, where to hide when the gang came round to take me along with them on an evening's rampage?

Mother wrote to her sister Margery who lived with Granma at Tigh-na-Rosan and Margery found two dominies who were willing and able to keep my education going as best they could. Only one of these was a real dominie – Mr Rae, who had been a schoolmaster all his life and had recently retired from the headmastership of Alton Burn, a prep school just outside Nairn. The other was Canon Ballard, minister of the Episcopal Church – or Kirk as he preferred to call it, not liking the English connotation of the word 'episcopal' – Canon Ballard whose boring sermons I had sat through for many years. I was to visit blind Mrs Grimmett in the Fishertown for lessons in Braille. The worst part of the whole arrangement was the idea of living with Granma, but my mother reminded me that Margery would be there all the time; if anything went wrong, tell Margery and Margery would write home for me and say whatever I wanted to say. She would, I knew, and yet it is not the same; a letter must be private between two people only.

I spent the Christmas holidays at home in London and I remember liking it more than most Christmases. Mary and Joan were home from The Vyne, their school in Hampshire, and one of them brought a girl friend with her whose slanting Siamese-like eyes seemed lovely to me. Barbara, who always looked after everyone and became anxious when anyone was ill, took special care of me.

When all the school terms began, I set forth for Nairn. Mother had intended to come with me, spend the day at Tigh-na-Rosan and return to London by the night train on the same afternoon. But nothing had been organised in time for that. Mary and Joan were back at The Vyne and Barbara would get home from her day school long before Father could leave his office.

So I travelled alone. I was glad. To go alone with my mother by the same night train, 7.30 pm from platform 13 at Euston, that had brought us joyfully away from London for so many years, would have been a sorry travesty.

It was easy in January for Father to find me a third class carriage to myself. He hired a pillow and a blanket for me from the platform trolley, then walked all the way down the train to the guard's van to tell the guard where I was and would he keep an eye on me. Luckily, I knew nothing of this at the time, but I did wonder later why the guard kept opening the door of my carriage and waking me up during the night. Mother, who had given me plenty of sandwiches and ample spending money, said that if I felt hungry in the early morning I must hold out until the train crossed the border – not waste my money on English food trolleys, such as those of Carlisle which sold rubbish, but to wait at least till the train stopped at Carstairs; better still Perth where the platform trolley sold hot mutton pies, which with a bap and a cup of tea would last me until Margery made a real breakfast for me at Nairn.

My mother was kissing me and hugging me as I leant out of the window. My father looked shy and embarrassed. Barbara whom Mother lifted up to me, clutched me and seemed to be crying, or just about to cry. Then suddenly the whistle went, the two engines pulling the train hissed, and I was waving, absentmindedly, not thinking of Barbara or my parents anymore. And they were leaving. But they were strangers – those three growing further and further from me as the train gathered speed.

At Perth in the early morning I walked down the corridor and stood on the platform for a while, remembering how Father used always to walk to the guard's van there to make sure that none of our luggage had been put out at the wrong station during the night.

Perth platform had always been in daylight then, the summer sun long risen, but on the morning of my lonely arrival it was lit only by dingy hanging lamps. The platform was crowded, not so much by passengers as by people selling things from basket trays slung from their necks, from tricycle trollies on which the salesman rode, from double decker four wheeled trolleys pushed by a man and a boy who helped him to hand the stuff into the train. You could buy sweets, tobacco, newspapers, maps, ginger beer, lemonade, tea, cakes, sandwiches and the famous hot mutton pies. I fetched my pillow and blanket and gave them to the pillow girl who said,

—— Twas a braw nicht, I'm thinking, but ye were on your lonesome?

—— Aye.

—— Well now, you're a canny loon, or look to be. Next time ye travel north, send word for Meg o' Perth and she'll go south to bring you. Mind my name well now. Meg. They all know Meg. And Meg will share your pillow wi'ye and we will travel couthie warm togither.

She laughed and pushed her barrow further up the train. The mutton pie man came next. I took mine and two baps and a mug of sweet tea and put them into my carriage.

There was still plenty of time by the station clock for me to walk up the platform and watch the engines being changed, for now we had left the LMS and joined the old Highland Line with its yellow carriages and red engines. There were a few through coaches from England stuck on to the back of the Highland train and I did not have to move from mine. We had had two engines to pull us out of Euston up that steep incline known as Camden Bank. One of these had been taken off at our first stop – either Watford or Rugby and one had had sufficient power to pull the train over the Pennines, through the Lake District and the border hills to Perth, where the steepest climb of all began across the central highlands.

I had never seen the countryside in winter before – the trees and bushes leafless black, the frozen ploughed fields to the north of Perth and then, within an hour or so you could see nothing from the windows of the train except snow, in various shapes, tents of it covering trees, giant white tea cosies, long rolls of blankets lying on the ground.

As the train slowed down at Nairn, leaning from the window to watch the signalman and fireman swap their single line safety tokens, I saw Michie. He was crossing the iron footbridge towards the platform on to which I was about to step. How could he have known I was coming to Nairn? I would be ashamed to arrive by cab at Granma's; it was only twenty minutes walk; and sixpence would not nearly pay his fare. Besides, he had often told me that it wasn't worth his while to harness up his horse in winter to meet the night train from the South. The day trains from Aberdeen and Edinburgh were the only ones that carried winter passengers who could afford a cab.

Michie reached the platform just as the train stopped. I could see no one else and heard no doors banging to show that people had got out. Crouching low along the corridor I locked myself in to the WC determined to escape from Michie by travelling on to Gollanfield Junction and walking back to Nairn. But of course I had left my suitcase in the carriage. Michie saw it at once and got in to fetch it expecting to find me. I heard the station master speaking to him anxiously. The train was already almost four hours late for Inverness and he did not want another second's delay. Then I heard my aunt Margery's voice and knew that my plan had foundered.

—— Yes, that's his case. I know it. And anyway look at the label.

—— Then maybe he's down on the platform, ma'am.

—— No one got off the train. I was watching from the waiting room window all the time. Margery began to cry,

—— David? David! Oh, the stupid boy, where is he?

At this I slid the WC bolt silently back and walked down the corridor towards them.

—— O, there you are, I said. O, it's nice you came to meet me!

It was she who had ordered Michie and his cab. A well meant act, I know, but for me the first of a long line of humiliating acts. From now on I was an invalid incapable of achieving a twenty minute walk along flat roads.

What puzzled and alarmed me was Margery's choice of Michie as the one to drive us. If I was to be coddled for the rest of my life, I thought one of the motor cabs would do better. And then Granma hated Michie. Margery, absent-minded as she was, with her thoughts only on her book, must have known that well, because no one could live at Tigh-na-Rosan without hearing the tirades with which Granma assaulted Michie whenever she caught him at the kitchen door wooing the cook with one of his 'bit gifties'. Granma drove him away, threatened him with the police, accused him of poaching the salmon and trout with lamps and nets at night, of snaring the hares on the game preserve of Achareidh, of trapping the birds with birdlime.

Therefore I did not relish the prospect of our arrival at the house. She would hear the horse's hoofs far off, I knew, and be standing like a judgement at the gate.

But suddenly as Michie opened the cab door for Margery to get in, and just as I was about to step in after her, everything changed. I understood why she had sent for Michie, the only person she knew who would really welcome me on my solitary arrival, who could ease the desolation that lay before me – that dreary prospect of living alone with old people in a town that had once been enlivened by adventure, crammed with excitement among boys and girls of my own age. Everything suddenly changed because Margery, turning back towards me with one foot on the step, said, 'Why not ride on the box with Michie, David? May he get up with you?'

—— Most certainly he can, Mrs Walker. And I'll gie him the reins and he can drive for my fingers are numbed with the cold.

—— O, you better drive, said Margery laughing as he shut her into the cab.

As soon as we had emerged from the traffic of the High Street and crossed the perilous Inverness Road into the straight length of Albert Street, he did give me the reins and I drove, making only one mistake as we turned a sharp corner and a hind wheel hit the kerb. Here Michie put his hands over mine and pulled the horse's head sharply out from the pavement.

—— Ye maun take your corners wide, Davy loon. Ye have four wheels under ye, mind. It's no like Duncan's milk float ye are used to. Two wheels winna snick a corner.

At the next corner, knowing that once we turned it we would come into Granma's view – What possessed you Margery to let the boy sit out there? In this weather, and just out of an overheated train? – I pulled the horse up, gave the reins to Michie and climbed down to sit with Margery inside the cab.

Granma was standing in the open gateway as we arrived. I got out first, wondering what to say to her, but it was she who spoke.

—— Ladies first, she said. Why did you not let your Aunt Margery leave the carriage before you?

I knew she was wrong. Perhaps she was maliciously trying to fault me or perhaps having been for so many years without a male escort she had forgotten that the only doors through which a gentleman should precede a lady are those of vehicles – motorcars, railway carriages, even the step of a bus. It is so that he may turn and hand her down. My father had taught me this years before. I knew instinctively that Granma knew it. I looked at her hatefully. Then took Margery's hand as she stepped out of the cab.

*

I suppose Granma had kind and gentle qualities – she was my mother's mother – and I suppose she could speak in an ordinary calm voice and have conversations with friends – she had after all brought up three daughters and a son renowned for their liveliness, intelligence and wit – yet after those three years of living with her, from the age of eleven to fourteen I can remember nothing but acerbity issuing from her tight mouth. Perhaps the premature death of her husband had sunk her spirits so low that during the ensuing years they became entirely hidden, until by the time I knew her they were lost to her entirely, buried deep in her unconscious mind as a protection against pain.

I cannot remember ever hearing her use my Christian name in the vocative once during those three years.

—— Do not take so much salt to your meat. It is uncomplimentary. Janet's cooking is adequate.

—— If you must take salt, do not splatter it. Place a half a spoonful on the side of your plate.

—— Does salt cost a lot then, Granma?

The granite stare. Grey granite.

—— I cannot bear to sit beside you. You have not washed your hands.

—— I did wash them, Granma. It hasn't all come off.

—— Then leave the table and wash them properly.

The dung from the byre and stable had come off easily before dinner with ordinary soap, but there was no green soft soap in the lavatory and yellow grease and black oil from ploughs and harrows were indelible; and then, from grooming horses, every pore on my fingers and the backs of my hands was ingrained with fine, grey scurf; and as I never bothered to wash after milking my hands began to smell sour soon afterwards. Sour milk wins against hurried soaping.

Cleanliness is godliness, love is a paltry ridiculous joke, sex, even thoughts of it, are wicked and filthy; dance, song and pictures are the work of Satan. Scotch morality is filled with such perverted notions and even though Granma adhered to the Episcopal Church, which is said to be less puritanical than the others, she abode by them all. The vice of meanness, condemned in every other country, is in Scotland translated into a virtue called 'thrift'. Granma was thrifty. The downstairs rooms of Tigh-na-Rosan were lit by gas, by wall bracket lamps that gave a good light. But the only light in my bedroom was one candle which burned in an ordinary saucer-shaped candlestick. I was supposed to bring it down every morning and put it into the pantry so that I could put a match to it in the evening and light my way upstairs to bed. But often I forgot to bring it down.

One evening when I went to the pantry and saw I had forgotten it, I remembered that I had used my last match on the night before. I went back into the drawing room to ask Granma for a new box.

—— Bring your box, she said.

So I had to grope my way upstairs in the dark and feel

about my bedroom till I found the empty box. Granma unlocked a drawer of her writing table, took a full box out and placed four matches in my empty box.

But I had my revenge a few weeks later, or I should say that God avenged me, bringing me by His subtle vengeance the only happy experience I had ever had with Granma. She had been out to tea with friends and was late in coming home. I had let the drawing-room fire get low and was sitting in the dark reading *The Mill on the Floss* in Braille. On the mantelpiece she always kept a vase full of spills which she made out of old envelopes for lighting the gas from the fire. She never would waste a match on the gas lamps. But this evening someone – probably Margery – had moved the spills from their usual place. I watched Granma feeling along the mantelpiece till she found a piece of paper, which she folded neatly into a spill. This she lit from the embers of the fire which I had allowed to die. She put the flaming end to the two gas lamps and brushing it out against the fireplace let the half-burnt end drop into the fender. She left the room without looking at it, but I idly picked it up. It was a five pound note, which in those days were large white sheets of paper, beautifully inscribed in black italics, with a printed number on the top left hand corner and the same number on the bottom right. People used to cut them in half for safety and send each piece in a separate envelope by post, but unless you had the two numebrs to match it was worthless. Granma's note had only one number now; the other had been burnt away.

I wished I had not seen it. It was embarrassing and, to my surprise, I felt sorry for her. I thought of throwing the remains of the note on to the fire but dared not, first because she might accuse me of wasting a perfectly good half spill and secondly because she was bound to remember some time soon that she had lost £5. Or could it have been Margery's? It was most unlike Granma to leave as much as one farthing lying on the mantelpiece.

I made up my mind that she must see it. I unrolled it and laid it flat on the mantelpiece, putting some small ornament on it to hold it down, and sat down again pretending to read, but my fingers were trembling at the thought of

Granma's reappearance, and the Braille dots meant nothing to me.

She came in. She picked up a letter and an opened envelope. When she saw the burnt £5, she held it up against the lamp without a word, then folded it and put it into the envelope with the letter. Neither she nor I ever spoke about it.

*

The invisible wire joining Granma and me, became so taut that it had to snap or slacken. I guess it was Margery's softening inflow that slackened it, but that also was invisible and had to work hard against me, who was doing my best to tighten the wire, to snap it once and for all.

If Granma and I had seen more of Margery we would have been much happier together. I liked her and admired her because she was a writer. But she was ill and often had meals by herself, often spent the winter evenings upstairs in her room and always, summer and winter, snow, rain or shine sat working in a specially made hut in the Tigh-na-Rosan garden. Her little dog Puck was always out there with her. The hut was piled with books and papers, and she typed on a large German typewriter which had three banks of keys and no shift key. Margery, who had started her book in London when she worked as a doctor's secretary at University College Hospital, had been advised to go home to Nairn because she had TB, and to get as much fresh air as she could. She had worked for Lord Rhondda during the war who, as food minister, had successfully established rationing from 1917 to 1918. When she was applying for that job she had asked Uncle Robert to write to Rhondda recommending her. His letter included the phrase, 'My niece, Mrs Walker, is an excellent typewriter' – which became a family joke although that word was ordinarily used for 'typist' in his youth. I suppose it was through Lord Rhondda and the interest of his ministry in Public Health that she made many friends in the medical profession – our family tradition in medicine must have made her known to them too. She was certainly respected – my mother used to tell me jokes about how shy she was, often mistaking compliments for criticism – and the names given to acknowledge personal help in the foreword to her book are impressive.

It is a good book called *Pioneers of Public Health*, containing twenty-one biographical essays starting with Thomas Sydenham, who died in 1689 and ending with Lieutenant General Sir William Leishman who died in 1926. The subtitle of the book is *The Story of Some Benefactors of the Human Race*.

Unfortunately for Margery, it was published in 1930 not long after Paul de Kruifs' *The Microbe Hunters*, a similar book which quickly became a bestseller.

I have just taken Margery's book from the shelf to look at it. The preliminary pages sadden me.

It is dedicated to my cousin Ronald who died or was killed in a mysterious way in South America in 1928, two years before the book came out. Ronald often came to stay at Tigh-na-Rosan to be with his mother. He was five or six years older than me and had a motorbike. Another hero.

To the
BRIGHT MEMORY OF MY ONLY SON
RONALD B. WALKER
B.A. of King's College
Cambridge
WHO DIED IN THE TROPICS
MAY 1928

And then at the end of her preface Margery puts

M. E. M. WALKER
Tigh-na-Rosan
NAIRN, 1929.

These simple words would not make anyone else sad. But Margery died a few years later in a London hospital and I was alone with my mother when she received that news. And 'Tigh-na-Rosan, Nairn, 1929' is of private significance to me, marking as it does the end of a period unique in my life. In the autumn of 1928 I had left Nairn for London and, except as a holiday-maker, was never to live that life again.

I have no doubt now that her book, and probably even the fear that she would die before she had finished it, kept her aloof from the wire – that taut wire of enmity between Granma and me. If she had intervened earlier in our often silent quarrels my hatred of Granma and her exasperation with me would have faded, instead of lasting all our lives. What Margery did in the end to slacken the wire was more by chance than design, for she overheard one of her mother's provocative remarks to me. What I did next morning in asserting my first quarter inch of independence arose by chance, too, for I overheard the rebuke she made to her mother and it gave me courage for the act, which was minuscule physically but morally powerful enough to lead to others which made my life at Tigh-na-Rosan tolerable and even, I suspect, engendered in the crevices of my grandmother's sealed heart some secret respect for me.

Ours was a great quarrel conducted not by open government but by the secret services. Between two nations it would have led to war. Great quarrels are born of great issues: possession of land, possession of woman, the dividing up of inherited jewellery. Ours was born of a pinch of salt and a speck of cow dung.

Margery was for once spending the evening downstairs in the drawing room, sitting reading by the fire in the chair I usually sat in. Granma's chair was empty. We could hear her moving about upstairs. I was sitting at the card table – still reading *The Mill on the Floss*. I was a slow Braille reader and the books are so heavy and bulky that it speeded me up a bit to lay mine on a table rather than balance it on my knee. Suddenly I heard my grandmother's voice.

—— Margery! Is David in there?

—— Yes.

—— Send him out to me at once.

Margery smiled to me as though to say – Don't burst with rage. But what she said was

—— Granma wants to speak to you. She's in the hall.

Granma was holding a candle to the carpet, but as the shadow of the candlestick hid what she was trying to show me I found it difficult to respond to her questions.

—— What is this, do you suppose?

—— I can't see in this light.

—— You must have an idea, I suppose.

—— I can smell it all right. It's cow dung, I'd say. I'm sorry.

—— Do not use that language in this house. If it is manure, then what makes it black? Test with your finger if you can't see. I felt and looked at my finger in the light of her candle. It was oil. Always humble and afraid, I apologised to her profusely, explaining that the hobnails on my boots caught up the mucky straw and then if you trod in some oil by mistake it all stuck together, and the doormat doesn't work with hobnailed boots.

—— Why do you wear them, then?

—— All the men wear them.

—— You are not a man. You are a thoughtless, careless, little boy. Fetch soap and water and a scrubbing brush and clear it up at once.

—— It's too dark, Granma. I'll do it in the morning.

I knew that Janet would do it for me early before anyone else was up, but Granma said the morning would not do; the oil would have sunk further into the carpet by then.

The drawing room door had been standing ajar all this time and Margery had heard everything. She now came into the hall.

—— Come and sit down, Mother. I've something to tell you. David, it's long past your bedtime. Don't forget your book.

On the way to fetch my candle from the pantry, I stopped to eavesdrop.

—— You forget yourself sometimes, Mother. Janet or I will clean the carpet.

—— No. He must clear his own mess up.

—— He is not allowed to stoop.

—— He can kneel. If he can kneel to mend his bicycle puncture, he can kneel to scrub the carpet.

Cowdung, even when laced with oil, is not enough to make a Great Quarrel. No explosion will take place without a pinch of salt. This I supplied at breakfast next morning. I could not have consciously known at the time any more clearly than I now know whether I did it on purpose to provoke Granma, and by that provocation purify the ugly negatives that had governed our relationship ever since the moment when she accused me of dismounting from Michie's cab the wrong way; or whether it happened by chance, as our other quarrels about salt had happened. For she was right, I did put too much salt on my food, partly from habit – the more you get used to the more you want – and partly from nervousness, for something to do with my hands as we sat in crabbed silence over meals, my mind bursting with things I longed to tell her about the farm and horses, the splendid herring catch that week, the gipsies' encampment on the carse, but afraid to tell her anything for fear of sacrilege. Over the high and holy joy of my offering she could walk with cloven hooves like the Devil, crushing my spirit, pulverising the temple in which I sometimes dwelt. Meanwhile she kept glancing at me, throughout meals, at my fingernails for blackness and bitten-ness, my ears for accumulated dirt, my tangled mop of curly hair that looked just the same before or after a brushing.

Porridge for her, as for most Scotchwomen of her class and generation, was a peripatetic course. I sat down to mine but she wandered anywhere with her bowl in one hand and spoon in the other, round the dining room table to the window where she would stand for some seconds looking out at the weather but making no comment on it, out into the hall, through the drawing room and music room and sometimes into the kitchen to speak to Janet about lunch. I suspected her of taking these porridgy walks as a government inspector looking for dust or stains on the carpet, but I felt safe that morning because Janet, who would always do anything for me, had cleaned my messy boot mark away. Not even the stark naked eye of my grandmother could detect a trace of oil.

The reason for our quarrel had been removed. And yet making sure that she was watching I sprinkled salt on my porridge. The porridge tureen was on a hot plate on the sideboard, milk, salt and things on the table. Granma had helped herself to porridge and was standing watching me

as I sat down to mine. To enrage her still more I did not even
use the salt spoon. I picked up as much as I could between
finger and thumb and sprinkled it over my porridge till the
plate looked as though it had been kept out all night in the
snow.

—— That is deliberate! said Granma. I have been con-
sidering some course of action during these last weeks.
From now on you take your meals in the kitchen.

—— I like eating with Janet. You get more.

—— Take your plate into the kitchen.

—— No, Granma.

She left the dining room. For once, for probably the only
time in her life she slammed the door behind her.

There was a delicious smell of kippers from the hot plate
on the sideboard which almost quenched my pride. I
stuffed all the toast into my pocket instead, without waiting
to butter it, and peeping to make sure the old woman had
gone to the back of the house, seized my coat and ran to the
fuchsia bush where I kept my bicycle. The bush was a snow
house, an igloo, its white roof and walls visible from Tigh-
na-Rosan's front windows in winter, its leaves and red
drooping blossoms forming a curtain all summer, under
which I kept my bike. One tyre was soft, but not flat. I
decided not to waste time pumping it up. It was my
courage, so speedily deflated immediately after the incident of the salt, that needed pumping up, and I knew to my
shame that if Granma opened the front door and called me I
would go to her like an obedient dog. Not daring to look at
the windows or door, I pushed my bike through the snow
to the gate. The snow was soft and deep in the garden. I
feared I might not be able to ride at all. Then, when I
reached the front gate, still in full view of the windows, I
could not open it. Its latch had frozen into its socket during
the night. I had to kick the snow away till I found a stone to
bang it with. All this took time, noise and terror. But I got
safely away.

I had two or three falls on the way to Sandwood Farm.
Ruts in the snow had frozen hard during the night and my
front wheel caught in them as in tramlines. In my hasty
escape I had brought neither cap nor gloves. I could not feel

the handlebars with my fingers, clutched them clumsily with the palms of my hands, and my ears felt as if someone had burned them with a red-hot needle. But it was a joyful ride. I was free and proud and for the present oblivious of the future at Tigh-na-Rosan, which had to begin, unless I risked the fuss of a search party, at lunchtime, half past one.

The sky was snowy, blackish and dusky to the west before me, but lighter overhead. I knew it was too cold for any more snow to fall, the frost too hard, the east wind blowing me towards Sandwood far too fierce for snow, and I felt it on my neck as though I had never felt an east wind before and I looked at and listened to the country as though I had never travelled through it under snow before.

Snow makes all the land silent. Individual sounds are startling, lonely, clear.

At the edge of the Tradespark woods where they open on to wide fields about halfway between Nairn and Sandwood I heard two shots near me and a scream a second away. I knew of course that the shot came from a man hiding in the trees and the scream was a hare's but as I could see neither of them, it was like hearing sounds in the dark. As I stopped and put my foot on the ground to look, I likened the sound of the double-barrelled shotgun to two small dynamite shots in a stone quarry, and the scream to a girl's in pain or fear.

Further on, just beside me, a lark rose from a whin bush where it had probably taken shelter from the snow, for usually when they take a rest from flying they stay on open land. I did not see it but the loudness of its song made me know it was near me and I heard it as it rose and rose into the sky, twirling its notes like little bells and whistles round and round, and every second more distant from me. It was separate and alone. In summer its song would have mingled with many sounds.

Snow had smoothed the fields and bushes and all the branches of the trees; the dark, sharp ridges of newly ploughed land, the rough tussocky pastures which I knew to be there were flat and pure beneath a white tablecloth. Even jagged rocks were round and white and the strands of barbed wire above the stone dykes were dotted with blobs instead of spikes; the rectangular tops of the posts that held them were cushions; the thorns of whin bushes were shielded, the blackthorn's blackness was invisible, its thorns blunted. Near Sandwood there was one peewit crying 'pee-weet, pee-weet'. It was large enough for me to see.

The cart track from the Inverness road up to the farm was impossible to ride on. I half pushed, half carried my bike up the hill to the shelter of the steading. Githa, who was washing milk cans, heard me and came to the dairy door and when she saw my bare head burst out laughing, which annoyed me.

—— Davy! What happened to your bonnet? Did ye lose it on the road this weather?

—— Where's Duncan and Bob? Where's the horses? Out this weather?

—— They went before light for timber to the mill. What else can a man do in the frost unless lie abed. But ye are gey early yourself. I doubt something's amiss.

I put my bike into the cart shed without replying. If she was in, and all the men out, her younger sister Ireen would probably be at home. Two more women. Why cycle all the way from Tigh-na-Rosan to hear them chatter?

—— You look to be famished, said Githa. Come in to the house and I'll make the tea.

As she filled the kettle, I saw the black porridge pot standing on the stove.

—— It's stiff standing there those two hours. I'll make ye a rasher and eggs. What is it then, Davy, did ye have a bit differ wi' Mrs Finlay, the day?

—— Aye. Gie' us the porridge Githa. Never heed the rashers.

—— 'Twas your mucky boots, I ken it well. Didn't I tell ye a hundred times – get your feet out o' them at the door and keep a pair of soft shoon there ye can slip into.

In their little house, two up and two down, every movement, almost every word could be heard up or down and now we could hear Ireen singing and clattering about above our heads.

> Aunty Mary
> Had a canary
> Up the leg o'her drawers:
> It whistled for hours
> And frichted the Boers
> And won the Victoria Cross!

Ireen took two jumps to reach the bottom of the stairs and burst into the kitchen.

—— I heard your voice, she said, and came over and ruffled my hair and sang

> I've got a teddy bear
> Blue eyes and curly hair!

– which annoyed me, or I said to myself that it annoyed me but the truth was that the affectionate teasing of these two sisters made me happy. They were older than me – Ireen fourteen, Githa sixteen – but they treated me as an equal. But all the same, what were they? Two more women, who in spite of their welcome and jokes could be ready to find fault at the drop of a hat like any other woman.

—— Is your father away to the sawmill, as well?

They both burst out laughing. I did not know why. They were usually laughing and their laughter often ended in a quarrel, which was that morning about who should muck out the byre, as the men were away, who did it the last time, who lay a-bed while the other was working.

As their voices rose against each other like two frenzied moorhens I left the table and walked across to the byre.

I always avoided mucking out the cows unless I was sure there was no one to watch me. The thick pancakes of dung bedded on sodden straw were too heavy for oculist's rules. The graip, as the four-prong fork was called, was heavy too, and wide; to raise it loaded and tip it into the wheelbarrow stressed me and brought blood to my face. So, believing that their quarrel would keep the girls away from me, I assumed the ridiculous posture I had invented for this kind of work, lifting the dung a little at a time with my eyes on the rafters above me and my legs bent at the knee in an awkward curtsey.

I had planned to muck out five cows, which was half of them. After the third I knew I would be late for lunch which would harden the quarrel with Granma in which I was already regretting my part. I had no watch in those days but possessed an instinct for the time, so when Githa came in to tell me to go home I was not surprised.

—— Be quick, she said. Never fash Mrs Finlay more the day. It's me she'll be blaming for holding you and your dinner cold on the table.

She took the graip from my hand. I felt myself blushing, speechless, ashamed, confused, for the snow had silenced her footsteps and I was only aware of her presence when she was inside the byre. I believed she had seen me curtseying. I ran to my bike without a goodbye and pedalled all the way down the hill. It was still freezing hard even in the middle of the day and I made myself later still by letting my front wheel get caught in the rigid narrow rut of a pony cart. I fell with the bike; the chain came off and lay in the snow while I scrambled to my feet. My fingers without gloves were already numb and now, after pressing against the snow as I disentangled myself from the fallen bicycle, they were powerless. With cold and frustration and fear of Granma, I was almost in tears as I fumbled with the chain and cogs when the pony cart which had caused my misfortune rescued me. The snow had silenced its tyres and the pony's hooves and with my head bent down – against the rules – I was not aware of it till I heard the driver's voice crying 'Stand!' I stood upright.

He was telling the pony to stand still, a command familiar to me because I used it myself on the milk round – and Flossie like most of the horses responded to the voices so readily that one could have driven her without reins – but such was the guilt and the fear of my eyes going wrong again that I stood upright and looked at him as he jumped to the ground. He crossed the road to me and looked at me laughing.

—— No bonnet, no mittens! Did your mother let ye oot like thon? Ye are frae Nairn?

—— My mither's doon sooth, I said crossly wishing to be addressed as a man. She disny live in Nairn. I stretched out the town's name as broadly as I could into something like 'Nay-errain', but he was not deceived. He changed his

accent into what he thought was English and said
——  You'll be Lord Finlay's grandson,
I shook my head.
——  I know you. I know. You are Colonel Thomson's
son. A grand man your father, a braw man – I know him
well. Is he in good health?
——  I suppose so.
He fixed my chain on and went back to his pony, saying
'Come and warm your hands.' I watched him slide his
hands one by one underneath the pony's tail, just below
the crupper, and hold them there. 'Come on,' he said, 'it's
the only warm place on the road.'
I wanted to, but stood there watching till he put on his
gloves and drove off. Then I rode away like an outcast. I
had rejected Newton and most of the qualities it stood for. I
privately wished to leave Tigh-na-Rosan and go to live at
Sandwood but Githa had rejected me that morning by
mentioning 'Mrs Finlay' several times as though I was tied
to my grandmother's bootlaces. She and the strange rough
pony cart man by their kindness to me pushed me away
from them into the frigid class I had been born into. The so-
called upper middle class into which I had been born does
not now seem frigid to me, but then it did. The life on the
farm, the readiness with which Githa, Ireen, their brothers
and father said aloud what they felt and meant, their
laughter and unrestrained quarrels released the constric-
tions that Tigh-na-Rosan bound me with. If anyone at
Sandwood shouted angrily at me, I would shout back and
all would be forgotten next minute.
As I was about to pass the tradesman's drive to Newton I
saw Shetland ponies gathered by the fence. That roadside
field had been let out for grazing and their keeper had
thrown their hay over on to the snow at the corner nearest
to me. One of them stood eating with its hind quarters to
the fence. I slid my cold fingers under its tail and feeling
about found it to be a mare. It felt warm, but it was not only
the relief from cold that pleased me.
When I reached Tigh-na-Rosan that day I went straight to
the kitchen by the tradesman's entrance, but that did not
hide me from the dining room windows on my right. I

glanced in, saw Margery and Granma at the table and wheeled my bicycle quickly out of sight, knowing they had seen me. Janet opened the kitchen door and said

—— Your dinner's spoiling in the oven this half hour. Go through to the dining room and I'll bring it. You can wash your hands here at the sink.

—— I'll eat it here.

—— I'm not having you here in the kitchen. What would Mrs Finlay say!

—— It's what 'Mrs Finlay' said. I pronounced her name spitefully and sat down at the kitchen table without washing my hands. Janet was flustered and did not take my dinner out of the oven.

—— Master David, she said, looking out through the window with her broad back to me, you are as good a loon as ever I saw and there's no cause for you to be thrawn.

—— I'm not. I was told to eat here.

Then Margery rescued us and I, obedient as her little Cairn terrier, followed her fearfully into the dining room with Janet as our rearguard, my dinner in her hand. There was no one in the dining room, no need for my fear. Margery sat by me as I ate.

—— Where's Granma?

—— In the drawing room. I wish you could be kinder to her.

—— Kinder?

—— At least not so cruel.

—— What? I said, and when she did not answer, I said What did you say just then?

—— You provoke her. It's as though you enjoy it. You are cruel.

I gaped at her, holding up my knife and fork. I was shocked by her judgment, so suddenly contradicting my opinion of myself. I was shocked but said nothing. How could she call me cruel when everyone else thought me kind?

She took up a pile of books and said she was going to her 'Summer House'.

—— Let me carry them, I said, and we went out on to the white lawn where the snow was unmarked except by her

footsteps and Puck's, to the Summer House. She sat
writing her book in it all winter but always called it her
'Summer House', which I suppose its makers may have
called it for it was intended to be used in summer. It was a
beautiful wooden hut with a sloping roof and one open
side, furnished with table and chair. Within there was a
little room with windows looking out on to the open part,
and into this Margery sometimes retreated, but only in the
wildest stormy weather for the hut was mounted on a
swivel. A light touch would turn its open side away from
the wind or towards the sun.

As she laid out her books and papers, I lingered by her
anxious to make her say more about my cruelty but not
daring to pronounce the word I said only,

——  It's all right for you, you're always writing.

——  You can write in Braille.

——  No one can read it and there's nobody in Nairn to
type it out.

I did not tell her how I hated the fiddly Braille writing
machine with its six keys and stiff brown paper that
slipped.

——  When your eyes are a bit better you can learn
typewriting. Professionals learn blindfold – all by touch.

I thought 'the lawn is blindfold' and when I said

——  The garden's lovely, all smooth and white, she gave
me a look that frightened me, and said

——  In some diseases the patient's skin looks smooth and
healthy. You can't see what's underneath. When's Mr Rae?

——  Not till three.

——  I must do some work. It will soon be dark.

Nairn is far enough north to be blackened by nightfall
between three and four in winter. At mid-winter there was
no daylight until about ten in the morning. There were no
street lamps in our part of the town.

*

Mr Rae lived only two streets away in a stone house
somewhat like Tigh-na-Rosan but smaller with a smaller
tidier garden and no view of the sea. It was his wife who
kept the garden; he was not tidy at all. He wore baggy

knickerbockers and a jacket like a rat-eaten sack frayed at the cuffs and elbows and with charred holes in the pockets which came from his hastily hiding his lighted pipe whenever he heard a hand on the doorknob of his study where I had my lessons. Mrs Rae brought us tea, bread and butter and a cake every time I was there and once after she had gone, when I told him his pocket was kindling, he said that she did not like him smoking in the house. It seemed that, so long as the pipe was invisible, the thick smoke that hung about the bookshelves and ceiling came from some-where else, perhaps from the fireplace which often smoked when the wind was high or the coal damp.

She, who spent most of the year in the garden, was pale and he who spent most of his time reading or writing indoors, taking only an occasional stroll on the links or beach, had a farmer's complexion as if reddened by sun and wind. This puzzled me when I saw them together. The farmers' wives and daughters whom I knew all looked reddish brown – robust – like Githa and Ireen. But of course it is different for country schoolmasters and their wives. As headmaster of Alton Burn School, an isolated house a mile to the west of Nairn bounded on three sides by carse and fields and on the other by the sea, it was he who spent long hours out of doors at games or on walks with the boys and she who made the beds, cooked the meals and washed the linen. The impression made by weather on Mr Rae's cheeks had been deep enough to last until, two years after his retirement to Nairn, he began to teach me. Alton Burn is now a hotel. When I went to look at it recently I thought how much happier my prep school years would have been had my father's work not taken us away from Nairn. Alton Burn was the only preparatory school nearby and, even if I boarded there, the carse and the beach and the sea and the sight of the Black Isle across the firth would have remained with me as part of my life at home. Also, as I discovered when I began to have lessons with Mr Rae, both he and his wife were intelligent and kind, the opposite in character to the people at Dotheboys Hall.

Mr Rae taught me history, mental arithmetic, geography without maps, English, Latin and French – but after the formal part of each lesson was over he read aloud to me, often with passionate excitement, shouting during the dramatic passages, whispering the emotional and sometimes bursting into tears, which embarrassed me greatly although it strengthened my love of him. I read a good deal in Braille during the long dark evenings and I specially liked Braille at night with the book on my thighs and my hands warm beneath the bedclothes, but Mr Rae's speed and mobility were a relief. The startling expression of his voice and face, quick and lively, held my attention even through works that would have bored me and most boys of my age, for he never stooped to me. In the reading, as in the lessons, he treated me as a man who though skilled in some arts wished to learn new ones, stretching my intellect and emotions far beyond the limits that my previous teachers had set as suited to my age. When I told him I had finished *The Mill on the Floss*, he plunged me into *Middlemarch*; when I told him that Walter Scott's novels were boring and how I had crawled through *Ivanhoe* at school he at once took *Guy Mannering* down from a shelf and began to read it aloud to me. We spent almost a year on *Moby Dick* and another on *Les Misérables*, and usually he broke off at a moment of suspense so that I longed for our next meeting as one looks forward to the next episode in a serialised magazine story.

Mr Rae's subject at Oxford University had been Modern History which with literature remained as his most active interest throughout his life. He kept his knowledge of history flexible by borrowing new scholarly works from libraries in Edinburgh and London and buying those few he liked and could afford. Except for the chimney breast which had rose-patterned wallpaper on it all the walls of his study were hidden from wainscot to picture rail by books, and never having seen real tapestry I imagined it to be like this, a warm, faintly varied pattern of leather, gold, black, red, greens, blues and yellows divided into strips by the shiny dark mahogany edges of the shelves. The carpet, which had once been red, harped on one regular pattern which ran away under two armchairs and a sofa. It was probably as old as Mr Rae, but in the growth of hair more

worn, for his head was covered with thick white hair. The
floorboards which surrounded this lovely old carpet were
black like the bookshelves and shone with polish.

When I first went into that room, feeling shy and unable
to speak, I at once remembered Uncle Robert's study and
that made me unable to hear, as well, for my mind had left
Mr Rae's house for Newton, left the awkward, foreign
present for the familiar past. But really the only resemb-
lance between the two rooms was the books. Uncle
Robert's was twice the size and smelt only of ink and
leather bindings. Mr Rae's room was comparatively crowded with furniture and had a pleasant mixture of smells
which I have never forgotten; tobacco smoke, coal and
wood smoke, floor polish and the warm soft air from the
chimneys of paraffin lamps. In summertime when the fires
and the lamps had been quenched the scent of flowers took
their place; it is roses, sweet williams and night-scented
stock that I remember best, for Mrs Rae adorned the house
inside and out with the abundant blossoms of the garden.
Bees flew into the study by the open windows; the smell of
newly mown grass came in too.

But it was in January, a day or two after my arrival, that I
first entered Mr Rae's study. I hated it. I was afraid to look
at him and was utterly possessed by my private thoughts. I
could hear his voice but at first I did not take in a word he
said. He began by trying to find out what I had already
learned at school and despairing, I suppose, of getting
more than a submissive grunt from me he resorted to
practical commands.

—— Recite the multiplication tables.

I said them with some stumbles but no mistakes up to
twelve times twelve.

—— Latin declensions.

I managed the first and second declensions, then got lost.
The same with the verbs.

—— You have a good memory, he said. What did they
teach you of history?

I seized on thoughtless recitation again and gabbled
through the names and dates of the Kings and Queens of
England, without a mistake, from William the Conqueror,

1066 to George the Fifth, 1910. But when he asked about
Scottish Kings I had only heard of James the Sixth.
—— Do you like lists?
No answer.
—— They have a life of their own, a pleasing rhythm, but
they live apart from language, apart from people. Do you
see the royal dates in a vertical line or horizontally? and
when I could not answer he said
—— It doesn't matter. You can put them in a circle or
jumble them. It's all the same. They are all there. Tell me,
Thomson, of some important happenings in your own life.
I could not think of any and he would not prompt me.
The silence was more unmanageable than what had gone
before and to ease my torment I told him how my aunt had
come with Michie to meet me at the station.
—— Why did you hide? he said and, when I told him,
laughed
—— Well, what else?
I told him about the 'two young bears' and the slaughter
of the hens, about how I was kicked on the head in a rugger
scrum, how Pidgy's leg was cut off at Sandwood, how
Uncle Tom fell down the Newton front steps, but when he
asked me to give dates for those incidents I could not.
—— You've peopled those events. That's the main thing.
Can you people your list of Kings?
I shook my head, remembering only that King John had
died of a surfeit of lampreys and that Henry the Eighth had
six wives, and I felt my face blushing when I thought of my
answer to an end of term exam question which said 'Who
was Marlborough?'. I wrote 'A very good Queen' because
all I could remember was a picture of him with long hair,
and my answer was read out to the other boys of my
Dotheboys School. Mr Rae rescued me.
—— The study of history can be, like your own memory,
in a jumble. Any happening that interests you can be
studied first. Dates are important only when one happening is the consequence of another. And as for place it is
probably better to start with the history of a place you know
well than to struggle with the history of Tibet. The Battle of
Culloden is distant in time but near this room in place.

Cumberland's army was encamped at Nairn on the night before the battle.

I frequently imagined the Battle of Culloden because we had often walked and had picnics on the moor. My father had shown me the positions of the armies, described the horses and wagons, the soldiers, their weapons and their dress. It was vivid in my mind and once I had burst into tears as I read of the Jacobites' defeat. But at school I had learnt nothing of it or any other battle except the date and the superiority of the English.

—— Let us start even nearer than Culloden, said Mr Rae. Let us start half a mile from this room, in the middle of Nairn between the river and the High Street. Tomorrow, if it is a fine day, let us have a peripatetic discourse. Come at two, before it gets dark, and we shall learn more on our walk than by sitting in the study.

—— What about the snow, I said, hoping to frighten him off, for the prospect of being seen walking with him down the High Street shamed me.

—— You have good boots and I shall put on my snow boots.

No more snow fell that night or next day. The frost remained hard and although the streets and paths were slippery where they had been trodden, he never hesitated or slipped. One end of the Tigh-na-Rosan road, which has only six houses in it, was blocked in those days by a stone wall built to protect Mrs Newbiggin's gardens from intruders. Yet, in the daytime she never locked the wicket gate that led through it and not only Granma, who was a close friend of hers, but everyone living nearby, used it as a short cut to the High Street shops. Even the messenger boys rode their carrier bicycles through Mrs Newbiggin's park to and from that wicket gate. I see now that Tigh-na-Rosan's street is called Viewfield Street. I never knew that as a boy. The name plate, if there was one, was hidden by a honeysuckle bush and on letters people simply put 'Tigh-na-Rosan, Nairn'. I knew Viewfield only as the name of Mrs Newbiggin's house and park.

—— How would you like to be called Mr New Building?

said Mr Rae as we walked from the wicket gate along the snowy path towards the house and I laughed for the first time in his presence, for though I knew the meaning of the name I had never translated it into English. We stood still near the house, by the drawing room windows. I hated that. I was afraid Mrs Newbiggin might see me. But we had to stand still whenever his pipe went out.

The gates of Viewfield open on to a sloping road that curves down towards the links and the Fishertown. There were houses on the opposite side of this road but, so far as I remember, no front doors. Only windowless gables faced the road. The windows and doors of the rows of houses looked on each other across narrow alleys which led from Viewfield to the High Street. Mr Rae chose one of these and walking side by side we filled it till we met a fat woman with a basket and had to draw into a doorway to let her pass. I knew her, and from her basket and the empty creel on her back I knew she was taking a short cut to Newton to gather fir cones, for the thick trees there kept the snow off the ground. And even if I did not know her well, I knew her china milk jug with the flowers on it which Joan and I filled every August morning from the churn. I pulled the peak of my cap down on to my nose and looked at the ground. She said something formal to Mr Rae and did not recognise me.

He was talking all the time about windowpanes – how you could tell their ages by the type of glass – about doorknobs and knockers, thatch, slates, building stone, stone used for the corner posts which protect the end houses from cartwheels. He said that in his father's day no houses or shops opened into the High Street. Their fronts were in alleys like the one we were in. When we emerged into the High Street opposite the Constabulary Gardens he said

—— Thank God we came through safely.
—— Surely there aren't robbers, Mr Rae?
—— No, no. But we could have been run over. That sonsie wifie was as broad as the Inverness bus.

When I laughed he made me laugh more saying 'When you hear it coming, lean in against the dyke or die' and laughter and the many things he said, so shortly, took my self-consciousness quite away. I walked with him among many people, even passing boys I knew, without discomfort.

The Constabulary Gardens are now a public park. I do not know whether they were public in those days but Mr Rae had the courage to tread anywhere and was well known. No one would stop him whatever he did. So we went in through the double iron gates and across a wide gravel forecourt to the big house which stands square like a fortress set back about twenty yards from the High Street and surrounded by terraced lawns that step down at the back of it to the precipitous bank of the river. There are plenty of flowerbeds in the garden but on that day the snow had made them invisible and level with the lawns. Only the stems of shrubs and the trunks of trees broke the whiteness. We walked to the low fence at the river's edge and looked down on to the river, a brown ruffled stream with clusters of foam settled near the banks which looked like tawny soapsuds.

—— The east wall of the ancient castle of Nairn was here where we are standing, said Mr Rae. There were postern doors on either side. The main gate faced west, where the High Street now is, near the top of Castle Lane.

I pretended to be interested. He went on about it for a long time and, standing still, I felt cold. But suddenly he drew my attention to him again by speaking of an underground passage which was supposed to have led from this castle to another one which had been built in the sea on the rocks below the swimming baths near Tigh-na-Rosan. He did not describe the underground passage. I did. But to myself. For days and days afterwards. And I 'peopled' it. And I went down it by myself and came back again. From the sandy grassy hillocks below the baths looking out to sea between clumps of whins I could see the castle itself especially on still evenings when strangely shaped shadows darkened the water. It and the tunnel were phantoms alive in the imagination and as strongly held in mine as the Culbin church steeple sticking up from the sand.

*

There are two beautiful golf courses at Nairn, the Dunbar
Links on the east or Forres side of the river and the Newton
Links, as it was then called because Uncle Robert had given
part of his land to the Club, that stretch from the west of the
town towards Fort George and Inverness. Both lie along the
edge of the sea and to play golf on either or merely to walk is
an unearthly experience which stays in one's soul all one's
life. The sky seems limitless and has nothing to do with the
sky you look up at from the garden or street. The colours of
the sea change all the time. Nothing has been tamed in the
rich greenery beyond the inland boundary of the links; no
houses or hedges are visible. Beyond the end of the
Newton course the carse begins and that looks endless too,
a long wide expanse of short grass dotted with white stones
and the bleached skeletons of animals. At the far end of the
Dunbar course there was in my boyhood, before trees were
planted, nothing to be seen except sand.

During those years with Granma I went on long walks,
sometimes with the dogs sometimes alone, almost always
by the sea edge of one of these golf courses or along the
beach itself. The Newton course is three miles long, the
carse beyond it about four, without trees, without hills,
without houses except for one salmon bothy which no one
could see from even fifty yards away because it looked like a
part of the ground, its low walls having been built of
unhewn boulders that lay nearby and its roof of grassy sods
on which in the spring and summer wild flowers grew
swaying in the wind, their colours flickering in sunlight like
those which grew on the ground. I had known this bothy
since the earlier years of my childhood. Bob MacDonald
lived in it with four or five other men during the salmon
fishing season and I sometimes went with Joan or Mary or
both to see him there, but mainly to see the great blue
salmon boat which they winched up on to the beach after
they had taken the catch from the cage-net. It meant more
to me than to the others because I had discovered it all by

myself in secret when I slipped out of a party in a sad mood
and ran away to the carse.

It is best to have an aim on a long walk, a bridge, a cairn, a
special tree or rock at which with relief you can turn back. A
stranger would find no such landmark on the carse. Mine
was the bothy. Even when there was no one in, its crooked
door was on the latch and I always went in to sit down for a
few minutes, not from tiredness but for respite in my battle
with the wind.

I suppose there are some still days on the carse but I can
remember none. When the leaves in Tigh-na-Rosan garden
were motionless as I set forth, there was a strong breeze
there; when the wind in the streets was merely blustery a
gale blew along the links and carse. It came almost always
from the west, from the snowy mountains of Sutherland
and Invernesshire. I think it was colder than the east or
north winds which blew less often. It was sometimes so
strong as to throw you back as you leant forward against it;
sometimes you had to turn your back to it because facing it
you could not breathe. On wild days the dogs were wild,
running ahead, running back to me worried in their minds,
and I with my head down like a butting ram took long
strides to cover the distance quickly.

In such weather no one could walk along the beach
towards the west. Flying sand stung your face, got into
your eyes and nostrils and clung to the front of your
clothes. When the tide was out I usually walked back from
the bothy on the sand or ran without effort as though
flying, for the wind blew me and the dogs back to Nairn.
But if you walk, the mysteries of sand and wind touch your
perceptivity more distinctly.

Down towards the sea on your left, dry sand blown along
the wet is caught in clusters like tiny snowdrifts against
pebbles half embedded in the wet sand. The dry sand
rushes past you, ahead of you not in one stream but
several, slanting, parting, crossing and rejoining. This
flying sand is pale. Some of it is white. Looking down
through it, through its thin veil towards your feet, you see
the dark wet sand you are walking on and that is so hard
and still, so immovable by the strongest wind that it

appears to be made of quite another substance.

As I turned from the salmon bothy towards Nairn I imagined I was wading downstream in a fast shallow river, the stream rushing over my shins and ahead of me. I thought of smoke blowing past me. In places where the sand was thick below me, it was like walking on clouds in a high wind that blew them ahead of me, that blew other clouds to me at the back of me.

Houses in the low-lying streets of Nairn being only nine feet above sea level are often flooded by high, stormy tides. They are pestered with sandstorms too, but these are merely a nuisance. In the seventeenth century sand was the greater danger; it does not subside like water, nor melt like snow; you cannot wade through it or be rescued by boat and it is impossible to shovel a passageway into a house through a large drift of dry sand, as one can shovel snow, because the more you shovel the more the sides fall in.

Alexander Brodie of Brodie, the Laird of the lands adjoining the Barony of Culbin, kept a detailed diary throughout the years from 1651 until 1680, when he died. His public interests were religion, politics and law. He had been MP for Elgin in the Edinburgh Parliament, representative in the general assembly of the Church of Scotland, Lord of Session and commissioner appointed to meet Charles II at the Hague, and it is, I suppose, his emotional and vivid account of such matters that led to the publication of his diaries nearly two hundred years after his death. But of equal interest is his daily account of local events, of his family life much of which is tragic, and of his management of the Brodie estate and farms. He worked by hand with his men on the home farm and at the peat cutting, until illness and weakness stopped him near the end of his life and it was that concern, I think, that led him to describe the weather in many diary entries.

Anyone can now explore the house he lived in, Brodie Castle, about ten miles east of Nairn, because it is now a museum owned by the National Trust for Scotland. The core of it was built in 1567 on or near the site of a thirteenth century castle belonging to Malcolm, Thane of Brodie who died in 1285, and in spite of much arson, sacking, storm and rebuilding, the principal parts of its structure are as they were in the diarist's time. It and his crops were exposed to storm only slightly less than the manor house and crops of his neighbour Kinnaird of Culbin who lived between him and the sea.

Brodie wrote,

The late harvest and inundation of water was 1653.
Die Sabbati, 11th September – A great speat [flood of the River Findhorn].
30th October – A great storm of snow and frost.
1655, 5 Julie – This day was a verie great flood, and delug of rain, which raisd all the waters to a great height. Let not the Lord destroy a land and a people that are drownd in sin and ingodliness.

Except for the pages written during long absence from Brodie Castle, his spells in Edinburgh and London, his diary is spattered with disastrous Acts of God. Once or twice he mentions sandstorms, but only severe ones. His estate was far enough inland to escape the driven sand that flattened the crops and spoiled the pastures of Culbin and the lower land of Nairn. But it is evident from reports of the great sandstorm which happened fourteen years after his death, and from earlier accounts, that sand had been shifting for centuries between Whiteness Head and Findhorn Bay, a distance of about twenty miles, and from Findhorn Bay to Burghead, another ten miles or so. Hector Boece says that 'in the year of our redemption 1097 . . . the land of Moray in Scotland . . . was desolated by the sea, castles subverted from the foundation, some towns destroyed, and the labours of man laid waste, by the discharge of sand by the sea; monstrous thunders also roaring, horrible and vast.'

On April 11, 1663 Brodie wrote,

I heard that Nairn was in danger to be quitt lost by the sand, and by the water . . .

The sand governed the water. Each great sandstorm

changed the course of the rivers Nairn and Findhorn, swamping farms and leaving the harbours dry. The lands of Culbin were, in the seventeenth century, watered by the Findhorn which flowed through them to the sea and by its tributary the Muckle Burn. There is a medieval reference to 'the rough carse of Culbin', but in Brodie's time the whole estate was called the 'granary of Moray'. It was more populous and much more fertile than his estates. It had sixteen rich farms on it, crofts and labourers' cottages scattered over it, a fishermen's clachan on the Hill of Findhorn and many fishermen's bothies on the banks of the river. The land was flat, easy to plough and in the middle of it, surrounded by the fields of the home farm stood Culbin House, a stone building with gardens, lawns and trees about it. There were abundant orchards too. 'A stone-built doocot – the privilege of a barony – stood on a hillock.' Like other prosperous lairds, the Kinnairds had a church or family chapel at which some of their people worshipped with them. It must have been the church whose spire my father warned us not to trip upon.

Only one of the sixteen farms, Earnhill, which is there to this day, survived the great sandstorm of 1694. It came suddenly from the west on an October day that year, a high cloud of sand, two miles in width. It is described as being like a river flowing at great speed. Men reaping barley had to run from the field and within a few hours the sheaves they had made and the standing barley not yet cut were smothered. A ploughman, almost suffocated by sand, had to leave his plough half way up a furrow, untackle his horse and lead it away. The Mill of Dalpottie, to which the Laird and his tenants had always brought their grain, was buried and the waters of the Muckle Burn which drove its wheel were shelved away from it to the east together with the greater waters of the Findhorn, which found a new outlet to the sea.

On the first night people stayed in their houses, believing that the walls would keep them safe, but the sand as it hit each obstruction piled up into sloping mounds, such as those I have so often seen in miniature against pebbles on the beach. Only a few sheltered houses had doors or windows facing east; most faced the west winds. And in the morning almost everyone woke in darkness. All doors and windows were blocked with sand. They had to break gaps in the back walls of their houses to get out. There was a lull in the storm that morning and they drove their animals inland, hoping, I suppose, to reach common grazing or find charitable neighbours who would share pastures with them, for there was no grass on Culbin now, no greenery of any kind, no yellow corn, only miles of sand and a horrible sandy marsh made by the river Findhorn in the night, when its mouth was choked.

On the marsh, as the water drained away during the next few days, lay the corpses of hens, rabbits, hares and even sheep and when the wind dropped there was a pestilential stench of rotting flesh and vegetation.

During the lull, the people went back to their houses, hoping to rescue some of their things, but the storm began again as roughly as before and with more danger in it, for the huge sandhills it had created during the previous day and night were now shifting; the westerly gale lifted them and blew them along in massive, blinding clouds. The sky darkened. The people, believing this was the end of the world, ran for their lives, taking with them only some small things which they could carry.

Next morning there was nothing to be seen but sand, not even the tops of trees, nor even the chimneys of the laird's big house. The church had been deeply buried. The Culbin Estate looked to its inhabitants then much as it looked to me in 1921, except that the sand dunes and sandhills had long been coloured by bent grass, when I first went there with my sisters and parents.

For two and a half centuries, until the nineteen-thirties when newly planted trees grew strong enough to break the wind, the sands kept moving. The desert landscape changed with every storm. Large sandhills were blown away and new ones raised. Dead trees were exposed from time to time, and once the west wind tore the sand off living fruit trees which blossomed and bore fruit until they were smothered again for ever.

About the year 1798, one hundred years after the great

sand drift, the old laird's house reappeared like a skeleton, the sandy top of its tomb torn off by the wind. The main chimney was the first part to be seen. A man climbed the sand and shouted down it. A voice which was probably the echo of his own answered him from the hollow room below and he ran away.

The Laird of Moy who then owned what was left of the Culbin Estate sent men and carts to demolish the house and bring away load after load of building stone. The remains were soon buried by sand again and people who knew the district in the nineteen-thirties could point to an oddly shaped sandhill which, they said, covered the house.

At times and in flat places, the wind took the sand quite away from the old fields. Ploughed and half-ploughed furrows, the whole shape of the rig could be seen, and on the head rigs, the place where the oxen and horses turned before starting on the next furrow, hoof marks two hundred years old were visible. The plough abandoned on the first day of the Great Sand Drift was also found. Part of it is now in the Elgin Museum. But neither the wind nor any searcher has discovered the most precious treasure known to the Culbin people at the time and, by tradition, to generations of their descendants, to have been hidden one night behind a sandhill near the shore.

Smugglers had landed a cargo at night which included, it was said, silk, tea, wine and brandy, goods much in demand in the north of Scotland but too scarce and highly taxed for anyone to buy from lawful merchants. It was too late to rouse carters and in any other place as remote as the Culbin shore, the cargo would have been safe till daylight. But during the night the west wind blew and when three of the smugglers went back at dawn to divide the goods into cartloads, the sand had shifted; the whole landscape had changed; there was nothing to be seen but sand. For hours they searched and tried to dig trenches but were hampered by flying sand until in the evening the wind dropped. News of the loss spread through the countryside and when the carts arrived they were accompanied by dozens of men who joined in the search, scraping with their hands, digging with spades, plunging their arms up to the armpits into the slopes of the sandhills. The carters probed with the long handles of their whips.

My encounters with Nairnshire sandstorms have been slight and not alarming but they gave me a hint of the terror and physical distress that caught people long ago. I have walked back from the Culbin Sands to Nairn, facing the west wind and sand, when there was no one in sight, nor beast, nor seagull, nor lark, nor insect, no earthly sound or sight, no ground under my feet. The river of dry sand that covered my feet made the solid sand I was walking on invisible, and sometimes even that gave way, clenching me up to the shins until I struggled out of it. The hills of the Black Isle, seven miles away on my right were raised above the sea by mist. There was no sea between me and them. I was aware only of the sky above, the powerful wind before me and the sand flying at me, past me, catching to a halt in my clothes. It was stimulating. It was spiritual. It was cold. Cold and excited, I reached Nairn, crossed the harbour footbridge near the gasworks and walked through the Fishertown, sheltered by low houses into The Brackla, the Fishertown bar, where the world was, where the earth was peopled with men huddled close to each other in the warmth.

J. F. S. Gordon, in his gloss on Shaw's *History of Moray*, third edition 1882, describes an experience much more frightening than mine, and from it one can better understand the sufferings of the Culbin people in 1694. For one of his visits to the Culbin Sands he chose a day when a westerly wind was blowing and made his way with his eyes shut, 'like one blindfold', through 'waves of sand which had a sensible weight.' At times the sand was pouring down in torrents, and sometimes masses, from the heights above. At times it lashed him 'with great force around the body like thongs.'

No sooner had I got beyond the fierce influence of the sand than I felt something about me which was quite unaccountable . . . a pressure of weight on my body which had the effect of dragging me down and retarding my progress, as if the power of gravitation

had been increased ten-fold . . . Every pocket about
me was filled with sand, and my clothes were completely saturated with it, and my shoes were like to
burst, and my eyes, my ears, my nostrils, and my
mouth were all partakers, more or less of it. On
moving about, I observed the minute particles of sand
pouring from my clothes as thick as when a drizzling
rain falls from a summer cloud.

The sandstorm seemed to Gordon to be 'a work altogether beyond the common of nature . . . I could not help
thinking that the furies must have leagued together to
punish me for entering upon their domains.'

Neither Gordon nor I saw the hand of our God in the
sandstorms we walked through, but the calamity of 1694
came to the Culbin people as a punishment for their sins.
The wrath of God was in everything, in war, arson,
robbery, storm, flood. It was used to punish man for his evil
thoughts or actual sin; and every emotion, every pleasure
was a sin.

In the month of May, 1656, Alexander Brodie, then
thirty-nine years old, wrote

In going about the fields, I found the heart apt to rise
with carnal delight in fields, grass, wood etc. This I
desired the Lord to guard me against, that such
decaying, corruptible, poor comforts, steal not away
my heart.

In January,

It was a great flood of rain; by which I saw how great a
God He was that did hang up these bottles above, and
squeeze them forth upon our heads at His pleasure. I
looked on the water as I went forth to the field, and
saw the trees, they could not resist the waters, albeit
strongly rooted . . . I observed the water taking away
much of the ground, young trees, corn, land and

grass.

I desire to note it among the remarkable passages of the Lord's providence towards me, that, in my passage to Edinburgh, 6th December, 1657, the horse, falling in the water of Urie in the evening, where the water was so deep, the frost so great, the difficulty so insuperable, that yet, 1. The same did not befall myself, for I was near to it, and why might He not have reserved it for me? 2. That the boy who was at the same time on the ice, and had that same horse in his hand, yet he was safe. 3. That the beast also was safe; and being on a Sabbath day, and I travelling, it was a matter that might give offence . . .

June 4, 1672. Young Cromarty came here, and Mr Urquhart, the minister. I spoke sharply to him, for his travelling on the Lord's day.

July 29, 1676. I did beat Abel for sleeping in time of prayer and my heart challenged me for passion, perturbation, inseasonableness, and questioned if that were the right way, but rather by admonition and reproof.

In 1640, on Thursday December 28th, this Alexander Brodie was one of a party which included my ancestor, the Laird of Innes, that came to the grand old cathedral of Elgin and destroyed every object in it. The party was led by the Reverend Gilbert Ross, minister at Elgin. They tore down and ripped medieval paintings, smashed the screen which was beautifully carved, probably gilded like most ancient screens and adorned in patterns of blue, red and green. The screen and the ornamental woodwork of pulpit, font lid and choir stalls they chopped up for firewood. All this they did to please God, who had since the foundation of the Christian Church, been plagued by the gaudy contrivances of man.

It is difficult to find out what the common people felt about such acts of destruction, nearly all of which were instigated and carried out by the educated gentry, but it is probable that they thought it wrong and that they feared it would provoke God to take vengeance. For education destroys tradition, weakens respect for ancestral beliefs, and although these peasants, unlike those of England, had had parish schools since the early seventeenth century the effects were slight. In the few Highland schools, this kind of education had no effect at all because the appointed teachers knew no Gaelic, a language that was said to be 'the chief cause of "the barbaritie and incivilitie" of the inhabitants of the Highlands and Islands.' In the Lowlands it was compulsory education, compelled not by law but by the moral power of the Church which administered it. Brodie and his friends continued theirs at the university and did not end it there, for in the great libraries of their castles they read not only the classics but contemporary works on theology, philosophy, politics, law. To them, I guess the generations of their kinsmen who had worshipped in Elgin Cathedral were to be pited as all misguided and superstitious people are to be pitied. But not all educated people approved of destruction.

In 1640, two years after the event in the cathedral, the historian John Spalding wrote:

Mr Gilbert Ross, minister at Elgin, accompanied with the young Laird Innes, the Laird Brodie, and some others, broke down the partition wall dividing the kirk of Elgin from the choir, which had stood since the Reformation, near seven score years or above. On the west side was painted in excellent colours, illuminate with stars of bright gold, the crucifixing of our blessed Saviour Jesus Christ. This piece was so excellently done, that the colours nor stars never faded nor evanished, but kept whole and sound, as they were at the beginning, notwithstanding this College or channonrie kirk wanted the roof since the Reformation, and no whole window thereinto to save the same from storm, snow, sleet, or wet, which myself saw, and marvellous to consider. On the other side of this wall towards the east, was drawn the day of judgment. All ways all is thrown to the ground.

It was said this minister caused bring home to his house the timber thereof, and burn it for serving his

kitchen and other uses, but each night the fire went
out that it was burnt, and could not be held in to kindle
the morning fire as use is; whereat the servants and
others marvelled and thereupon the minister left off
and forebore to bring in or burn any more of that
timber in his house. This was marked, spread through
Elgin and credibly reported to myself. A boldness, but
warrant of the King, to destroy churches; yet is done at
the command of the Assembly, as was said.

Spalding makes it clear that the mass of people saw
sacrilege in the destruction of Elgin Cathedral. For proof,
there was the uncanny death of the minister's fires each
night.

In England at that time, and for generations afterwards,
yeast for baking bread was kept alive, a small piece from
each baking being kept for the next. I, myself, having often
stayed in the houses of the poor in the Highlands and
Islands of Scotland, have seen that the domestic fire itself
was holy. Like the sacred fires kept alight by the Vestal
Virgins and by the Parsee priests of India, the domestic fire
was never allowed to go out. To revive it every morning
from the embers of the night before, to keep it alive from the
day the house was built, often for hundreds of years, to
carry burning embers to a new house when the old one falls
down still has, even now, a meaning derived from religions
older than Christianity. Prayers for 'smooring the fire', as
covering the embers with ashes at bedtime is called, are
now usually Christian. Or at least those which I have heard
as a guest are.

> The sacred Three
> To save
> To shield,
> To surround
> The hearth,
> The house,
> The household
> This eve,
> This night,
> Oh! this eve,

This night,
And every night,
Each single night.
            Amen.

*

Dr Eric Wilson, our Nairn family doctor, examined my eyes
from time to time and wrote to Mr MacLehose about them;
and one day news came from London that I could go home,
that my sight appeared to have steadied itself and was
unlikely to change for better or worse until I had stopped
growing. Mr MacLehose wished to see me before confirm-
ing his opinion. Meanwhile no plans should be made to
send me to school again; he wished to obtain a second
opinion. My parents were to make an appointment with
him for me as soon as the day of my return to London had
been determined. But Mr MacLehose could not express too
strongly his conviction that in the meantime I should
continue to adhere to the regime he had prescribed – not to
use my eyes for reading, nor to subject my person to any
physical strain, not, in particular to stoop, whether it be to
retrieve an object from the floor or to retie my shoe lace in
the street.

    When Dr Wilson read out a letter phrased somewhat like
that, Margery, who always accompanied me on my visits to
him, said

——  Now that's lovely. You never expected it, did you.
And took me straight to Rose Bros. to buy me a slab of my
favourite chocolate, the bitter French cooking kind –
*Chocolat Menier* – which she did not share my taste for.

——  I'll telephone Annie tonight, she said.

    I said,

——  It's better to write. I think Mother will want to
decide.

——  Decide what?

——  She may not want me to go home so soon.

    Margery looked at me and seeing, I suppose, a look of
doubt and gloom in me, let her own face droop in
bewilderment. On our way back to Tigh-na-Rosan, I lagged
behind her at each of the houses to which I delivered milk

every morning, looking carefully at them as though for the last time; the last time with the pony's reins in my hands would come soon, the last time in the stable, grooming the farm horses, the last of the byre, of feeding and milking the cows, of running by the river, of fishing, of wandering on the carse and distant beaches where no one saw me; the last time of gathering the sheep into their fold, the last time of feeding my beloved pigs. The last of Jeannie.

To my relief, my partial relief for I longed to be with my mother again, I was not invited home immediately. To uproot me, and try to replant me in London where I would have neither friends nor routine, to withdraw me from Canon Ballard, Mrs Grimmett and Mr Rae before it was certain that I could go to school again seemed to my parents unwise. When Margery read out my mother's letter, addressed to me and telling me this, I was utterly dejected, as dejected as I had been when I heard the news that I could go home. She put it on the mantelpiece and left the room. I took it down and read it to myself.

The long separation saddened me only when her letters came. They began 'My dear David' but those words came out of Margery's mouth. Their ending – 'Love from Mother' – strong in ink on paper was diluted by Margery's voice, which ran away with those three words as though they did not matter. I cheated the MacLehose rules so as to come near to my mother, to see with my own eyes her hand-writing, to be held in her arms symbolically by her words which were meant for me and no one else.

My trouble and Mr MacLehose's trouble was that my eyes were working well enough for that. It took more resolution than I possessed not to use them for reading, whenever I felt sure that I was alone. And yet I never read in a carefree or dare-devil way. The only letters that tempted me were my mother's, the only books, those thrilling ones, and sad ones, which aroused in me, as soon as Margery's reading aloud broke off, a passion of desire and curiosity.

After each lapse of this sort my spirits sank and my body sank into a chair or on my bed. I cannot remember any other secret activity that aroused in me a sense of guilt. I took care that no one could watch my sensual exploration of the private parts of horses and pigs, but so long as I felt safe from observation I felt no shame at all.

My other trouble, which was also Mr MacLehose's though he knew nothing about it, was the affected manliness I had acquired in self defence at Dotheboys Hall where boys and schoolmasters tormented me for what they called my girlish ways. It was my hair that started the jeering, for however short I had it cut no amount of Brilliantine would flatten it, and then I suppose that having lived at home with Mother and three sisters until the age of eight and seeing little of my father who did not get back from work till after we had gone to bed, I had learned feminine gestures. But by now I was taller than most boys of my age; the Merrytown dairyman thought I was fifteen; and my life at Nairn, bicycling, swimming, riding horses, had made me strong. Whenever I was with men or other boys or when I thought Githa or Ireen were watching me at work I behaved like Samson. Such boastful actions gave me each time a sense of guilt, a knowledge that I had broken my promises to my mother.

*

Jeannie, her governess and little sister had no special pew in church. The Camerons of Lochiel, and other great families, had theirs which no one ever usurped. But most of the congregation sat in almost the same place every Sunday, not by right, but by habit which was respected by the others. In summer our family filled the whole of the fourth pew, on the left, below the pulpit; for the rest of the year it was empty except for Granma, Margery and me. Jeannie, whose name I had learned from her governess's anxious cries after church when she ran away playing with her sister, usually sat in front of us in the third or second pew, which gave me a good view of her reddish yellow hair in forms that changed from Sunday to Sunday – a long flowing stream like Flossie's tail, a waterfall rushing over her shoulders, one thick pigtail with a black velvet bow, below which, at her waist, there was a spray of unbound hair which I longed to seize and brush my cheeks with, or two tight thin pigtails which showed the nape of her neck. Her hair when loose did not run smoothly like the deep river Ness which has no rocks to ruffle it. Her long curls twining, running underneath each other and out again, made its stream like the Nairn or the Findhorn whose stony beds make ripples.

Of all these forms, I liked the waterfall best; in bed at night it flowed over my face and chest, flowed down my hips and lay in a moving coil between my thighs. But except rarely when she knelt leaning forward to mutter a prayer with the rest of us, the waterfall hid her ears. At prayer, her hair sometimes split into three, two streams ran forwards over her shoulders showing part of her ears. Sometimes I waited in vain all through the service for that moment, but I always carried her ear in my pocket and felt it with my fingers or put it secretly into my mouth pretending it was a sweetie, for everybody, except Granma and the men, sucked sweeties in church. It was a shell I had picked up on the carse, about the size of a florin, pink, flattish, translucent with white marbled rays. When I was alone I used to look at the sun through it.

In one of his long sermons Canon Ballard told us to remember when we lay down in bed at night the happenings of the day, and to ask God's forgiveness for the sins we had committed. I tried. He had spoken forcefully from his austere pulpit above me. His own austerity streaking down from it had probed me in a place where the usual loose slop that he allowed, without thought, to drip on to us left me bored but unhurt.

When I snuffed my bedside candle out that Sunday night, I searched my mind for sins but could find none except the usual upset with Granma. And this was tiny; she said I had been fidgeting in church, and staring at the people in front of us. We escaped the usual quarrel because, afraid that she knew about Jeannie's hair, I said 'Sorry Granma', and nothing else.

Before I went to sleep Jeannie's hair covered me. Then suddenly the memory of a real sin took every pleasant sensation away. The sin had happened on the day before, in the morning of Saturday, when Ireen asked me to lift two

stones that were too heavy for her and carry them to the
threshold of the house. She wanted to place them one each
side and whitewash them. I stooped. I heaved the first one
on to my knees, then up against my belly where I held it as I
walked with it, she in front of me to show the place where I
was to lay it down. Stooping again, I laid it down carefully.
Neither she, nor anyone on the croft, knew anything of the
MacLehose rules. I had more trouble with the second
stone. Perhaps it was heavier, perhaps I should have rested
for a minute to regain my energy, perhaps it was more
firmly embedded in the ground than the other; and then, if
Ireen had not been watching, I could have taken my time.
    Instead, she shamed me – not meaning to of course.
———    It's too heavy for ye, she said. Let me gie ye a lift wi'
it. Which drew from me an extra show of strength. Yet on
the Sunday no amoebae appeared in my eyes. In bed I
thanked God for keeping them away and told Him I would
never do such a thing again.
    This was in the month of May, a month more wonderful
to the people of Nairn and north of it than to anyone living
in the south. Our long dark winter did not end till May, or
so it seemed to me. I remember making a snowman in
Tigh-na-Rosan garden on the sixth and although it seldom
snowed so late the hard and wintry look remained. The sun
gave little warmth until late in May, but the very sight of it
was joyful, for in midwinter we had only five hours
daylight. Even when the sun comes back in strength to the
Highlands and their Nairnshire foothills our spring leaves
have an autumnal look because, besides the usual fresh and
lovely greens, many trees have pale red leaves and many
have pale yellow.
    It comes back suddenly, this sun so long kept secret.
Those who can measure natural growth, light and heat, will
prove me wrong, but I believe that our spring came
suddenly in the middle of May. That was the feeling that
flowed into me every year, like a revelation which brought
grass, leaves, lambs, foals, dozens of yellow newly hatched
chickens all at once. There were suddenly too many eggs
after months of too few. Only calving was spread throughout the summer so as to spread supplies of milk over the

barren months, when no cow was to be seen in any of the fields.

I used to plead with Githa to be the first to let the Sandwood cows out, and I remember that ceremony more distinctly than any of the other pleasures of the farm; for although there were no emblems, no rhythmic waving of leafy branches, no formal dance nor music, as there had been in the past, it was a ceremony to us. Githa and Ireen did sing and dance.

First I opened the field gate which was at the far end of the yard. Its hinges had long since rusted away and so you had to lift it, a dead weight which I took under my forearms as I brought it over to the dyke. This seemed no sin to me because I did not have to stoop. It was an ordinary gate, with five straight bars and one diagonal, as like any other farm gate as one human face is to another; but in a stack of thrown-away gates I would have known it by two neat holes at the top bored for a purpose long forgotten, by a splintered gap low down made, I suppose, by a heavy boot impatient at the mud which hindered it from opening, by two smudges on the third bar where someone had once cleaned his tar brush, by the shapes of the moss on the top bar which hung like a fringe or eyebrows.

As soon as I had managed to get the gate to lean against the dyke, I walked back to open the door of the byre, which when I compared it to that ancient field gate seemed primeval. Its outside was studded with nails which had no practical purpose, but which now that I know more about the old religion I believe to have been hammered in for magical reasons. These nails and the outside of the door were clogged with tar. They were tarred every autumn and sometimes again in spring. That black cover and the leathern hinges of the door, as thick as the rings that held the shafts of the milk float, were the only parts that had been renewed since the Virgin Mary's time.

The inside of the door was never touched with paint or whitewash, though the walls of the byre were white-washed summer and winter every month. The bare boards of it, polished by shoulders, hands and the flanks of cattle, were three inches thick with bevelled edges between them which, crowded with spiders' webs, dust and corpses of insects, formed the only smudged parts. The upright boards were strengthened by three horizontal battens. I think of it as primeval because it came into my dreams. I had seen doors like it in ancient churches, and at castles, which had sometime kept the cattle of Brodie, Kilravock and Cawdor safe from marauding bands of Englishmen and the plundering of Highlanders. Even our byre door had been used long ago to keep cattle thieves out. All kept the wind and the snow away.

The cows passed out of the byre one by one, as I loosened their chain necklaces, starting with the one nearest to the door. They gathered absent-mindedly in twos and threes outside until I followed the last of them out. Then we watched them wandering slowly as though without purpose, but we knew they knew their purpose, cows dazed by sunlight after seven months in the murky byre, cows lame with claw-like hooves grown long and misshapen from standing on straw, their skinny thighs caked with dried dung – for however diligent we were in mucking out there was always more for them to lie on – cows walking slowly through the yard, turning their heads to lick their flanks or gaze, lowering their muzzles to smell a green weed. At the gate where there was sometimes a jam they showed no haste, no striving. Sometimes one would have to raise her head and swing it over the neck of another to let her companion pass without clash of horns, but they did not push like pigs or sheep. Pigs, thrusting through a gateway, are rough and strident. Sheep huddle fearfully but patiently until their leaders have made way. Nor did the cows scatter as horses do, galloping and kicking their heels high when they see the freedom of a wide green field about them, lying down to roll on their backs and getting up again to shake and shudder before beginning to graze. The cows began to graze at once within the gateway, spreading on outwards and forwards step by step so slowly that I had to push the hindquarters of the last two or three aside before I could close the gate. We gazed at them, Ireen and Githa still holding dairy clouts or cans or whatever working things they had had in their hands at the beginning, I as silent as they were, thinking, if I thought at all, how sweet the spring grass tasted, for I often imagined myself as an animal, sharing its tastes and sensations, and often plucked a sprig of grass and chewed the stalks.

Except at plough time, hay time and harvest, the Farmer was alone in the steading doing odd jobs between the morning and the evening milkings. His sons worked at the salmon fishing, as motor mechanics or at one of the sawmills nearby.

One morning soon after the cows had been let out for the summer, he asked me to go with him and a young cow to the bull.

—— She is a bitty wild, he said, and she will run before me and there is fear for her with the motorcars on the road.

The bull lived in Tradespark, the old Muir of Nairn which had long since been drained and turned into farmland. It is about half way between Sandwood and Nairn. The cow, Githa told me, had been in season for two days. They had been annoyed at night by her anxious bellowing and were pestering their father to bring her quickly to the bull. He had waited for me.

We both took our bicycles and long ash sticks. I was to ride beside her, keep her in to the left, race her if she galloped and turn her back towards him. The cow knew the way – she had been there twice before – and as soon as we turned into the main road she began to trot fast.

—— Easy, easy! cried the Farmer, who had slowed down to prevent her feeling she was being chased, and I managed by waving my stick in front of her to bring her to a walk. But when we turned into Tradespark, which was a muddy track in those days, she broke suddenly into a gallop. The wheels of my bicycle were hampered by ruts and she escaped me. I saw her turn into the driveway of the bull's farm and when I caught up with her she was standing, panting, in the steading cow yard.

There was no gate to the drive or yard. The only nearby field was occupied by bullocks which would interfere with courtship and possibly get gored by the jealous bull. Before the Farmer let the bull out of his stall in the byre, he told me to go back to the end of the drive and stop the cow if she ran towards me.

—— They'll play for a wee whilie, he said, she'll pretend
she doesna wish for him. She'll run from him and if I canna
hold them in the yard he'll likely chase her doon the drive.
There is no need to strike her, just wave your ash before her
and she'll likely turn and he will turn wi' her, up again to
me.

He gripped my shoulder and glared sternly at me with
his one eye.

—— If she winna turn, let her gae. Let the bull gae after
her. We'll get them somewhere on the bicycles. Dinna
come between her and the bull. D'ye understand me, Davy
loon? Or I'll find ye dead on the road.

I was frightened and flattered, and very frightened as I
waited at the end of the drive; but when the cow ran
towards me, a yard or two ahead of the bull, I was not
afraid. I walked slowly towards her, speaking strongly to
her and whipping the air with my stick which made a
swishing sound. She hesitated, then turned and galloped
past the bull back towards the yard. I was ready to leap the
dyke, but without a glance at me, he turned and chased
her. I followed them keeping my distance but excited,
wanted to watch what would happen next.

When I reached the yard she was standing still with her
tail raised upright like a calf at play and he was licking the
place below it, covering it with white foam. Then he reared
and put his front hoofs on her back. He licked her neck. His
scarlet penis seemed to me at least a yard long and he kept
on probing it at her without success until the Farmer, telling
me to stand back, took it in his hands and guided it into the
proper place. Then the bull plunged and plunged. She was
small for an Ayrshire cow and he was the largest Ayrshire
bull, with huge upturned horns, that I had ever seen. I
thought he was killing her.

When at last he withdrew, his penis shrank a bit and a
long silvery stream hung down from it until his whole body
shuddered and the stream fell on to the ground.

The Farmer guided him to his stall while I watched the
cow. He came out of the byre breathing heavily and
clutching his chest. The bull had given him a hard knock on

the ribs while he was fixing the halter.

—— He meant me no harm, he said, on our way home. He never turned a horn on me, but the creature doesna ken the weight o' the side o' his head.

As the cow walked slowly homewards I said,

—— It didn't work.

—— What way did it no work, Davy?

—— All that stuff that didn't go in to her.

—— God gave him teems of it. He could cover twenty more coos this day if he'd be let run wild wi' them.

*

About a week later Duncan asked me to go with him to Nairn and help him with two loads of sand. I said 'Yes' very loudly and then I said 'Aye' which is a word less forceful, less prone to expose emotion, and he looked at me inclined to laugh but not laughing, for, as I now suppose, he could see no reason for joy in the long journey by cart to Nairn and the work of loading there. To me it was something more, this sudden invitation; his words were like those of a priest at an initiation ceremony. His brief invitation had made me a man. I knew of course, or at least I guessed, that he had tried to get a neighbour to go with him and asked for me only when he had failed but that knowledge did not spoil my pride.

May on the farm and in the town is a time for building and repairing buildings. There were two litters of pigs that May at Sandwood which brought nineteen little ones crowding into the rooms of the old wooden sties that were already filled with mothers, a boar, three gilts and about a dozen stores. There had been dissension in the MacDonald family about how to make more room. Duncan planned two concrete sties. His father said there would not be enough money until the autumn, until after the Lammas sales. Alec said 'Build nothing. Keep the stores on the midden in the byre.' And Githa said he could do the milking, then, for she was not going to sit down and milk with a crowd of pigs behind her.

But Duncan had a friend at Croy who had bought more cement than he could use; it would go hard with the damp. He wanted no money for it, nor did the builder in Nairn who had landed himself with the two loads of leftover sand which had to be removed from the drive of the house he was working at.

Going in to the West End of Nairn was a rare thing for Duncan and needed preparations that no other journey on the road required. People at the distillery, stone quarry, sawmill and smithy saw him and the horses and carts just as we saw them at work on the farm but for Nairn he put on his second-best clothes, polished the harness, washed the mud off the cart and gave the horse a special grooming. It was Bessie that day. He had wanted to take both horses and bring two loads home at a time but Bob was working with the other one. And Bessie was slow, better natured but old. I was insulted when I looked into the stable, impatiently wondering why Duncan wasn't ready to start, to find him grooming Bessie. I had groomed her as usual half an hour before, and I thought she looked ridiculous when he had finished with her. He had plastered her shaggy mane down with oil or something so that it hung flat on one side of her neck as if she were about to compete at a show. When I came in he put the dandy brush on the window-sill and began to plait the hair of her stubby tail, which was not long enough to make a good plait. Then he made a ring of it and tied it up on top of her tail. I laughed.

—— Does it no look well, then, Davy?

—— It's grand. Only . . .

—— Which way will I fix it, then?

—— Will I harness her, then?

—— Aye. Do. While I get my bonnet from the house. He was wearing a bonnet. He meant a better one.

My laughter and my 'Only' came because of Jeannie's governess. He had shaped Bessie's hair like her bun which stared at me every Sunday in church.

When we were ready to start, Duncan asked whether I would like to bicycle on and meet him fornent the Newton gate lodge.

—— Are we going to Newton? I was ready to withdraw from the whole expedition rather than be seen loading sand at Newton.

—— No, no. The Seabank Road. But at Newton ye could pass the time until I'm with ye.

I lifted my bicycle on to the cart and sat on the side board opposite to him. When we reached the main road he gave me the reins while he lit his pipe and I held them all the way to Nairn. There was no risk in that. With Flossie I had to be alert, stop her from shying into motorcars or making a wild turn for home, but Bessie would have plodded along by the side of the road with no one on the cart behind her. I knew it of course but any trust Duncan put in me flattered me absurdly. I watched the way he was sitting, knees wide apart, one arm resting on the side board, and copied it, holding the reins in the other hand. I watched his face. It took more than an hour for Bessie to walk the two miles into Nairn.

Duncan kept looking at the fields and telling me about them – the short dark green wasn't grass, he told me, but winter oats sown last autumn, the lighter green was meadow grass sown last spring with oats that had been reaped in September; there was newly ploughed land, mostly sandy, some loamy, ploughed well or raggedly depending on who ploughed it.

—— Ye are looking at thon, he said, but dinna look hardly, for thon was ploughed by a loonie only two years older than ye. I was at his father's funeral before Easter.

—— The fields in Canada, he said, ye canna see the edge of them, north, south, east or west. Everyone is like a county in itself.

As we passed through the dark pinewoods of Tradespark, I asked him to tell me again about how he got lost in a forest in Canada, he and the men working with him, his team of six horses and the long load of timber they were pulling which got stuck, its wheels in the mud above the axles, because he had chosen the wrong track.

—— How old were you?

—— Eighteen when I started logging.

—— How old would I have to be to go to Canada?

—— Twelve or thirteen, I dare say. Ye'd need to have finished with school.

I was excited by everything he said on that slow journey and, as I nearly always was by everything around me, by sights and sounds, by the thought of which house in the

Seabank Road we were going to, of what would happen next. There must have been boredom in my life at Nairn, encounters that lowered my spirits, but I cannot remember those now. I remember love and hope.

I loved Duncan more than Bob or the girls and yet, when I now think of them, Bob had a more friendly face. His was round and he smiled more often. Duncan's long, lean face was stern, except when he was talking.

I knew most of the houses in the Seabank Road and who lived in them and I kept looking at them as we plodded along towards the sea where it ended in a rough steep hill – the Sea Bank, I suppose. I wanted to ask Duncan which house we were going to, but he was gazing at the fields on our left. There were no houses on that side of the road until you got near the sea. So I did not ask him. I gazed in that direction too and beyond the fields to Newton whose upper floor and tower, grey against the light sky, showed stiffly above the trees. The flagpole was bare which meant that Uncle Robert, Lord Lieutenant of the county, was away.

When we passed the little road that led to Newton on our left and went down the slope towards the sea I had enough courage at last to ask Duncan which house we were going to, but he was lighting his pipe and did not answer.

It was here that the only houses on the left of Seabank Road began – four or five large villas with lovely gardens round them. On the right there was only the Golf View Hotel, in front of us the sea and beyond it the Black Isle just as I saw it every day from the Tigh-na-Rosan garden.

Duncan took the reins from me and turned Bessie into the wide open gateway of 'Kevin', the last house, the end house perched on a slight cliff that went down to the sea.

I had been driven into a trap, worse than my imagined visit to Newton where only servants would have seen me, into Kevin, The O'Toole's house. I could see his tricycle beside the front steps. I knew that his granddaughter Rosalind was away, but he often came to Tigh-na-Rosan and all the time, wherever he went, he talked. I could also see the heap of sand by the side of the drive in full view of the dining room windows.

Duncan jumped off the cart, telling me to keep the horse

off the lawn while he went to the kitchen door to say why he had come. I jumped off too and took cover behind her huge neck and shoulders. I could hear their voices. The cook's was shrill and excited, as though he was telling her that the church was on fire, but afterwards she laughed a good deal. They were at it so long that I was bored. I dared not start loading without Duncan because I knew that sand must be skilfully placed on the cart to keep the weight off the horse's back and yet not tip the shafts up by putting too much near the tailboard.

I looked at the sand and pushed some of it aside with my boot. Of all the heaps of sand I have seen in my life, in different countries, this is the only one which has stayed with me like a nightmare, like a horrid daytime vision. It looked beautiful.

The outside of the pyramid was reddish-blond and at every gust of breeze some of it flowed down in rivulets and spread, disappearing into the gravel of the drive. The toe of my boot exposed the dark, damp sand below this flowing mantle – in texture like coarse brown sugar, in colour like wet sandstone, but richer, deeper, as rich and deep as a chestnut. It was when we began to shovel it into the cart that I felt how heavy it was.

I could only just lift my first shovelful from the ground. I could not raise it over the rim of the cart which was about the height of my shoulder and, hoping that Duncan did not see me, I tipped half of it back on to the heap. From then on I tried various scoops until I found the amount I could throw on to the cart without spilling it. But still I was anxious to keep pace with Duncan. I liked it. I felt strong and thought, 'Next year when I'm thirteen I'll be able to lift as much as a man.'

Then suddenly as I stooped for a shovelful I could not see the shovel or the sand. The gravel at my feet, the lawn by my side, turned blood-red and when I stood up all about me was black as though I had been blindfolded. It only lasted a few seconds, and as soon as I could see Duncan who was beside me I interrupted his work intending to tell him that I could not go on, that I must go back to Tigh-na-Rosan. But instead of making a simple statement which he could understand I gave him the whole history of my eyesight with a long and abstruse glossary on Mr Mac-Lehose's rules. He listened to me, leaning on his shovel, and although I could see in his face that he did not know what I was talking about I went on and on.

—— Aye, David, aye, he said when I gave him the chance. Ye must tell me more at tea time. But now we must work to get the two loads home before dark.

I went on shovelling.

A ton of sand, which was the most that Bessie could pull, was so small a pile in the middle of the cart that I could not believe we had finished, but Duncan, after a lifetime with horses judged a load not by bulk but with an eye for weight, and this sand, having been rained upon, was heavier than it would have been earlier in the week. He climbed on to the cart and said

—— Go home now to your dinner. Leave your shovel in the sand. I'll no be back here until three o'clock.

I tried to tell him I would not come back, but instead I told him I had a lesson with Mr Rae at two and it might be five or ten past three before I returned to Kevin.

On my bicycle, at dinner and all through the lesson my eyes were normal but my mind was distraught; I knew I should not put them through another trial. Five seconds blindness was blindness. The next spell of shovelling might cause five weeks, months, years, or all years like Mrs Grimmett's. From moment to moment I thought of not turning up or of going to Kevin to tell Duncan I was ill or of staying there a little while and shovelling gently. Mr Rae said

—— Are you listening? He kept me late.

When I left him I did not know which way to turn – towards the Cawdor road where no one would see me, to Tigh-na-Rosan to hide in my bedroom, towards Kevin to confess to Duncan. In a torment of indecision, I went down one street and another and back again until a firm plan came to me – to go to Duncan and tell him I could not work, to reach him in time for him to find someone else to help him, the gardener of Kevin perhaps, or one of the men in the nearby villas.

I bicycled quickly down the Seabank Road and found him at work and instead of saying what I had resolved to say I said
—— I'm sorry I'm late.
—— I'm a wee bitty late myself. There's your shovel. We'll need to make haste.

I took up my shovel and went on shovelling until the load was filled. When he put back the tail-board, threw the two shovels in and climbed on to the cart I felt happy. My eyes had not been affected and I had helped him and pleased him.

*

Next morning at half past four, when I lit my candle, its flame was green. I shut my eyes and looked at it again and it was red. I blew it out and got into my clothes. By the time I reached the garden the sky was lightening and the lawn had purple patches on it. I jumped down the steep bank into the kitchen garden and out by the wicket gate through the whin-bushes to the beach. From there I could see the sunrise, red with moving green and purple shapes on it. About an hour later I walked back through the town to meet the Farmer on the Inverness road.

The milk cans had lost their shape, blurring into each other without edges like a grey cloud. The bottles were clearly defined but the doorsteps were invisible and on the same level as the pathways that led to them. I stumbled as I went to put the bottles down.

When we did the milk round together the Farmer and I walked to different houses leaving Flossie unattended by the kerb; in that respect she was well trained, though she always started off when she saw one of us returning to the float. It was usually I who returned first and took the reins to stop her till we both got on but today I was slower than the old man. I found him sitting on the float waiting for me.
—— You drive, he said.

It was daylight when we finished the West End, a clear morning with a pale blue sky and a few thin clouds streaming on it. It was not till then as we trotted back up the long Seabank Road towards the High Street that I saw amoebae. The Farmer often thought, and this time said, that I drove the pony too fast. The cans were jangling. I pretended not to hear him. I urged her on almost into a canter till he laid this hand gently on mine.

—— Davy, he said. Did ye wish to make butter? He laughed and that made me laugh and pull the reins to slow the pony down.

Near the end of the Seabank Road as we approached the Parish Church where the Farmer left his bicycle and usually left me to go to the town and the Fishertown, the pony slowed down to a walk. I let her walk. It was only then, without haste or anger, that I looked about me and knew I could not drive down the High Street. It was as if the kerb on our left was part of the road. It and the road were covered with a green film that moved about as though formed by tiny green weeds blown back and forwards by a breeze on a pond. The weeds moved in patches over the wall and windows of the church as well, blotting out each part as I looked at it but moving with me so that, as soon as I ceased to look directly at it, a window or cornice became clearly visible in the corner of my eye. I remembered learning this in London when my eyes first went wrong – that I could see any object by looking to one side of it; but the High Street was often crowded at that hour of the morning with motor-vans and horse-drawn lorries which edged in and out of each other leaving narrow lanes for me to guide Flossie through. One side of those? Which side?

—— Are you in a hurry to get home? I said to the Farmer as I pulled up opposite the church where he usually left me.

—— May be, he said. And may be not if that is God's will.

I told him untruthfully that I had an early lesson that day with Canon Ballard and would not have time to drive back to Sandwood. When I gave him the reins, he looked at me firmly with his one eye but said nothing to show his surprise. I said nothing to expose my shame, but the feelings of surprise and shame were strong in both of us, for on occasions when he had forgotten to let me drive I had sulked in anger, and when sometimes, seeing the High Street traffic tangled, he took the reins out of my hands, I felt that he had publicly shamed me.

When we had finished the milk round he left me at the Parish Church, put his bicycle on the float, and drove away slowly towards Sandwood. I suppose I looked glum. I know he waved 'Goodbye' to me with a stiff, false gesture.

It was too early to go home to breakfast and I was determined to do nothing unusual, nothing that would evoke questions, so I walked down past the front gates of Viewfield to the Links and across the grass to the beach.

All strain left my eyes, all anxiety left me as I crossed the green Links; only the bandstand had a blotch on it and I passed it without looking at it again. The whin-bushes near the sea were properly dark green, their yellow flowers yellow, uncontaminated by ghostly, moving specks. The sand and sea were pure too but I found it was as well not to look closely at the rock pools and seaweed.

We got through breakfast without questions and I went to the drawing room to read St Luke's gospel in my Braille bible, which Canon Ballard had set me for homework. I always kept my eyes shut while I was reading Braille and when Margery came quietly into the room, as was her way, her voice alarmed me.

—— Aren't you going to the farm today?

—— They're killing a pig and don't want me there.

I looked at her. She was covered with pond weeds. She went away.

Canon Ballard was all right. I knew enough about St Luke by then. But after tea I heard his car approaching Tigh-na-Rosan. His car distinguished itself from others by going bang-bang-bang as it went along. I ran upstairs and stayed there until I heard him leaving. Both Margery and Granma were in the drawing room when I came down and the gas was lit. I took up the Bible as a protection. I did not want to read it, but there was no other Braille book in the room. Margery interrupted me.

—— Nothing's happened to your eyes, has it, David?

—— No.

—— You must tell me.

Granma sprang her lorgnette at me.

—— A collision between your person and Canon Ballard's escritoire cannot have been caused by the escri-

toire's losing its sense of direction.
—— What did he say, then?

Margery asked me upstairs to her room and told me that Canon Ballard thought I was not seeing as well as usual. I had fumbled for the doorknob and as he watched me crossing the road, he saw me feeling for the kerb with the toe of my boot.

Margery said this kindly. I did not receive it kindly. I waited for her to go on, but she was waiting for me. At last she said

—— David, tell me!
—— Have you got a book about moles?
—— Moles?
—— To read to me.

I had seen many dead moles and picked them up and some live ones as they ran at the sound of my footsteps towards a hole that went down to the dark tunnels in which they lived. I liked the feel of their soft, dense hair. I had learned at school that they had no external ears and that their eyes were minute. When I examined dead ones and pushed the fur of the head aside I could find neither ears nor eyes, so close was the fur, and this was hard to understand, for owls and other creatures that see well in the dark have large eyes. Moles, I guessed go by touch and smell and quick hearing; they were probably short-sighted and only needed their tiny eyes when they ventured into an open space, like the Links.

*

Margery bicycled to Dr Wilson who telephoned to an oculist in Inverness and next morning we caught the train there, my train with pictures in frames above each seat which I remembered although I could not see them clearly. From the corridor Margery looked into one third class carriage after another; every seat had crumbs and stains and crumpled newspapers on it, the floors were scattered with orange peel and empty bottles which began to roll as the train moved off. The carriage Margery chose was as smelly as the rest. The train, now near the end of its long night journey, had dropped most of its passengers here and there and was carrying their rubbish on to its terminus at Inverness. I could see the country well enough and until we came to Gollanfield Junction where a branch went off to Fort George I knew every mile of it, woods, fields, farm steadings, the roads that went over the railway line, the burns that ran underneath. As we passed through Delnies I knew exactly where Sandwood was, although it was hidden by trees, and I raged in silence as I remembered how stupidly I had behaved about the sand. It was the sand and only the sand that had put me out of the byre and into this smelly train that morning.

I cannot remember the oculist. I can remember what he said, which was what I guessed he would say, that I was to go to bed in a darkened room. On the way to the station to get the afternoon train I asked Margery. How long?

I had heard him say 'six weeks', but wanted her to soften it. She took my hand and said 'A month or so. Perhaps a bit more. It's not long really. And you'll be up just in time for Newton. Mary, Joan and Barbara, and Annie and your father will be here for the holidays in July.'

Inverness was black and gloomy, as it had been on my first visit to it at the age of seven when we were taken there to buy clothes, as it is to this day when I am seventy. The pride of the Highlands, their so-called capital, seems a dark prison to me, shutting out the open beauty of the mountains and the sea which are only ten minutes walk away.

*

It was a room I had never been into. I think it had been used as a boxroom and that Janet and Margery cleared it in a hurry to make it ready for me. So far as I could judge, the curtains being drawn, one wide window looked over the garden to the sea, and the other to my left, as I lay in bed with the top of my head towards the sea, gave on to the side garden and the gardens of the next door house which had been built in the middle of a wide green space. My new room was large and long and seemed vast to me because the only furniture, two chairs and a small, low table, was beside the bed. There was no candle on the table. I asked Margery not to read to me, put my spectacles on the table, lay awake for a bit, then slept till the dawn showed through the curtains.

When I felt for my spectacles they were not there. I got out of bed and swept the floor with my fingers. They had been taken away. I knew it was part of the treatment. It angered me. It humiliated me. Without them I needed help from other people.

The carpet had also been taken away and had left behind it a pale dusty strip of floor. The pictures – two – had gone from the walls. The door was open or shut or not there at all and at the far end of this long room I could just see a hole in the floorboards large enough for me to get through. A black hole.

My memory of those six weeks in bed at Tigh-na-Rosan is not precise, nor is it lost to me, but its quality resembles the quality of dreams which when described aloud lose their essence. The essence, the blur, the vivid but edgeless impression cannot be enclosed in words. So when I say that my whole body turned more than once into sand, once into water and several times into wind I hope that people who dream vivid dreams will recognise experiences similar to their own.

Sand flies with the wind, drops with the wind and runs with the wind before you or behind you and against you, buffeting, soothing, stinging. It drives its sharp way through pinholes, through cracks in the walls, between the window and its casing, underneath the door. It is as boisterous as the wind on which it rides, and as peaceful afterwards. It goes where the wind goes. Water makes it powerless and still.

When I touched my face with my hand one night it was smooth and rounded as a buttock, without nostrils, mouth or eyes and as I stroked my cheek the tips of my fingers made grooves in it and although I was not pressing my hand became filled with a substance which trickled be-

tween my fingers on to the sheet. When I stretched my arm
out and opened my clenched fist the breeze from the open
window blew the stuff away. It was a warm night. I threw
the sheet and blanket off me and tried to sleep, but the
breeze took me up, spread me over the room; parts slid
through the chinks in the floor boards, parts under the
door, a great part into the fireplace, up the chimney and
away through the sky. I was loose, dispersed, and lay still
only for a few minutes at a time, as when I settled on
chimney stacks, and early in the morning just before the
church warden came ran under the church door and
covered the altar steps. When he came to sweep me up he
closed the door behind him against the wind and then as he
opened it to empty his dustpan I and the wind blew back
into the church.

*

Every Saturday and Sunday evening and sometimes on
early closing days during the week Mina came to see me. I
had seen little of her since the early years of my childhood,
not because I loved her less but because I had so many more
interesting things to do than going to her house to learn
how to make gingerbread. When I went for sweeties in the
shop which she kept with her husband on the High Street
brae she had no time to talk except for the business of 'Is
Mrs Finlay keeping well? And Mrs Margery?' It was
Margery, I think, who told her about my imprisonment,
and she came at once in her long blue dress and floppy grey
tam-o'-shanter.

She walked into the room as gently as she spoke. Her first
words on her first visit were 'You are well here, David.
There are many who would wish for your bed.' She kissed
me and stroked my hair. She went to the window and held
the curtains open a chink.

—— Come and look at the moon.
—— I'm not supposed to.
—— A few steps will do you no harm.

It was a full moon. Like the earthly lights seen without
spectacles it was covered with holes and bubbles like a pail
of milk during milking.

—— Lochiel's lantern, she said.

—— Why is it his lantern?

—— It gave him light for his wicked deeds.

—— He comes to our church.

—— I am speaking of those Lochiels that went before him. Will I tell you a story?

I went back to my baby days when she was with me; perhaps because I was lying in bed, a yearning for her old bedtime stories came to me on those evenings. She sat on a chair beside me as she had sat long ago, her skirts overflowing it, hiding it, as though she was crouching with nothing to sit on, her long-sleeved arms resting on her knees, her white hands loosely clasped. When I asked her for a new story, one I had not heard before she said

—— I doubt but you have heard every one I have since you were three years of age.

—— Tell me about the witch in the old Kirk of Nairn by the river.

—— What is that, dearie?

—— How the Devil was there and bit her shoulder and poured the blood into the palm of his hand and made the sign of the cross on her forehead with her blood.

—— What has taken you my child? I never told such a shocking thing and if I had heard it myself I would not tell it.

She was as near to anger as I had ever seen her and I felt ashamed because she was truthful. It was a story I had read secretly in Uncle Robert's library, while he was out at golf, in *The Criminal Trials in Scotland* which has a long section on witchcraft. Mina left the room with an excuse and I thought she would not come back, but she did and sat down looking sadly at me. I touched her sleeve. I said I didn't want a story, just to talk. She looked at me, not believing me, and said

—— My grandfather's grandfather knew a witch. Maybe I told you that?

—— What, Mina?

—— The witch with a pony. She was in Sutherland just over the county boundary from Caithness where I was born. Well, she turned her daughter into a pony and her name was Janet Horne. She took this young filly to the smith to have her shod and she rode her and the filly was a girl the same age as you.

—— How did she get a saddle and bridle to fit?

—— Janet was a poor woman, David. She wouldn't have money for the like of that.

—— She'd need a whip if it was a girl. Mina almost laughed. She said

—— You're a terror. And then told me how the daughter was 'lame in her hands and feet' for the rest of her life from the nails the smith had put in when she had hooves. The mother died a cruel death inside a lighted tar barrel in which the people rolled her down a hill and it was cold weather and the poor creature sat warming her hands at the fire they were getting ready for the barrel.

—— Was the pony blue?

—— Blue, did you say?

—— Blue roan.

—— Indeed I never heard what colour it was. It is long, long syne.

—— Then tell me about the blue filly.

—— Now I know what you're after. Not tonight, dearie. It is time for sleeping and the story is long.

I often asked her for stories she had told me when I was small. She sat down and told me the Blue Filly on another evening and I am sure it lasted a whole hour. Blue Filly was my name for it. She called it The Widow's Son. It is about a boy who was always out stalking creatures on the hills, for his father was dead and he and his poor mother had little else to eat. One day when he was crouching 'at the back of a knowe, before the sun and behind the wind, there came his way a youth like a picture riding a blue filly.' The youth slid down off his filly and he and the widow's son played at cards, and the widow's son won. The youth got on to his filly and said 'What is the stake of our gaming?' 'The blue filly under thee.' The poor widow's son took the filly home and she changed into the finest woman that man ever saw. Next day he went stalking again and when he came home in the mouth of the night his mother told him that the big giant had taken away his sweetheart. The widow's son went out to search for his blue filly, his fair lassie.

As he made his way over the hills he met the blue-eyed falcon, the brown otter and the grey dog of the mountain. Each one changed into a man and spoke to him saying 'It was late when the big giant went past with your sweetheart on his shoulder.'

At last he climbed down into a desert glen with no life in it and no houses except one big white house, and there on a rock outside it he saw his sweetheart with a golden comb in her hand, and she would take a while at combing her hair, and a while at weeping and when she saw him she said 'My sorrow! What brought you here? The giant will kill you.' But the widow's son said to her, 'Two shares of fear on him, and the smallest share on me.'

She hid him. She had a long talk with the giant when he came home and laid it as crosses and as spells on the giant not to come near her for a day and a year, and she and the widow's son were together in the giant's house until the evening of the next day.

Then she spoke a long time with the giant, and tormented him and at last he told her that he kept his heart in an old oak stump on the bank of the river. She and the widow's son split the oak stump with an axe and a hare leaped out of it. 'There goes his heart away,' she said. 'Now he will come and kill you. And then he will kill me.' The widow's son called the grey dog of the mountain and he came. He had caught the hare and he brought it to them by the throat. The blue-eyed falcon and the brown otter came, and the giant came roaring to the sweetheart of the widow's son, pleading for his life, but the widow's son struck him down, as he would fell a tree, and the giant fell dead. And the widow's son and his sweetheart stayed in the giant's house and on the land of the giant, and their children's children, and their children's children were there when I was last in that glen.

Mina often began and ended her stories with the words her father and grandfather had spoken. She once said that the last of the giants in Scotland had been killed some years before the last wolf. It was a man called MacQueen who killed the last wolf, just over the hill from Strath Nairn.

—— Did they kill all the fairies too?

—— Well! Now! The fairies turned against Our Lord and no man or woman that held Him in their heart ever was touched by the fairies. Maybe they were afraid to show themselves when the faith grew stronger in the land. They live underground. My father saw them one or two times milking his cow, but I believe it was only in his mind he saw them. We hear so much about them that we see them, just the way we see creatures in a dream at night. The Lady of Daviot was a person to be taken by the fairies and it was that same MacQueen who saved her with his magic candles.

This was one of her old stories and I liked it even more now because I knew that lonely place where Uncle Robert had sometimes brought us on visits to his friends at Daviot House which stands close to, but high above, the left bank of the River Nairn about halfway between its sources and Nairn harbour. After tea we were let loose to clamber down the precipice and along the river in bare feet, half in, half out of the water, to the stony place where you can climb up the cliff through the dark trees to the ruin of the Castle in which the Lairds of Daviot once lived.

Mina said,

—— It was in a house by the river Findhorn at the edge of the Hill of Pollochaig that the magic candles were and it was in the hills of Daviot by the river Nairn that the Voices of Daviot were heard. Indeed they are heard to this day. I believe you have heard those voices, dearie.

I told her how we used to shout and sing for the echo to come back to us below the Doune of Daviot. It was called a double echo, but we thought it more than that because it came from every side repeating itself in several voices.

—— Well, the man who owned the magic candles was a MacQueen and he was a tacksman. He owned no land but paid his rent for house and land to Mackintosh, the Laird of Daviot, and he had great thought for the laird and whatever Mackintosh asked him MacQueen would do.

Well, Mackintosh went south for a wife and the people did not like it. When he brought her home, she had no Gaelic and could not speak to them. She had foreign dress and foreign manners. And she was beautiful. People would stop working to gaze at her. Horses stood still when they met her on the mountain path and birds sang as she passed, in places where they had never sung before. The fairies of the Doune of Daviot saw her too. MacQueen saw her once. Everybody thought her beauty was uncanny and that she belonged to another world, that she would bring misfortune to the House of Daviot and unhappiness to their laird.

On her first Christmas at the castle, the laird planned a feast and he invited many people to it from far and near and the best musicians came, for she loved music and she loved dancing. But before the feast began she told her Highland maid that she was going for a walk on the Doune to 'have one more look at the mountains and the sea and the Nairn valley before this Christmas sun had set.'

She did not come back. The cooks watched their fowl, fish and venison spoiling for an hour, lifting them from the fires and on again as they cooled. The guests grew sulky in the great hall. The dogs whined and yelped. The laird said, 'My lady will soon be home. She has gone for a short walk.' And thinking to make them lose the time he told them stories, but they were saying between themselves, 'It is a long walk,' and whispering, 'We came to a feast and found a fast.'

—— Didn't they get anything to eat then? I asked Mina. I was beginning to feel hungry for supper and was thinking of the miles and miles those people had walked or ridden. There were no roads near Daviot Castle long ago.

Mina thought that the tenants and poor people would get plenty to eat in the kitchens and grander dishes than they had looked for, for the lairds and ladies and the gentlemen and women had none of the dishes that had been cooked for them. Not one of those invited to feast in the great hall would take a bite without their hostess at the table.

That night men with lanterns and torches searched the Doune of Daviot from below to the top, from one slope to the next. The laird sent his men to the east as far as Nairn, to the west beyond Inverness and into the high mountains to the south. But no one had seen her. No one saw her for a year.

Three days before the second Christmas Daviot's cousin, Captain McGillivray came home from Africa to Dunmaglas which is not far from Daviot. He was the Laird of Dunmaglas.

In his wide journeys the Captain had uncovered mysteries of other worlds and as soon as Daviot told him how his Lady had disappeared he said 'She is in the dark. She has been kidnapped by the Fairy Prince. Bring me one of MacQueen's candles and I shall find her. We have only three days till Christmas and then she will be with the fairies for ever.'

They sent a messenger. The night was black. The wind was wicked. Both rivers were in spate. When he crossed the ford of the Nairn the water came over his waist. When he swam across the Findhorn the raging torrent swept him downstream and he reached the opposite bank half drowned and had to walk an extra mile back to Pollochaig.

When he came to the house he was told that MacQueen was away across the river but would be home that night, so he waited and after waiting long his ears were dinned by a whistle from the opposite bank. A horse, all saddled and bridled, galloped out of the stable – no man with it – and plunged into the Findhorn. It swam back through the flood with MacQueen on its back and when he had dismounted walked quietly, unattended, back into its stable. When the messenger saw this enchantment he was afraid.

MacQueen gave him one of his three wax candles because he knew that without its light the Lady of Daviot could never be brought up from under ground.

—— Carry it home to your master, he said, but never look back on the way. Never look back, do you hear me?

The messenger heard him, but in the Pass of Pollochaig a thunderstorm came on him and at each flash of lightning the rocks cast fearful shadows. A host of demons chased him, crying out, and he looked back. The candle melted in his hand.

Next night they sent another messenger through the flood and storm. He looked back too and the second candle melted.

On the third night the third messenger was carried away

by the flood as he tried to cross the ford of the river Nairn and was nearly drowned. When at last he reached Pollochaig, MacQueen refused to give him his last candle. The three had been in his family since heathen times when the Priest of the Temple of Carnach, among the stone circles of Clava, nearby, gave them to them. The fairies, said by some to have taken refuge from the Christians underground, had loved the MacQueens and protected them ever since.

—— I would rather part with the best bullock in my herd, said the tacksman to the third messenger.

Then he thought of the Lady of Daviot, remembering her beauty and the grace of her walk as she, only once, had passed by on the hill. He gave away his last candle.

The demons pursued the third messenger too, but he did not look back.

The Laird of Daviot gave the candle to the Laird of Dunmaglas who, holding it at midnight walked by the river Nairn till he came to the path the lady had taken on her way up the Doune. There was a green circle among the stones beside that path. He had found it long before as a boy and walked round it and over it fearfully, daring the fairies to grasp him. Now, he stabbed the green turf with his dirk until it struck stone. He pulled the turf away and came to a slab with rings set into it, by which he raised the slab. He slid in to the deep, dark passage below and slid until his feet touched a level floor. Then he lit the candle. He saw that he was in a lovely cave with 'marble baths fed by a marble fountain' and he saw a dark opening beyond the baths, just in time, for the candle was guttering in the fountain's spray. Near the end of a long, dark, winding passage he heard music. Then he saw brilliant lights. He took off his bonnet to shade the light of his candle and stood looking into a banqueting hall more magnificent than any he had seen in all his courses round the world. It was all green, its malachite pillars flickered back the lights of ten thousand candles, tinging them with green, the rounded walls were draped with darker green and a thousand dancers moved like the leaves of trees in spring, casting green shadows on the floor. The most brilliant and the tallest of the dancers

were two dressed in gold and green who whirled like the
wind among the others, who parted as they came near and
closed when they had passed.

The Laird of Dunmaglas knew that the tall man in gold
and green was the Prince of the Fairies. He took his bonnet
away from the magic candle and it shone on the hall and
quenched all the other candles. It melted the dancers, all
except one, into a green mist which vanished leaving him
alone with a lady dressed in green and gold. Now he knew
who she was and said

—— What are you doing here, my Lady of Daviot?

—— Am I late for the feast? Have I done wrong?

—— Do you know what day it is?

—— It is Christmas Eve.

—— Which Christmas Eve?

—— I was invited to this dance by a beautiful youth. Is
Daviot angry? I thought half an hour would do no harm.

—— You were bewitched by the Prince of the Fairies. This
is your second Christmas Eve under ground. Come with
me now or you will never see the face of the earth again.

She went with him. He brought her home.


After Mina had gone and I had had supper, after Janet had
taken my plate away and Margery had come to say
'Goodnight', I crawled in the darkness to the hole in the
floor. It was not a hole. It was a trap-door with a ring set into
it. I pulled this up and slid feet first down through a long
pipe that perfectly fitted my body. The descent was long
and frightening. The pipe grew hotter and hotter and every
second I expected my feet to plunge into the molten core of
the earth. But, suddenly they touched a floor. I stretched
out my arms but could find no walls. As I thought of
climbing up again for my bedside candle, I fell into a warm
lake; fell deep, could not breathe; struggled and writhed
and at last emerged into a narrow slippery passage which I
crawled through till I saw lights glimmering and fading
through curtains of seaweed which parted and closed with
the movement of the sea. Their soft look deceived me, gave
me false hope, for to make my way through them into the
light beyond was the most difficult part of my journey.

When at last I pushed my head through they clung to me like snakes entwined and held my shoulders back. As, time after time, I felt them tighten and close in an uneven rhythm I learned not to push but to be passive, waiting for the moment when they parted. As soon as I caught one such moment in the nick of time I used all my strength and broke out into the open gasping for breath. The air was salty, the light was brilliant, though where it came from I could not tell, for looking up I saw a roof from which dark seaweed hung black and brown, on long tapering strands like bootlaces, in flat leaves with bubbles on them, some with bunches of brown berries, some shaped like hands, the fingers paler than the hand.

When I stood up I was one of an immense crowd of people who were holding hands in twos and threes and swaying, rhythmically, parting and closing in groups like the strands of seaweed curtains which hung down the walls behind them. Through gaps at one second or another I saw in the centre of the hall a huge round table burdened with food in wooden dishes and whisky in crystal jugs. The people seated round it were all old and ugly except three. A man about twenty years old with a crown on his head sat facing me, furthest from me. On his right sat a girl with long fair hair and on his left a girl with long black hair. Both wore circled garlands in their hair. I looked again through another gap and then through another. I saw that the fair haired girl was Jeannie and the dark haired Patsy.

In the middle of the table there blazed a tall thick candle made of amber-coloured wax and around it in widening circles rings of smaller candles flickered, each ring lower than the next. The candles in the last and widest ring were shorter and slighter than birthday cake candles. It was from all these, which I could not see from the floor, that the brilliant light spread over that vast chamber.

I was shorter than anyone in that assembly of smoothly wafting people and taking chance by chance and step by step whenever I saw an opening I reached the round table without being observed. I stood quietly between an ugly monster with a grey beard and a horned helmet and an old woman who looked like Lady Tin-Opener – both guzzling.

When I drew a deep breath they looked round. But not in time to stop me. I blew the great candle out. Smoke poured from its wick and kept on pouring as if from the funnel of a ship. All the smaller candles went out too and belched their smoke until the chamber, now in darkness, was filled with a honey-smelling fog.

By the candlelight I had judged my distance from the two girls well enough to find them in the dark. I was guided too by their smell which was earthly and warm, and then they were moving their heads and talking to each other across the Prince. By mistake I put my hand on his which was watery and cold as a rock exposed by the receding tide. Standing behind him I stretched my arms out taking Patsy's hand in my left hand and Jeannie's in my right. I pulled them after me through the swaying people who were now closing in on me with a threatening manner. Behind the seaweed arras, circling round the rocky jagged walls, we came to a large black opening and soon we were running in a tunnel hand in hand and three abreast, wet underfoot and dripping overhead. It was pitch dark for the first half mile, then as we came round a bend we saw faint daylight like the first glimmer of dawn. The floor of the tunnel began to slope upwards and was soon so steep that we stopped running. We were out of breath. The air grew warmer as we climbed the slope and the stones of the tunnel were dry.

—— But where does it lead to? Jeannie said in a frightened voice. She was trying to pull me back.

—— It leads up to the world, I said, and she kissed me. When Patsy saw that she tore her hand angrily from mine and ran ahead.

The daylight ahead of us shone down from the top of a stone stairway which we climbed. At first we could see Patsy's bare feet, then her legs, then her skirt, then the whole of her standing on a wide slab at the top of the stairs, her arms above her head trying to push an iron grating up. It was lovely to see the sky through its bars above her head. The grating was rusty and as it had not been opened for a thousand and twenty-six years its hinges were sealed by grass and its flanges clogged with earth. I pushed it up with one hand and we climbed out into the Constabulary

Gardens, by which I knew that we had come up from the old castle of Nairn to the later one.

—— O, thank you, said Jeannie.

—— For what?

—— For waking me up. She was overjoyed when she saw where she was and called me a hero and kissed me.

I wanted to make friends again with Patsy but she ran away shouting

—— You might have waited till after the pudding!

*

That morning – I think it was the same morning – Granma came into my room. My misfortune had softened our feelings towards each other very slightly; she had ceased to criticize and I had begun to feel something approaching affection for her, but her brief visit that morning annoyed me. She said she had had a letter from my mother.

—— What did she say? Will you read it to me?

—— I have left it downstairs. Mrs Grimmett is coming to see you this afternoon.

At the door she turned and said

—— How are your bowels?

—— Granma – please tell Mrs Grimmett not to come.

—— It is arranged. You must keep up with your lessons.

I liked Mrs Grimmett in her own Fishertown house but hated the notion of having a blind person in my room.

It was all right when she came. She brought a new large scale map of Scotland embossed with clear lines and bumps, for rivers, roads, railways and mountains, all pleasant to feel and explore with the fingers, and she told me what to feel for and described each place in an excited way as though she had just discovered it herself. But just before she left she shamed me. She felt my face with her gentle fingers and kissed me, first on the forehead and then on the cheek, and said

—— Don't be unhappy. Think of me. I am six times your age and I've had a good life. When I was twenty I was asked to go to London to teach blind children. I had never been out of Nairn before. My sister came with me – the blind leading the blind. We took the train to Aberdeen and the boat from there to Tilbury. It was the cheapest way. And London is a big and muddly place. Even sighted people lose their way, but we never asked one soul. We won through to our rooming house alone together.

Much embarrassed and wishing she would go, I said something meaningless.

—— After school I took the children home by bus. I put them off in ones and twos at different stops where somebody was waiting for them. I never made a mistake in all those years.

Next day I was loitering in the High Street on my bicycle trying to decide how to spend my pocket money: on sweets, cakes or crayons, which would last longer. My indecision was prolonged because my sixpenny bit that week was a beautiful Victorian one, thin but with a clear impression of the Queen when she was young. I did not want to part with it. Behind me I heard a tinkling of little bells and there across the road outside Rose Bros. I saw a strange pony and trap. Kenny Cameron was holding the pony. I knew every outfit that came into Nairn and this was too rich and trim to belong to a farmer.

I sat on my bicycle with a foot on the pavement opposite the shop watching till a boy came out with brown paper parcels stacked up to his chin. Kenny with the reins in one hand took the smaller parcels from him and put them on the seat. The other boy stowed the rest at the back of the trap. Then Jeannie came out of the shop. It was Jeannie! She too was carrying parcels and when she had thrown them in – she threw them in – she jumped into the cart without using the step and drove off down the High Street at almost a gallop which she soon had to check because the Inverness bus came roaring up the brae towards her. I followed her and overtook her as she pulled up by Asher's, the baker's shop. I passed her and stopped to look back.

—— Laddie, she said in her lowland way which I had heard outside church, can you hold my pony a minute. I'll give you a penny, she said as I came towards her. She did not recognize me. I put my bicycle against the wall.

I had plenty of time to look at the pony. It was a blue roan, big and strong with black mane and tail. Its mane was short and plaited in a row of little knots all down its neck. Each knot had a round silver bell on it and from its plaited forelock hung a larger bell. Its harness, black and brilliantly polished, with silver buckles and rings, was decorated with small flags. The Royal Standard of Scotland with its red rampant lion flew highest on the peak of the collar, the upright hoops on the saddle through which the reins passed each bore a *fleur de lys* and, fixed to the breeching where it joins the crupper, there was a golden dragon passant on a blue field. Even the pony's tail had been trimmed to look like a flag on a short thick staff. The trap had flags on it too, one on each lamp holder and two on the back rail. It was all too fanciful for my liking and the pony wore a gilded basketwork muzzle which looked like a miniature, old-fashioned cage for a canary.

Jeannie came out of the shop with her arms full of pokes and cake boxes. She had a chocolate éclair sticking out of her mouth like a cigar. I took the parcels from her and put them on the seat. She pushed the whole éclair into her mouth and said with bulging cheeks

—— Don't squash the meringues.

Then she took a penny from a little purse which hung from her neck like a locket and held it out to me.

—— Keep it for next Sunday when the plate comes round, I said. She looked at me.

—— I've seen you in church! I didn't know you with no specs on.

—— I only wear them in church.

—— Would you like an éclair, then, or a cream cookie? I don't want to open the meringues. Would you like to come for a spin?

I chose a cream cookie and a spin, and gave her the reins.

—— Better hold his head while I get on. He'll dash for home when he feels me. Which was what the pony did. I scrambled on to the moving cart and sat beside her. Ahead of us I saw a railway lorry plodding across the narrow bridge and a car coming towards it. She could not slow down. We plunged past the lorry, scraping the stone parapet on our right. The car stopped and we squeezed through on to the Auldearn road which was steep enough to make the pony slow down to a trot.

—— It's my turn for a cream cookie now, she said. Can you drive a horse?

—— Yes, and a motor.

—— But Tweedledum's so naughty.

I drove while she rummaged on the floor where most of the parcels had fallen as we crossed the bridge. Asher's cookies were so tall and thick that they needed two hands. She broke hers in half at the layer of cream and ate that first.

—— Do you like my pony?

—— Yes.

—— Would you like to have him?

—— How could I?

—— Get my uncle to take his shoes and socks off and tell me what his feet are like.

—— Why?

—— Chrissie says she peeped into his bedroom and he's got hoofs, cloven like a goat's. But it's a taradiddle don't you think?

—— Does he like bathing?

—— He likes the girls on the beach. If he sees a pretty one he goes in after her.

—— If I keep near the pretty one . . .

—— He always swims in sandshoes.

—— I'll watch him changing.

—— Impossible. (She pronounced it the French way.) He changes in the machine with the door shut. What's the cure for freckles?

—— Mare's milk at night. Rose water in the morning.

She looked at me making a funny face and laughed.

—— But Tweedledee's only just in foal. Eleven months. Next April! That's too late.

—— I like your freckles.

—— Coo, it's hot. Do I smell sweaty?

—— Yes, it's nice.

—— What's your name?

—— David.

—— Davy, Davy, fie for shame

Kissed the girls in the railway train.
—— Jeannie, my queanie

> Ate a heap o'neeps.
> Tammy Piddle kissed her
> And now she's his for keeps.

—— How did you know my name then?
—— That lady calling you and you won't come.
This made her laugh more than ever.
—— Fräulein Nein, she said, and when the pony slowed down at the top of the hill and sneezed,
—— Nein, Tweedle. Nevvair in company. And if you cannot your sneezink suppress, then your hoof, mit handkerchieve, before your nose raise.
—— Not if you're wearing a muzzle, I said.
—— Oh, I forgot. We can take it off now.
I got down, took it off and as we moved on asked her why he had to have it.
—— He's carni-voorous. He eats the boys that hold him in the High Street. Did you see those chocolate cakes?
She rummaged on the floor again and found them.
—— It's lucky you've got a big mouth, I said.
—— Kolya says I'm pretty.
—— Who?
—— My cousin. He doesn't like my freckles. Can cousins marry?
I was too jealous to answer, and sulked for a while. We had long since passed through Auldearn and were on a rough road, strange to me, steep, twisty, narrow, leading south towards the mountains. The loneliness of it and being with her in the loneliness excited me as all explorations did, and frightened me a bit because I knew every side road between Nairn and Forres and this was as strange to me as she was. I was exploring both and both seemed dangerous. She seemed not to have remembered our encounter under the sea. She sang songs and rhymes in different languages as we went along and was quick to find out that I did not understand the words.
—— You don't know much do you? What school are you at?
—— Eton.

—— But it's not the holidays yet.

—— They let me off the summer term to let the other fellows catch up with me. Oh, look at that hawk!

She could not see it. Even to me it was just a speck against the blue of the sky, but I knew it was a hawk by the way it held its wings. Then I saw a small leveret lying in its form far from us on the moor.

—— That's what he's after, I said, but she said

—— Where? You're pretending. But the hawk stooped and got it and then she saw them both.

—— My eyes are supposed to be good. But yours, David! Then why do you have specs in church?

—— To look holy.

—— Davy, Davy, stick him in the gravy.

—— Jeannie my queanie lost her seamie

Tammy Piddle kissed her . . .

Then he kissed her little sister

Made a bulgy blister

Tammelly Tummellie, Pebbellie, Pommellie

Piss, Pot Hot.

—— I'm dying of thirst. Can you see a spring?

I saw a burn just ahead on our left flowing out of some rocks in a waterfall but she wouldn't drink from it. She said there was probably a dead sheep lying in the water above.

—— It's the blasted heath, she said, I'll drive.

The pony seemed nervous and as we came round a bend he shied and tried to jump the dyke, which was low, on to the moor. She pulled him back too hard and he reared, tipping the cart up backwards. I grabbed the reins and hit him on the head with the whip between the ears. To make things worse, she screamed, but he put his forefeet down and at last I got him to stand still.

Before us, blocking the road, stood three old women with creels on their backs and baskets over their arms.

—— Witches! she whispered. What shall we do?

—— They are fishwives, that's all – out for fir cones.

But the first one said,

—— Davy, turn hame. Let the quinie go her ain!

The second raised her arm and, pointing to the hill before us, said,

—— Thon gait will bring ye tae the years that will be.
    And the third witch said
—— Tae the boneyard ye run
—— Turn back ere all's done.
—— Turn back! whispered Jeannie whose face was white as linen.
—— I must take you home.
—— I'll get a taxi from Nairn and you look after the pony. But when I looked from her, the women had gone. We caught no sight of them on the open moor on either side of the road and the brae before us was clear. It was long, straight and steep but the pony trotted all the way up without my urging him and the apple-ie colour of Jeannie's cheeks came back.
—— You saw them too?
—— Yes. There they were.
—— Oh good. I just thought . . .
    At the top of the brae the pony slowed down to a walk. His flanks were heaving and his nostrils blowing.
—— Let's give him a rest, she said. There's a grassy place soon. Do you really like him?
—— Yes. He's braw. But not all those flags.
—— It's Chrissie's birthday. They're for her. That's why I went to Nairn for the messages. I got nice messages, didn't I? D'you think she'd mind if we opened the meringues?
—— We'd better leave something.
—— Just one each. Please! There won't be many people at her party.
    We came to a yellow hill where the flowers of the whinbushes clustered in a million posies so closely that we could not see the leaves or thorns. As we gazed at them she chanted the old rhyme
—— When the whins are out of blossom
—— Then kissing's out of fashion.
    The tune she put it to was sad. I tried to kiss her but she turned her head away and I could only see her hair.
—— I like your hair, I said.
—— I'm going to have it bobbed.
—— Don't.
—— Dum's going to have his tail bobbed too. He likes to

look smart.
—— But it is bobbed.
—— He wants it shorter. No tail at all like an English sheepdog. People can't see my earrings now. Do you like them?

I pushed her hair aside. There was no earring. She put her hand to her ear and shouted – Stop! We'll have to go back. Asher's! It must have fallen off at Asher's. Like this one, look.

She took a ruby earring off her other ear. She was distressed. They were real rubies, she said, set in gold but with screw pins because her uncle would not let her have her ears pierced.

When I found the lost one on the floor of the cart she kissed me on the cheek and we went on.
—— Will you pierce my ears?
—— I don't know how to.
—— You just heat up a needle and push.
—— I could put a ring in your nose.
—— How d'you know that then?
—— Pigs. She laughed at that and said
—— Good. But a gold one. When will you do it?

Before we came to the grassy place we were stopped by a man on a horse which stood still in the middle of the narrow road. The horse was black. The man's brogues were black with silver buckles and the stirrups they were lodged in were gold. He wore fine black leather gloves but all the rest of him was hung with green, a plaid from chin to ankles hitched in folds at the waist, and between his knees and the saddle and on his head a green Glengarry sharply pointed at the front like the prow of a boat.
—— Turn back, said Jeannie, it's Uncle James!

I knew he would follow us if we did that and I made our horse stand still as his came towards us at a walk. He shouted
—— Your money or your life!

I shouted
—— Unbonnet to the lady.

Jeannie whispered
—— Don't provoke him, and I promised him my silver

sixpence, but only if he lifted his bonnet and put both hands on his bare head. He lifted it. There was another one under it and another and another. I went on at him. There seemed to be no end to them. He put them on the pommel of his saddle until they started falling off and then the road was strewn with his green bonnets. When he took off the last one a jet of white smoke gushed up from the top of his head and he put his hands up as though to staunch it. I told him to keep them there and promised to slip my sixpenny bit into his brogue.

By the time I reached him, his head and shoulders were shrouded in smoke and there was a cloud of it above us in the sky but I could see by the points of his elbows that his hands were out of my way. I unbuckled the brogue on his near side and pulled his hose down to the heel. His shin and ankles were covered with black hair. As I pulled everything off I touched something hard like an inner shoe. Then I saw his hoof, cleft in the middle like a goat's but beautifully polished like Tweedledum's. There was a smell of linseed oil. I pulled his hose up quickly, dropped the sixpence into his brogue and did the buckle up. Then I ran back to our cart and took the reins from Jeannie. We could see nothing, for the fog had come down to the ground and the sky above us was black with it. We went on cautiously at a walk, listening for the hoofs of the devil's horse but we heard nothing and there was nothing in our way.

Jeannie leant close to me as we came through the fog, silent and clutching my arm, but when we emerged from it into the bright summer, she looked at me happily as though nothing had broken our journey. When we came to the grassy place Tweedledum tried to go on to it, but, seeing a wider, greener stretch ahead, I would not let him.

—— Let him, said Jeannie, he wants to piddle. Nein, Dum, if you wish to leave the room you hold up . . . And as he was doing it, she whispered to me

—— It splashes on his legs if he does it on the road. That's why he held out so long. How about you? I've wet my knickers.

On the grass we had Chrissie's baps and cheese and two bottles of ginger beer from Rose Brothers parcels, and then I

told her that her uncle had goat's feet.
—— I told you so, she said, did you see his tail?
—— No.
—— Do you know what penis means?
—— No.
—— It's Latin for tail. I looked it up. But when I put it in
my composition, Miss No got cross and said 'No, the real
word is *cauda* – always write *cauda*. This verd you write
already is low Latin.'
—— I've remembered *cauda*, now you say it.
—— What gender is it, then? She's always finding fault.
—— The Gender of a Latin Noun

> By meaning, form or use is shown
> A man, a name of People and a Wind,
> River and Mountain, Masculine we find
> A woman, Island, Country, Tree
> And City, Feminine we see.

She laughed while I was reciting this, but said
—— Where does *cauda* come in?
—— Pay attention, Miss Jean, or I shall keep you in. Fifty
lines after school unless I perceive an improvement in your
conduct.
—— Yes, sir.
—— The endings denoting the gender of nouns differ in
accord with the five declensions – thus:

> Feminine in First, a, ē
> Masculine, as, ēs will be
> Abstract Nouns in iō call
> Fēminina, one and all:
> Masculine will only be
> things that you may touch or see,
> (as curculiō, vespertiliō,
> pugiō, scipiō, and pāpiliō)
> with the Nouns that number show,
> such as terniō, seniō.
>
> Echō Feminine we name:
> carō (carnis) is the same.

—— That's lovely. How can I learn Latin like that?

—— Kennedy's Latin Primer. Q.E.D.

—— What?

—— Quite Easily Done.

I taught her 'Abstract Nouns in io call' by repeating it and within five minutes she chanted it to herself without a mistake.

—— What's vespertilio?

—— A bat.

—— What's papilio?

—— There's one – look.

—— A butterfly! How lovely!

After we had been through the whole thing again, she said

—— Then *cauda's* feminine and penis is masculine like Dum's tail and you, but whatever Fräulein Nein says, *cauda's* no good for me.

—— I think she's right about penis. It's very old Latin, perhaps.

—— But I haven't got a tail.

I kissed her. The lovely pressure of her lips on mine took everything else away. When our lips parted and she lay with her head on my shoulder, and my arms round her, I said

—— Why wouldn't you kiss me before?

—— I didn't want to have a baby, which made me laugh a little, and I said

—— It doesn't happen just by kissing.

—— Fräulein Nein says it does. How then?

—— Like animals.

She gasped. Then she burst out laughing and said

—— That would kill me! She had hidden in a forbidden place and watched Tweedledum mounting Tweedledee.

She jumped up and ran to the pony which, though we had not untackled him, was grazing quietly, pulling the cart behind him step by step. She snatched all the flags off. I ran to stop her but she said

—— He's yours now. You don't like flags.

I thought of Chrissie's birthday but had no control over this sister of hers whom I loved. I watched her clip with her nail-scissors the flag-like hair which hung from the pony's stubby tail, and shaping what was left into a knob at the end.

—— Isn't it trig, David? Like a stalk with a bud on the end. Do you know, she whispered, Kolya once showed me his stalk.

We untackled the pony, changed his bridle for a halter and led him down into a grassy valley which, once you were in it, seemed to be enclosed on every side by hills. If we had been taken there blindfold we would have believed there was no way out, for the river rushed into it down a waterfall from a rocky ravine and flowed out through a narrow gap between cliffs which turned sharply, obscuring its course. It ran wide and shallow through the valley, black water rippling white here and there over stones making a sweet sound, high notes and low notes, trickling, bubbling, melting into a lullaby that made us drowsy as we lay by its bank in the sun.

Jeannie woke up and searched the parcel for more ginger beer, but we had finished it. She pulled out a large bottle and unwrapped it.

—— Uncle Jamie's whisky! He'll never notice. Just a little. Have you got a corkscrew? There's two more bottles here.

My folding knife had everything on it – corkscrew, and screwdriver and a thing for taking stones out of horses' hoofs.

We had a little each out of the bottle and it choked us, making us cough. I spat most of mine out but she swallowed hers gasping.

Next minute she jumped up and danced the Reel of Tulloch, her toes moving fast, her skirt swinging, flaring, her arms above her head with hands curved towards each other, her face serious but gleaming with enjoyment, all in the bright sun. The light and moving shadows cast by her dazzled me, took me out of the valley altogether. There was no sky, no world, no person except her. I was joined to her, dancing in my imagination against her while she danced.

Suddenly she leapt high and landed on her hands and knees, the soles of her bare feet towards me.

—— Now you can kill me! Now I'm ready!

I turned her over on to her back and we kissed.

When we woke up the grass we were lying on was faded and brittle, like hay but cropped bare by the sheep which had grazed on it all summer. As we led the pony out of the valley the wind was cold and the leaves of the trees by the roadside were red, brown and yellow; the whins had only a few flowers on them. We drove uphill and down and up hills so steep that the pony walked them. On both sides of the road, and ahead, there were mountains covered with snow. We came to a church no bigger than a bothy and got married. We came to a bothy whose door was almost blocked with snow and Jeannie had her baby there, a girl much smaller than a lamb. When we left the bothy the snow had gone, the birch trees were showing pink and red leaf buds and the blossoms of the whins were closer to each other. The weather was spring-like too.

We drove on a little way and the sun was as hot as it had been when we started out from Nairn.

——  Do I smell sweaty? What's the cure for freckles?

We saw some red deer. We came to a shooting lodge belonging to some laird. I broke a window and got in. She handed me the baby and climbed in after me. It was cool and shadowy. We liked it and loved each other.

We quarrelled. That was because I spoke of Patsy, wondering where she was. A cloud came down from the sky and in through the broken window. I could not see Jeannie, nor hear her angry voice which faded away like the walls and ceiling. I heard Mr Rae's voice instead.

——  I thought you would never wake up.

I told him truthfully that I had not been asleep but he was unable to believe me.

——  You were in a trance then.

——  No. I was wide awake with my eyes shut.

*

Fantasies sustained me, preserved me from boredom during those six weeks but the switches I had to make when anybody came into the room were like being thrown out of bed and told I was late for school. The quick change from fantasy to realistic talk led me, long before I learned anything about psychology, to a discovery which I believed to be my own. I unveiled my subconscious self. For a great part of my incarceration I was longing to write. Sometimes I did write on my Braille machine but the stiff clacking noise of it came between my feelings and their expression. The only good that did was to preserve some evanescent memories after the Braille script had been lost.

Mr Rae said that up until his father's time no distinction was made between sleep and other forms of unconsciousness – trance, fainting, concussion, or insensibility caused by extreme cold. A man called William Foxley fell asleep for fourteen days and fifteen nights in the last year of Henry the Eighth's reign. The greatest physicians were called in to examine him. Even the King came. He was tortured by pinching, burning and cramping but in the end he woke naturally in good health, as though he had only been asleep for one night. In the eighteenth century a girl aged nineteen slept for fourteen weeks without waking in spite of many cruel attempts to rouse her. When at last she showed signs of waking of her own accord she took three days to wake completely. She seemed in good health but felt faint.

——— But coma often leads to death, said Mr Rae lightly.

——— Why didn't you wake me up then, if you thought I was in a coma?

——— I hadn't a thumbscrew on me and I've lent my pilliwinks to your grandmother.

He often made me laugh. He no longer gave me formal lessons but told me whatever came into his mind while he was with me and usually his answers to my questions startled me, and yet he would not answer until he had finished saying what he wanted to say. When I asked him about Lochiel's lantern and Lochiel's wicked deeds he spoke of something else as though he had not heard me; then suddenly he said,

——— Lochiel's wicked deeds! I suppose Mina was thinking of the Black Ewen Lochiel. His hair was black, that's all. He was no more wicked than your father.

By this he meant that my father and Lochiel, separated in time by nearly three hundred years, had spent their lives fighting wars, killing hundreds of people, risking their own lives with courage, believing in what they fought for, getting almost mortally wounded and being loved and praised by their countrymen and kinsmen.

—— Lochiel killed a wolf with his teeth.

—— You are mistaken, young Thomson. He killed a man with his teeth.

*

The Camerons we played with at Nairn, children of Lochiel, lived at Achnacarry in Lochaber, not far from Ben Nevis near the shore of Loch Eil. Lochaber had been the territory of the Clan Cameron since the fifth century AD. They came every summer to Clifton, the house next door to Tigh-na-Rosan and on Sundays went like us to the Episcopal church.

Cameron, the name which seemed so romantic to me as a boy, means Crooked Nose or Wrynosed Warrior. The man so nicknamed, who became the first Lochiel, is supposed by one tradition to have been a son of a Danish King who helped to restore Fergus II to the throne. He was renowned for his prodigious strength, 'a monument of which is still remaining near Achnacarry, the seat of Lochiel; namely a large stone of upwards of 500lb weight, which he could hoist from the ground with a straight arm, and toss it with as much ease, as a man does a cricket bat: a ploughshare he could bend round his leg like a garter; and the strongest ropes were no more in his hands than twine-thread.' He was so proud of his strength that he challenged every champion in the south of Scotland to single combat and won, but once in a chance quarrel when both were unarmed his antagonist 'with a violent blow of his fist set his nose awry . . . had they fought with swords, he might have hewed it quite off, but this blunt blow only set it on one side; yet so, as that it could never be recovered to its right position. From this accident he was always afterwards called Cameron, or, the Knight of the Wry Nose, as that word imports in the Highland language.'

At the age of thirty-four this man went north to seek his fortune and a wife. He found both near Ben Nevis in the lands that later became known as Lochiel's. His fame had spread even to that remote place and Macmartin of Letterfinlay, who then occupied it, welcomed him because he needed someone fierce and strong to lead his clan against their neighbours, the Macdonalds of Glengarry, with whom he had had a long quarrel. He gave his daughter to Cameron who then attacked the Macdonalds and after much bloodshed annexed a great part of their land. That is how he won wife and fortune.

From then on the Camerons and the other powerful clans enlarged their territories by plunder and slaughter, just as the European nations were to enlarge theirs centuries later. From the tenth century until about the fifteenth the Camerons ruled all the land between the River Spey and the Atlantic coast. By Black Ewen's time their territory had been somewhat reduced by constant warfare, but the power of the clan was not whittled away until 1745 when the Duke of Cumberland defeated them and Bonny Prince Charlie on Drummossie Moor by Culloden. The Lochiels we knew in the nineteen-twenties had no more than a family estate, large by the measures of the twentieth century and ancient by any measure.

Black Ewen Lochiel, called *Eoghainn Dubh* in the language he first spoke, was born in 1629. The story of his boyhood lay in my mind so long that I imagined it to be my own. I wrote some of it in Braille but most of what I am writing now is, of course, derived from books I read later in my life.

He was sent away from home at the age of twelve, in 1641, to live at Inveraray Castle with Archibald Campbell, a relative of his mother's, the Earl and, later, Marquis of Argyll, who from his repulsive squint was known as the 'gley-eyed Marquis'. Argyll had engaged a good Covenanter, one who shared his political and religious beliefs, as tutor to the boy. The clan Cameron, most of whom were for the King against the Covenanters, had long arguments before deciding to send Ewen to Inveraray. They knew, for one thing, that Argyll coveted their lands. If he could win the loyalty of this young heir to their chieftainship they would become subject to the Campbells. Yet, in the end, they gave way to Argyll's persuasion.

Ewen did not, in the end, give way. In spite of the strict Presbyterian lessons arranged for him at Inveraray Castle, he rejected the Covenanter's doctrine when he was seventeen and then joined Montrose to fight for the King and the bishops.

His five years at Inveraray Castle were divisive from the start. He had never enjoyed learning anything except fencing, the use of firearms, bows and arrows, the broadsword and the dirk and, better than any of these, ways of hunting wolves, foxes, the wild boar and various kinds of deer. During his early boyhood in Lochaber he had excellent tuition in these hard and dangerous arts. His tutors, who were probably just as keen on hunting as he was, allowed him to neglect book learning. At Inveraray he was in similar country among lochs, mountains, forests abounding with the same wild creatures uncontained by fences, undisturbed by roads; for there were no roads in the Highlands. It was his second paradise, as untamed as the first and as untamed as he was. But an attempt was made to keep him from it, to imprison him in the castle library from whose windows he could see the huntsmen setting forth, to lead him thence in mental chains to the family kirk which rang with the sounds of the hunt from the hills above, and droned with the voice of his tutor within.

He soon began to play truant, creeping out of the castle before dawn to wait on his pony hidden in the woods until the hunt came by, returning late for lessons or not till night. His tutor, being of a lower rank, was afraid to beat him. His uncle was not afraid but had few opportunities because he was almost all the time at war. And also it is said that Ewen had endearing charm. His polite apologies, his convincing excuses quenched the rages of his tutor. But no doubt he felt guilty. No one can continue to do what he is forbidden to do without getting painfully torn, without resolving to reform his ways each evening and breaking that resolve next day.

Then there was war, and at first he did not know which side to be on.

I perceive other qualities, other mental struggles which I shared with him in my way and according with my times;

for it is a mistake to say 'I was born in 1914 and he in 1629', implying that there is an essential difference between people who lived centuries apart. No date of birth is in itself significant; no person's life self-contained. Character and memory, although we are unconscious of their origins, reach back through generations like the shape of face and limbs. No one's mind is an entity detached from history or from prehistoric mythology.

Black Ewen was born at the time when the history of Scotland was being irredeemably warped; I was born in the time when the history of Europe began to be warped. Both of us spent our childhood during years when our relatives and all adults were preoccupied with war, and our youths at the time when future wars seemed imminent. At about the age of fourteen we were both pulled two ways at once. In his youth the small wars between clans and groups of clans which had continued for at least ten centuries were enlarged into a great war, a war that was led on one side by the most powerful Presbyterians who had devised the Covenant in successive versions and signed it, and on the other by the King and his nobility. Hunger, greed, private quarrels or revenge were no longer the sole reasons for fighting, although those motives still played a great part. People on the Covenanters' side were no longer fighting solely in the interest of their chieftains or, amongst the Lowlanders, in the interest of their landlords. They were fighting for a faith. The Covenanters believed that the Reformation had been no reformation. They believed that the Established Church was ruled by prelates, filled with idolatry as bad as that which had filled the Catholic Church. They wished to make the administration of the church democratic so that every parish and community could choose its own minister, and the ministers would never be allowed to have authoritarian power over their congregations. The king's party wished to preserve the Church of England in the form that had been shaped during Queen Elizabeth's reign. People on both sides were devout and genuine in their beliefs.

The motives and purposes of war are always difficult to come at. Almost every religious war, and wars made ostensibly for political purposes, now called ideological, have always been partly materialistic in purpose. Consider the 200 years of the crusades: it is impossible to disentangle the genuine religious feeling of the people taking part from their materialistic greed.

The leaders of the Covenanters possessed large, valuable, estates which were threatened by excessive taxes and even confiscation unless they took the so-called Oath of Indulgence. The Royalist Episcopalians were required by law to provide armed and trained troops for the government. If they failed in this their estates, too, would be forfeited. The Covenanters favoured Cromwell against the King and in 1645 under the command of the English General Leslie routed Montrose and his Royalist army at the Battle of Philiphaugh.

Soon after the battle the Marquis of Argyll was summoned to London on affairs of State and he brought Ewen with him, intending to enter him as an undergraduate at the University of Oxford. They travelled very slowly in the cumbersome family coach. When they reached Stirling, intending to stay there for the night, they found the city afflicted by the plague. The Marquis was so frightened by this that he refused to leave his coach, but Ewen, getting bored, slipped out unnoticed and wandered through the city. When at last the Marquis realized that he was no longer sitting beside him he sent servants to search for him. They found the boy in a house where the whole family was infected by the plague, but Ewen did not catch it.

The Marquis of Argyll stayed long at Berwick, where his ward often ran the risk of getting his brains dashed out in quarrels which he was daily engaged in with the youth of that town. So soon did he begin to act the patriot and to employ his courage in vindication of the honour of his country which commonly occasioned these childish combats, and when that news reached the Marquis, Ewen was forbidden to stir out of doors without a guard of two or three servants about him.

Black Ewen never went to Oxford, for his guardian, hearing that Montrose had invaded Fifeshire on his way to take Edinburgh, went hastily back to Scotland. After the battle of Philiphaugh in 1645, at which the Covenanters defeated Montrose and the Royalist army, cruelties were committed in the name of God by the Covenanters upon their prisoners and on women and children who had taken no part in the movement; atrocities worse than any so far perpetrated in Scotland. Some of these were witnessed by Black Ewen and his revulsion made him turn against his guardian and side with the defeated Royalists. This was the second and last occasion on which he was torn both ways.

His change of heart became irrevocable during a conversation with Sir Robert Spottiswood who was in jail at the time awaiting execution, for, after winning the battle, the Covenanters had called a parliament at St Andrews and it was there that the most important of the state and military prisoners were kept. Lord Ogilvy, on the night before his execution was due, had swapped clothes with his sister and escaped. The others under sentence of death, of whom Sir Robert Spottiswood was one, had been moved into a fortress and denied the usual access to visitors.

Ewen was determined to see the prisoners on the day before their execution. He waited until he was sure that the Marquis was busy in his private room, slipped out and walked to the castle where they were confined. He called the captain of the guard who, recognising him and doubtful what to do, excused himself by repeating the strictness of his orders to admit no visitors.

'What,' said Black Ewen, 'I thought you'd have known me better than to fancy that I was included in these orders? In plain terms I am resolved not only to see these gentlemen but expect you to conduct me to them.' The captain of the guard acquiesced.

Old Sir Robert Spottiswood had been a close friend of Ewen's long dead father and hearing that Ewen had been put in charge of Argyll he expressed the greatest surprise that his family should have consented to that. 'Can they expect,' he said, 'that you will learn anything at that school but treachery, ingratitude, enthusiasm, cruelty, treason, disloyalty and avarice?' Ewen answered Sir Robert by excusing his family and saying that Argyll was as civil and careful of him as his father could possibly be, asked him why he charged his benefactor with such vices. They talked for several hours. Ewen heard for the first time the Royalist point of view and understood that the Episcopalians were not so wicked as Argyll and his tutor made them out to be. Perhaps the main thing that influenced his opinion was Sir Robert Spottiswood's loyalty to the King. Next morning Sir Robert and the others were taken to the scaffold.

Most of the articulate citizens of Saint Andrews were angered by the news of the proposed executions and, in fear of them the Covenanters had engaged two preachers who, for some days, 'endeavoured to prepare the people for the sacrifice, which, they said, "God himself required, to expiate the sins of the land." '

Black Ewen, now Lochiel because his old uncle had died, beheld the tragedy from a window opposite to the scaffold in company with the Marquis and other heads of the faction. He could not conceal his grief and 'indeed the exemplary fortitude and resignation of the sufferers drew tears from a great many of the spectators'.

Lochiel who had successfully concealed his visit to the prison, asked his guardian later that day what crimes had these people committed and why they had not been allowed to speak before their death.

'We expected,' he said, 'to have heard an open confession of their crimes from their own mouths; but they were not allowed to speak, though I am informed that the most wicked robbers and murderers are never debarred from that freedom!'

The Marquis, shocked and astonished, answered him, saying that 'common criminals could never persuade the people to follow them in their crimes but that the more intelligent and eloquent could. He said that the Provost did wisely in not allowing the criminals to speak and especially Sir Robert Spottiswood, for he was a man of very pernicious principles, a great statesman, a subtle lawyer and very learned and eloquent and therefore the more capable to deduce his wicked maxims and dangerous principles in

such an artful and insinuating manner as would be apt to fix
the attention of the people and to impose upon their
understanding.'

His Lordship then proceeded to open the cause of the
wars and accused the king and his ministers as the sole
authors.

Lochiel now made up his mind to go home to Lochaber,
but he dared not tell Argyll, knowing that permission
would be refused, so he wrote to his family secretly asking
them to demand his return on some pretext that sounded
urgent and necessary for the welfare of the clan. This was
eventually done and in 1646, when he was seventeen, he
went back to the Lochaber Camerons.

All the able-bodied men of the clan made a whole day's
journey over the mountains to meet their young chief. And
when they brought him home on the following day he was
received with almost royal pomp and festivity. He made a
good impression on them by his talk and manner but some
were disappointed when they saw how slightly he was
built; his slender form was not suited to a warrior; in
appearance he was the very opposite of their old warring
chieftains. Yet he was jimp and nimble, more nimble than
most warriors. His fearless skill in riding untamed horses,
his prowess in hunting wild animals and his agility soon
put away their fears. He is said to have killed with his own
hands the last wolf in Scotland, but MacQueen of Pollohcaig
and the Magic Candles were also said to have killed the last
wolf, near Nairn, many years later. News travelled slowly,
and news of the death of a wolf probably did not travel at
all. That is why so many people in different parts of
Scotland claim that one of their family killed the last wolf.

In 1654 and 1655 General Monk, who commanded Cromwell's army in Scotland, bribed and persuaded several of
the Highland chieftains to come over to the Republican
side. Lochiel remained his most powerful enemy, with the
whole of the Cameron clan. Monk offered Lochiel two large
and rich estates, the payment of all his debts and any rank
he chose in Cromwell's army. When Lochiel refused the
bribe, Monk was determined to reduce the Cameron clan

and its stronghold at Lochaber. He sent a large force and in 1655 rebuilt Fort William as their headquarters very near to Lochiel's castle. Lochiel, at that time a Colonel in the Royalist army, was fighting in the South. When he heard about General Monk's invasion of Lochaber he returned there with his troops to defend the place. He was expecting to meet Monk's army on the way between Loch Lochy and Inverness, but his preparations for a battle there were suddenly stopped by a Cameron horseman who announced that five English warships had arrived in the sea loch, Loch Linnhe, which forms a right angle with Loch Eil at Inverlochy where the two waters join.

Fort William was by then garrisoned by 2000 Cromwellian troops, but its new fortification had not been completed. General Monk's army attended by a large following of workmen, servants and their families were in full possession of Lochiel's native territory. The shores of Loch Linnhe and Loch Eil were at that time covered with trees, a part of the Highland forest which has long since disappeared. When he reached Loch Eil, Lochiel dismissed the greater part of his army, telling them to go home, remove their cattle to a safer place and get food for themselves. They were exhausted by the battles in the South and by the long march home. Lochiel from his hiding place in the woods with only 32 gentlemen to support him saw two ships moored in the loch: one near to him and the other on the opposite bank.

It had been on Argyll's advice that the English came round by sea to Inverlochy, where they landed safely with a year's provisions. To strengthen Fort William, they felled a large number of oaktrees and with these and the plentiful stone in the area they made the fort impregnable within 24 hours. Lochiel arrived the next morning. Five days later, from his hiding place in the oak forest on a hill high up, he saw two more English ships arriving. They contained soldiers, who landed and began pillaging the houses of the village below, stealing poultry and cattle. They outnumbered the few remaining Camerons whom Lochiel had kept by his side, by three to one, but Lochiel decided to attack them. His officers thought him imprudent. He and his younger brother Amman might be killed. leaving no chieftain in the line of succession. Lochiel ordered them to bind his young brother to a tree and, being unable to spare a man, left him in charge of a small boy. Amman was angry and as soon as he heard musket fire, showing that the fight had begun, he threatened the small boy and forced him to unloose his bonds. Amman found Lochiel alone, because the men had disobeyed his orders and run on too early to the attack. Amman saw an Englishman hiding in a bush with his musket aimed at his elder brother. He shot the Englishman dead and saved his brother's life.

These English soldiers had no experience of the Highlanders' method of fighting nor of their strange weapons, the broad sword and dirk, the bow and arrow and the target, or shield. The Highlanders had few musketeers. Drummond says that in one place you might have seen five Highlanders attacking double that number of Englishmen and in another two or three Englishmen defending themselves against twice as many of their enemies. The English were routed, leaving many dead and wounded on the shores of Loch Eil. A few fled into the oak forest. Lochiel followed them alone. The English officer in command of the troops also ran in that direction to escape. Lochiel did not see him. Suddenly the Englishman leapt out of a bush and attacked Lochiel, sword in hand. Both fought for their lives. At last Lochiel managed to knock the sword out of the English officer's hand and they closed together and wrestled. It seemed to Lochiel that his end had come, for the Englishman was very large and strong and he slightly built and not so tall. His nimble agility saved him for a while and they rolled over and over until they fell into a ditch which had steep sides to it. Lochiel fell underneath this heavy man and was bruised and cut by the sharp stones at the bottom of the ditch. His arms were strong enough for a while to hold the Englishman so that he could not move, but eventually the Englishman freed his right arm and managed to draw his dagger. Lochiel caught a grip of it and was not stabbed. In a last violent attempt to free himself the Englishman raised his head, exposing his throat. Lochiel seized his throat in his teeth and bit it out. Drummond's words are: 'The Englishman's extended throat which he used to say God had put in his mouth biting it right through and keeping such a hold that he brought away the mouthful. This Lochiel said was "the sweetest bite I ever had in my life." '

This was the part of Lochiel's story that I asked Mr Rae to read to me again and again. For me at that time Lochiel's story ended there, but months later, answering my questions, Mr Rae read an account of his death: 'Sir Ewen's eyes retained their former vivacity and his sight was so good in his ninetieth year that he could discern the most minute object and read the smallest print . . .'

But Pennant wrote that he became 'a second child and was even rocked in a cradle.' He was fed in the end on woman's milk and suckled like a baby before he died. He died in February, my birthday month, in 1719.

I did not wish to live so long. I thought twenty-one was the best age to die. You would be officially grown up then.

On his way back from the battle of Inverlochy, Montrose brought some havoc to Nairn, but a greater devastation was made a few miles further east, beyond Auldearn.

> . . . the place of Brodie, pertaining to the Laird of Brodie, the place of Culbin, pertaining to Kinnaird; the place of Innes, pertaining to the Laird of Innes, and Redhall, all burnt and plundered . . . Their salmon cobles and nets cut and hewn down . . . Thus, as Montrose marched, he sent out parties through the country with fire and plundering.

According to Lachlan Shaw, it was on this occasion (February 1645) that the old family papers in Brodie House were destroyed or carried off. The people and the lairds were terrified.

When Montrose reached Nairn a deputation of Covenanters headed by the Earl of Seaforth had been sent to plead with him to spare the County of Moray. His answer was the fire and slaughter which Brodie of Brodie described.

In May 1645 Montrose met the Covenanters at Auldearn, two miles east of Nairn, and although his army was worse equipped and less than half the size of the Covenanters' he won absolute victory, which he cruelly exploited, that afternoon. He shouted 'Give no quarter!' when he saw the battle was won. No prisoners were taken. Wounded men were killed. Two thousand Covenanters lay dead on the land of Auldearn.

*

Uncle Jamie gripped me by the collar, his fingers like ice beneath my chin, and said

—　I am moving rapidly towards my death.

He said it twice quickly in a matter of fact tone, staring at me, which frightened me but I could not shift my eyes from his.

——　You will hold my horses for me till I fetch my breeks in here.

We were outside Hay's, the tailor's shop. He was wearing a kilt when he went in and a new pair of riding breeches when he came out. He left me outside the tailor's for almost an hour while the final fitting and the final stitching went on but I was not bored. I loved my charges, two beautiful fillies, one black without a single white hair on her, one yellow as oat straw with dark chestnut fetlocks, mane, forelock and tail. Their close summer coats were sleek, and shining although we stood in the shade, their manes and tails had been combed smoothly, so that the manes hung like waterfalls with ragged ends entirely covering the offside of their necks and their long tails ended raggedly over their hocks almost touching the ground. Their harness was black and as highly polished as the silver terrets and buckles. They were well fed but jimp and firm to touch. I could not leave their heads – they were fidgety with impatience – but from where I stood I gloried in the four-wheeled dogcart to which their traces held them. No such equipage had ever been seen in the High Street of Nairn before and I had only seen one at horse shows far from me. The shafts, wheels and body of the dogcart had been newly painted in bright yellow, set with thin lines in scarlet and black.

Opposite us, underneath Dr Grigor's statue, a crowd gathered to stare. Even the squat, kindly figure of Dr Grigor seemed to stare. And instead of feeling shy as I would have on any other day I was proud.

When Uncle Jamie came out he said,

—— You will drive me to the station. Fast! Or I shall miss the train.

I had never driven a pair before, nor a four-wheeled carriage, except for that short way with Michie, but his tone was severe and I dared not confess it. Fortunately there were no corners where the hindwheels under my ignorant guidance would have hit the kerb. As we passed the Post Office he said,

—— You drive well. What is your name?

—— Thomson.

—— You will drive these ponies home for me if we catch the train.

I flicked the reins to make them canter but he said severely,

—— Not on the tarmacadam. Just trot fast.

They trotted as fast as any other horse would canter and as we approached the station yard we heard the train. He picked up his Gladstone bag and leapt off before I pulled up. As he hurried away at a dottle-trot, I shouted,

—— But where to? Where do you live?

He shouted back above the noise of the train as it slowed down by the platform,

—— They know the way! And he disappeared into the ticket office. Then I saw on the seat beside me a beautiful goat's-hair sporran with a silver clasp and chain, the thing men carry their money in when they wear a kilt. I jumped to the ground with it in one hand and the reins in the other and called out holding it above my head, hoping he or the porter would hear or see me, for I could not leave these restless creatures to gallop home alone. He came out of the ticket office for a second and said,

—— Let them gang their ane gait!

Then he shouted,

—— But Thomson! Never touch them wi' the whip. Beware!

He disappeared.

He had not seen the sporran I was holding up. I heard the guard's whistle. The ponies heard the engine driver's steam reply and got on to their hind legs, pawing the air with their forefeet. I scrambled on and turned them towards the High Street, but we had reached the Post Office and the sound of the train was faint in the distance before I managed to slow them down to a trot. As we passed Dr Grigor's statue and braved the crowded part of the High Street, I even got them to walk. I guessed the first direction of our journey: down the High Street brae, curve to the right, cross the river bridge on to the Auldearn road, the way I had travelled with Jeannie and Tweedledum. But now I was uneasy – firstly because the dogcart was wider than the trap and when motorcars came towards us I could not judge what space to leave to keep the hind wheels off the bank on one side and away from the car on the other. But two miles further on, as we emerged from the long narrow street of Auldearn between woods and wide fields which all looked the same, I had forgotten the look of the turning to the right which we had taken in the trap. That little road was narrow and dusty but all little roads were narrow and dusty, and the ponies were going so fast that I could not slacken the reins and let them swing across the road when they saw their turning; a car might be coming; they might take the corner short and overset the dogcart. When at last they saw it I managed them across with no mishap.

We passed the blazing whins, the green way into the secret valley, the wedding kirk, the bothy where Jeannie had her baby and climbed slowly, for now the fillies were sweating and blowing, up a mountain track which was frightening and strange to me. Rocky crags with skeleton trees growing in them shut out the sun on either side and we climbed through a dark twisty tunnel with no roof of its own, only a blue strip of sky above us. There was a sound of rushing water as we went downhill for a little way and we came to a black pool by the side of the track into which a white waterfall was tumbling. My urgent charges, now placid and exhausted, stopped to drink. I went with them holding the reins in one hand and scooping the water into my mouth and over my face with the other. With water streaming from their muzzles and mouths they turned slowly like cows back on to the track and stood so politely that I could not believe it of them – as though to give me time to get on to the driver's seat. But when I gathered the reins and called to them they did not move. I let them rest for a while, then flicked the reins on their backs. I said some encouraging words, then slapped the reins down, hoping that would hurt a bit. I shouted but they would not budge. At last, but fearing the Devil's stern words which came back into my ears, I took the whip from its stand and drew its lash gently across their backs. I did not strike them with it. The black who was the first to feel it raised her hindquarters and kicked. The blonde when she felt it reared up. Then both reared, biting each other's faces, and the sky turned dark as night. A cloud came down upon us. I saw nothing, but the carriage moved. All sounds were gone, no wheels, no hooves. We seemed to be sailing through the cloud. Then I heard the wheels on gravel, grinding. I had slackened the reins but sat there helpless with them in my hands. All was still and silent. We had come to a halt but I sat where I was. When the cloud blew away, the ponies had gone, the shafts were resting on the ground with the harness in its proper place between them. I jumped down, taking the warlock's sporran with me. I was in a large deserted stable yard, silent, no sound of horses or people. One side was in the shadow, dark, the other bright in the sun. I looked over every half door into loose boxes, starting on the bright side; all were empty; the coach house at the end was empty too and the long rows of stalls on the dark side had nothing in them but clean straw. I saw neither cat nor dog, nor cock nor hen. There was a ghostly stillness. I was afraid.

At last I came to a closed door. I knew it would be wrong of me to open it but longed to find the ponies safely there. With my heart in my mouth, thumping, I lifted the latch holding it with one thumb to stifle the click, and opened the top half just wide enough to let me look in. The hinges did not creak and in a few seconds when my eyes became used to the dusk inside I saw my two charges together in one stall with their heads down, feeding at the manger. Their long tails, the black and the blonde, swishing now and then, were the only parts I could see clearly. I was so pleased to see them, so relieved in my mind to find them, that I swung the lower half of the door open and went quickly into the stable to caress them and pass my hand down their legs to make sure they had not been injured after I had lost sight of them.

The sound of the door made them stumble and turn their heads towards me. The shadowy light which now reached them from it showed me that they were not ponies at all. They were laughing. They were hastily pulling on their clothes. They were Patsy and Jeannie doing up their stockings side by side.

—— Did you meet my uncle? Jeannie said.

—— Did you put the ponies in the paddock? Patsy said. Did you water them first?

—— Did you give them a feed? said Jeannie.

For shame I could not answer; then I told them how they drank at the black pool.

—— And then?

—— And then I couldn't see them any more.

This made them laugh at me more, shaming me more.

They got into their skirts and came with me over to the sunny side of the yard.

—— Don't look miserable, said Patsy.

—— There's black puddings and cookies in the house, said Jeannie, and ju-jubes.

We ate the things that were there and Jeannie went on eating long after Patsy and I were full. Then she said

—— You drove too hard this morning. You were fierce with the whip. But I don't feel a bit tired now. Do you Patsy?

—— Would you like to have a ride now? said Patsy. The fillies have had a good rest.

—— Ride the blonde one first, said Jeannie.

—— No, the black. The black!

Wanting to please Jeannie, I chose the blonde, which displeased Patsy.

—— Put these on then, she said, taking down a pair of spurs from a hook, you'll need them. She's so sluggish. We'll go and saddle up while you're fixing them on.

I put the spurs into my pockets, one each side, and went out after them to the paddock where I thought they would be catching the ponies, but the green paddock was deserted. I called. No answer. I looked into the stable where I had discovered them and there I saw the ponies saddled and bridled standing side by side in that same stall tethered to the rings on the manger. I patted them and stroked them, then called 'Jeannie! Patsy!' again. The ponies pawed the ground and pricked their ears up when they heard these names. Probably the girls had gone back to the house to fetch me, but how could they have brought these creatures in and saddled them in so short a time?

As I led the blonde one out, the black laid her ears back and kicked at me, just missing my knee. She was newly shod. She could have broken my knee. I spoke to her severely and rode off on her companion, who was not sluggish at all. I rode her over hills and into valleys, through woods and across a shallow river on to a plain where we galloped hard for a mile or more, and, though I had brought a small riding crop from the harness room I did not touch her with it once.

When we got back, I rubbed her down in the sun, put her into one of the loose boxes, took her saddle and bridle to the harness room and there put on Patsy's spurs – an old-fashioned pair with sharp rowels which spun like wheels at a touch. I swapped the blunt riding crop for the springiest long switch I could find and went to get Patsy. Not knowing the fillies' names I had begun to think of them as Patsy and Jeannie after their colours.

I spoke gently to Patsy, keeping to the side of her, well away from her heels, as I walked into the stall, and to my relief she seemed to be afraid of me, fearing perhaps that I would beat her for kicking as, I guessed, the warlock often had. I slid my hand under her mane and stroked her neck caressing her soft lips and muzzle with the other. I took deep breaths and blew up her nostrils. She blew her sweet grassy breath on to my face. She was gentle and quiet and nuzzled my hand and neck. She stood perfectly still in the yard to let me mount; Jeannie had fidgeted in a playful way; and when we came out into the open she trotted fast and beautifully as though she liked it even more than I did. She jumped a five-barred gate without my urging her – I had never worn spurs before and was afraid to touch her with my heels for fear of pricking her – and galloped up a wild hill full tilt. We went at a slow walk down the far side of it, but as soon as we reached a shady, secret valley she put her head between her legs and bucked. She took me completely by surprise. She had made me happy and calm, won me to her again, and after the long ride on Jeannie, her lively gallop had tired me a bit. Going down the hill I had rested on her gazing at the sky and hills. I had allowed her to pull the reins loose and had slackened the grip of my legs on her flanks, leaving only the tips of my boots in the stirrups. She bucked again and I lost the stirrups. Then she reared and, plunging down like a seesaw, with her heels in the air, tossed me over her head to the ground where I lay half-stunned for a second or two, but managed to cling on to the reins, with which, as soon as I was on my feet, I jabbed the bit against her gums in a way, so my father had told me, that was followed only by cruel or ignorant men. She reared again, lifting me off the ground by the reins. Now we fought. She tried to slash me with her front hoofs. I hit her with the switch, first on the cheek then on the tenderest part of her belly. When she turned to kick me I lashed the haunch nearest me again and again till I saw she was quivering. I mounted her again at last and dug the spurs into her rolling them as she galloped down the valley and across the plain until she slowed down exhausted.

At tea the real Patsy had a thin blue stripe down her left cheek as I sat opposite to her and two bloody spots on either side beneath her ribs showed through her white blouse. Her eyes were glistening with tears. I reached across the table for her hands.

——— It was my fault, she said, but I thought you had more sense of humour.

—— You angered me, frightened me. I'm sorry.
—— Then will you bathe my wounds?

Upstairs on her bed I rubbed her down all over. There was a thin blue bruise across her belly and several on her left buttock. I smoothed them all away with my tongue until she was the colour of rich cream again.

*

I had long periods of gloom on my own bed where no sunlight reached me, the curtains being always drawn. In the very depths of my sorrow, my yearning for life outside which I could hear distinctly all day long, I believed that the doctor had prescribed dusk merely to prepare me for perpetual darkness. During these hours I longed for my mother, to tell her, to hear her, to see her once again before nightfall, to feel her face and hands. I allowed myself to weep freely sometimes and felt calmer afterwards, but always stopped when I heard footsteps on the creaky stairs.

In the middle of one morning while the bare room was sinking with me in it unresisting, the stairs foretold my mother's presence by my bed. To me the creak meant Janet, with lemonade and biscuits, for Granma never came at that hour and Margery had been with me after breakfast before going out to her garden hut. But as soon as the door opened I recognized my mother by her smell. I could not believe it but knew it was she. She came running on her toes to me like a long leafy branch of syringa blown towards me by the wind, the delicate green leaves, swishing beneath sweet flowers, white, tinted rose, tinted orange. She had left the door open and I saw her in the staircase light. She leant over me, kissing me and raising my shoulders from the pillow. She did not speak. I could not. We stayed a long time like that, my hands in hers. Then she went quickly to the door, to close it, and then she gave me a miracle by opening the curtains of the garden window not wide but widely enough to let a band of sunlight in. It shone from the window away from me slanting towards the fireplace. Even without spectacles I could see the dust dancing in it and the amoebae kept away.

She sat on my bed with her arm round me asking me

about me, telling me about my father and Mary, Joan and Barbara, answering me about Kuti and Pidgy, the tortoises and guinea pigs. She made me laugh and wriggle away from her arm.

—— I must go to Granma, she said – I hardly spoke to her. I rushed upstairs from the door.

She had come on the night train from Euston, taken a motorcab to Tigh-na-Rosan and rushed upstairs. I remembered how Uncle Robert, when he was in London, used to ask the butler to send out for a 'licensed motor taximeter cabriolet'.

My mother came back carrying a tray with my dinner on it and hers. She stayed with me all day. I loved being with her but felt deranged and after tea which she also fetched, a boiled egg and scones and oatcakes for me, and only one scone for her, I even felt bored, ashamed to be bored but relieved when she went downstairs to have supper with the others. When she came up again, late, to kiss me goodnight I longed for her to stay.

Next day after dinner I asked her the time. Two o'clock. Only two hours left before the train for London reached Nairn from Inverness, and I wasted the two hours in anxiety, in my dread of being alone through the crawling weeks before me, for now that she was here no one else in the house, not even the thought of Mina's visits told. My mother counted seventeen days on her fingers, moving her lips as she did so.

—— You've done more than half and when the school holidays begin we'll all be here and you'll come to Newton with us.

When the moment came her eyes, close to mine, shone with tears which did not escape but her voice was soft and steady. After she had closed the door behind her silently as she had slowly walked towards it silently, I felt nothing. My heart was dead. When Janet brought tea I stared at it and did not touch it. When dusk fell, about midnight, I wished my mother had not been to see me. I remembered how on the train from Marylebone Station back to Dotheboys Hall after each holiday I used to want all school holidays abolished, because of the painful week I had to endure before my mind left home and settled almost happily into the other world. My mother's visit killed my fantasies. I was cross with myself for not treasuring her enough while she was beside me. For several days I was bored, sad, reg- ᵗful. The holidays at Newton seemed too far away to matter and whenever Granma came into the room I was grumpier than I had ever been before.

*

One day early in July Margery brought me my clothes and pulled the curtains open. I could eat in the dining room again, go to the manse and to Mr Rae's house for lessons, and do whatever I wanted to do in my spare time. But I was not allowed to wear spectacles, which changed the world around me for the better in some ways, and also for the worse.

I forget what I could see and remember what I could not see. There were no individual leaves on the trees but each green cloud was beautiful; the hairs of Flossie's mane were woven close like silk. I could not distinguish a single blade of grass on the Tigh-na-Rosan lawn. At night my candle and the moon took on the same shape; the tapering flame of the candle had spread into a flat disc; the crescent moon was indistinguishable from the full moon; like all other lights they were circular; like all other lights they were dented with pinpricks and tiny dark saucers forming a pattern within the circumference.

Sometimes when I heard an insect or caught a glimpse of a bird flitting past, my fingers would go up to spectacles which were not there, to push them closer to my eyes and find out whether it was a wasp or a bee, a thrush or a blackbird. I became accustomed to all this and within a week forgot it, accepted it as my normal way of seeing. The bliss of my release into the light and open air meant more than anything else. I rode my bicycle as before, but with more caution. I rode Flossie in the Sandwood fields without any caution at all, but was forbidden by Granma and Margery to drive her in the milk float. That would have been so public an exercise that I dared not disobey. I went without spectacles until the middle of August, I think, for I remember watching the Highland Games, seeing everything clearly, the circus too; the hermaphrodite at the fair I saw clearly, and everything that went on in the ring at the Newton Farm Show was distinct. The games, circus, fair and show were our special delights in August.

Everyone released from captivity, from prison, hospital, dungeon or attic, walks into a new world, familiar but new. In towns he remembers railings which he touched and passed by daily long ago but now a patch no bigger than a thumbnail where the black paint has blistered exposing the red lead undercoat appears for the first time. In the country he sees more than the wide field where he used to call the ewes; every mound, every bend and corner of its boundary appears to him as though he had never seen it before. Each cherry in a basket has its own shape and colour. I think of colour now as I remember my release. Flower beds, lawns, pillar boxes, blue and orange carts, front doors, thatched roofs, tarred huts, arrested me. I stood to look at them. For me they really were new. I saw masses of colour for the first time. No single flower appeared, nor any edge; roofs merged into the sky, flowerbeds into the lawn.

I counted the days of July in my head and on the night before my longed-for day, I kept on waking as I used to wake when I shared a bedroom with my sisters, restlessly searching on Christmas Eve for bulging stockings at the foot of the bed, and calling to each other 'Nothing. Better go to sleep again.'

I woke too early, walked across the lawn in my pyjamas and bare feet out through the back garden gate to the beach, went into the sea swimming naked for the first time in my life. It was cold.

I climbed into the station because the gates were shut, no porter, ticket man or station master to watch, ran up and down the platform, pushing barrows, riding on them when they got up speed, swung on the footbridge dangling my legs over the line, swarmed a rain pipe on to the waiting room roof. When the porter arrived he could not see me. I was down between the platforms laying my penny on the shining rail to wait for the engine to flatten it and make it larger than a half-crown. I stooped till I reached the end of the platform, then walked up the slope whistling a tune.

The first cab to arrive was Michie's, loaded with fish-wives and fish. Every morning he brought them from the harbour with their heavy loads of fish, which had been landed earlier from their men's boats, to catch the train for Inverness where they sold them. The fish were in creels and long boxes. At the station the creels, fitted with shoulder bands like knapsacks, were hoisted on to their back and with a basket on one arm, and usually a bulky parcel on the other, they walked quickly across the line and stacked their things in the place where they knew the guard's van would stop. Then they came back to the cab for the boxes, which Michie, standing on its roof slid down to them. The boxes were oblong with air holes in the lid and a rope handle at each end. It took two people to carry one across. Michie and I carried some. My parents had always forbidden us to cross from platform to platform in this way. We had to use the passengers' bridge, but I was no longer a passenger, a holiday visitor to Nairn.

The bell went, the signal flopped down.

—— She's left Auldearn, said Michie. She's crossing the river. I had no luck in it this morning. We want rain. Here she comes!

'She' streamed past us so fast that I thought she would not stop, a purple blur filling the dry bed below the platform with two old carriages in faded Highland railway colours clearly visible as they slowed down; for we were waiting near the end of the train where the guard's van was. Michie saw my father leaning out of a window and ran to him. I stood still for a moment wishing the train had not stopped, then ran after him. I was shy and flustered. I would not let my mother kiss me, did not answer my sisters' 'Hullos' or pat the scrabbling dogs. I climbed into the train and fetched suitcases from the corridor while Michie unloaded the trunks and bicycles from the van. Mary and Joan said they would bicycle to Newton but by the time we reached the cab Michie had tied the bicycles on to its roof on top of the luggage. Mother asked them to walk – 'It's too much for the horse, '– but Michie pushed them in and turned the brass door-handle which only opened from outside. I felt sure that the five of them, even with their luggage, weighed less than those fat fishwives. When the cab was out of sight and the train gone I went back into the station on to the line, but could not see my penny anywhere.

The cab was turning into the avenue when I caught it up, the gates wide open, the gate lodge people waving and arms from the cab window waving back. I waved as I overtook it but did not look.

Dark. Dank. Tall heavy trees blackened the gravel and shut the sky away. When I turned the first bend I stopped with one foot on the ground, waiting for them to come nearer. Huge rhododendrons ahead of me, bordering the avenue as it bent again towards the house, shut me in a cul-de-sac blocked from light at both ends. The sound of the horse's hoofs released me and I went fast between the bushes into the sunlight, skidding round the house on bright gravel and putting the brakes on so hard that I fell. I left the bike where it lay and sat on the front steps, hidden by the parapet.

The first thing I glanced at was Michie's horse. It was not sweating or blowing. The load had not been 'too much for it' at all. Michie had prospered since our early days and he and his horses looked well fed.

Then I saw my father getting out. He looked like someone else. He took my mother's hand as she got out, then turned to shake my hand affectionately. I rushed to Michie as soon as he let go, to help him with the cases, but my mother came and clasped me to her, kissing me. It only took a second but I began to cry. Then the lawn – running with the dogs and sisters, then the corridors and staircases, exploring the house. Then the woods and stables, running, climbing trees and roofs, walking high walls and jumping down, acrobaticking on the ropes of the swing which hung from the old beech tree beside the front lawn.

People said my sisters were pretty or bonny or beautiful or whatever they said, especially Mary who was sixteen by then and nubile, I suppose, rather plump and luscious with a round and pleasant face. I am imagining what other people thought of her – what I have been told since. I did not think of my sisters as girls at all. Mary was too old to like our antics and Barbara too young to reach roofs and tall trees. Joan was my Jonathan, inseparable, daring, more agile than me and full of ideas of what to do next, each of which made me say to myself, 'I wish I'd thought of it first.' I had always treated Barbara as a pet to be bullied and pampered by turns.

We played in the empty stables as before but now they were completely empty; our seaweed horses no longer followed us up from the beach for oats and a rest. The rosettes won at horse shows were still there, pinned to the wooden partitions between the stalls of the long dead horses – red rosettes for first prize, blue for second, green for third, yellow for 'highly commended', each with ribbons flyblown and tattered with age. We washed them. We dusted and polished the stable furnishings and swept the floors.

*

'What's the time, Mr Wolf?'
'Nine o'clock.'
'Ten o'clock.'
'Eleven o'clock.'
'Noon.'
'What's the time, Mr Wolf?'
'DINNER TIME!'

We had our dinner in the morning room at one o'clock, two hours before the others had theirs in the dining room, for Uncle Robert never returned from the golf course until after two, and then he took almost an hour to change his clothes with the help of Johnstone. He was over eighty-five.

Most large country houses had a morning room in those days, a room placed where the morning sun reached it. It was in this room that the people took their breakfast, and after breakfast when the tablecloth and plates had been cleared away, the ladies spent the rest of the morning in it, sewing or playing the piano or doing whatever they liked. When we were very young at Newton we had breakfast in it but nobody else did and somehow it became a children's room. Maybe it was the most pleasant of all the downstairs rooms at Newton. It was furnished with a round table and some little tables, including a card table, a few chairs, one or two armchairs, but no sumptuous sofas such as the ones in the drawing rooms. At one time when one of us had measles and had to be kept separate from the rest a small bed was brought in there for the invalid, and this bed stayed there forever after.

'Hickory, dickory, dock
The mouse ran up the clock.'

'Rumbildy, dumbildy, dum
My pudding's in my tum.'

'I spy with my little eye something beginning with C.
Comb. No. Cotton reel, camera, creepy-crawly. No, no, no.
Cabbage. Where? On Barbara's plate. She won't eat it.
Car. There's no car. Buke's car, I can see it from where I'm sitting and Catsy-Patsy getting out of it.
Crumbs, coal scuttle, carving knife, catapult, clock.
Chatterbox You!
How could I spy me?
In the mirror on the wall.
Crowsfeet. What? Sign of old age on Mary's eyes.
Shut up or I'll kill you – it's better than being a baby.
Chest, Calendula, calendar. Tell us when we're getting hot.
Card table. That's very hot. What is it then? I give up, let's all give up.
Catechism. In the prayerbook on the card table.
That's not fair. You can't see it with the prayerbook shut.
In my mind's eye, Horatio.'

I went through the billiard room to the conservatory to look for Patsy. Her father, Buke, always had his whisky there or on the lawn outside, usually with my father, when the Dick-Clelands were invited for luncheon. Granny called it luncheon, which seemed to me funny.
'The luncheon function is a munching junction where

gumption gets most glumption.' What we called supper, she called dinner.

'Love, honour and obey'. That was in the prayerbook.

When Patsy and I got married she would have to love me. But she wasn't there. My father called me.

Say 'Good morning' to Buke. Good morning, good morning, how are you today, nice day, bad weather, we need rain, have you been bathing this morning?

I leant back in one of the basket armchairs while Buke made jokes at me, and asked stupid questions about the winter in Nairn. I liked these chairs best of all the furniture at Newton. They were wide enough to fit Uncle Jim. Their springy basket work was fixed to bamboo frames. The upright back could be set to slope or let down to make a bed, and there was a footrest which could be pulled out from underneath. Each chair had wide basketwork arms, fitted with pockets specially made for everything anybody carried around with them. There were large pockets for books or newspapers, a round pocket for a glass, larger ones for decanters and a small tray for any odd objects such as cigars or cigarettes. You could have lived in one of these chairs; there was room for everything you needed. When we were younger we changed them into boats, motorcars, carriages pulled by four horses, railway engines, carts.

I liked Buke in a distant way but was afraid of him and hated his jokes. I think my mother felt the same. He was always making fun of his wife, her sister Edith, Patsy's mother. But although he was richer than any other member of the family except Uncle Robert, he was not grand or pompous in his manner. I don't think money made him feel superior to anybody, certainly not to my father.

My mother was a bit afraid of Buke, not for her own sake, but for what he would think of us. When we went to tea at Sandwood we all had to dress in clean clothes and I had to brush my hair. When we visited his London house in Grosvenor Gardens I had to put on my Sunday suit and brush my hair.

Patsy had two brothers, John, a lot older than she was, a rather fierce, rash and powerful boy, and Donald – younger, who was the only really good-natured, kind and gentle one among our Dick-Cleland cousins. There had been another, a little girl, who died of smallpox at the age of six. She died at Newtonmore, where she had been taken to convalesce in the good mountain air.

My mother's elder brother Robin came on his old bicycle up the front drive to join us, and I got up from the chair and sat on the grass beside him. We all liked him as one might like a funny looking animal and I think he regarded us as animals, that he thought of us as he thought of his horses and dogs, lovable creatures to be touched and spoken to but from whom no one could expect a sensible reply. He had a bad stammer and a large moustache which muffled the words which got through. He was tall and lean, and had a slight stoop, which made him less military looking than my father who kept his upright stance until old age. Robin's limbs and neck swayed about in a most unmilitary manner, yet he was Colonel of my father's regiment after my father retired. He himself had retired a few years later and come home from India; and the people of Nairn, I believe, put down his eccentricities to having spent all the years of his youth with no European company in the Himalayas and on the Afghan border, in lonely tents where he dressed for dinner every night. Colonel Robin Finlay is still remembered by the older people in Nairn in a way I think they would not have remembered a conventional army officer. And on my frequent visits to Nairn in the 1980s I had an eery feeling that I was regarded with the same sort of kindly half-amused respect. I wander about the High Street and the Fishertown as he did and I am now at about the age at which he died.

He and my father took the usual military care of their appearance, and as he sat down in the basket chair he said: 'The trouble with that night journey is that you cannot shave properly on the train. Do you use a safety razor?' 'Yes,' said my father, 'you can't use a razor on the train.' They meant the cut-throat razor which both of them used until the end of their lives. Robin had cut himself on his first journey from London, and being unwilling to arrive at Nairn station unshaven, he had bought his first safety razor which he much disliked. My father started singing,

And he played upon a razor, a razor, a razor,
And they ca'd him Aiken Drumm.

—— Sing the whole of it, Daddy.
The only times his native Forfar accent showed came
when he was angry and when he sang.

> There lived a man in our toon
> In our toon, in our toon
> There lived a man in our toon
> And they ca'd him Aiken Drum.

Buke, Robin and I sang the chorus with him:

> And he played upon a razor, a razor, a razor
> And they ca'd him Aiken Drum
> And his coat was made o' the gude roast beef
> The gude roast beef, the gude roast beef
> His coat was made of the gude roast beef
> And they ca'd him Aiken Drum.

Mary, Joan, Barbara, Patsy and Donald, hearing him,
came and we all sang the chorus loudly.

> And his buttons were made o' the bawbee baps
> The bawbee baps, the bawbee baps
> His buttons were made o' the bawbee baps
> And they ca'd him Aiken Drum.

> And he played upon a razor . . .

It is a long song. The gong for the grown-ups' luncheon
dinned and dinned but no one went in until my father came
to the end.

> And his hat was made o' the crust o' the pie . . .
> And his breeks were made o' the sheep tripe bags . . .
> And his cane was made o' the fat sheeps' tails . . .
> And his name was Aiken Drum.

> And there lived a man i' the t'ither toon
> The t'ither toon, the t'ither toon

And there lived a man i' the t'ither toon
And they ca'd him Willy Wud. [Willy Mad]

We all knew what he played upon and sang the chorus together:

And he played upon a ladle
A ladle, a ladle
And he played upon a ladle
And they ca'd him Willy Wud.

And he ate up a' the gude roast beef . . .

And he played upon a ladle . . .

And he ate up a' the bawbee baps,
The bawbee baps, the bawbee baps . . .
And he ate up a' the crust o' the pies . . .
And he ate up a' the sheep tripe bags . . .
And they ca'd him Willy Wud.

In the copy I still have which is in his handwriting, my father put notes on expression before the last two verses and he wrote 'gude tails' instead of 'fat tails':

(Slow and pathetic)
But he choked upon the gude sheeps' tails
The gude sheeps' tails, the gude sheeps' tails
And he choked upon the gude sheeps' tails
And there was an end o' Willy Wud.

(Very pathetic)
And he played no more on a ladle
A ladle, a ladle
Oh! He played no more on a ladle
There was an end o' Willy Wud.

——— You're coming to tea, Buke said to us as he went into the house.

\*

Our attitude to Newton had changed. Our attitude towards Uncle Robert's numerous guests who were different but still, most of them, of the legal profession, had become more mature. They were no longer gargoyles. They were people. The house itself had not changed. Probably the long carpets of the staircase and the corridors had faded a little and the curtains of the drawing rooms and billiard room, having been washed so many times, had probably faded too. But to me neither carpet nor chaircover nor curtain had any patterns on it any more. Of course Newton had changed as it had changed for centuries. That summer a sewage drainpipe burst and I watched the workmen dig up the old pipes, which were tree trunks hollowed and pointed like pencil points at one end, blunt at the other. These were fitted in together. The men replaced them with earthenware pipes.

Newton means New Town of course. But in old Scots 'town' meant any enclosed place such as a castle or a farm. The word is derived from the Gaelic word *Dùn*, which is the same as Doune – the Doune of Daviot, for example – and it usually meant a fortified place or castle. There are many Newtons in Scotland; in Nairnshire there is Newton this and Newton that, and all are farms. Our Newton was originally called Easter Newton, i.e. East Newton, as distinguished from Wester Newton, and originally it was a farmhouse, the remains of which could still be seen in my boyhood at the back of the house, where one stretch of stonework is very old and you can see the shape of a long low two storey building, the typical shape of a Nairnshire farmhouse. The house and farm originally belonged to the Roses of Kilravock Castle which stands by the river Nairn between Cawdor Castle and Culloden Moor. But in 1780 they sold it to Robert Faulkner, a Nairn man whose forbears had married into the Kinnaird family of Culbin. Everything in those days, most marriages and almost every exchange of land, was local. For the next 100 years until 1887 when Uncle Robert acquired it, it changed hands several times and each new owner enlarged and altered the building, until at last a man richer than the others built battlements all round it, and erected the tower which we loved so much, and to which we climbed with MacDonald up the winding staircase every morning when he went up to hoist the flag that flew above Newton House. Uncle Robert, although he was born in the south-east of Scotland had a local connection too. He had married Biba, the daughter of Cosmo Innes, and the granddaughter of Rose of Kilravock and descendant of the Laird of Innes who, with Brodie of Brodie and the others, had desecrated Elgin Cathedral in the seventeenth century.

*

'Goodbye, Robin, goodbye Buke. Yes, I'd love to come to tea at Sandwood; will Patsy be there?'

The best part of tea at Sandwood, next to Patsy, was being driven there in Buke's car, an old open Benz, large, with brass lamps and door handles. It was pale brown. The front seat held four people with a squash and the back seat which was higher, like a theatre dress circle, held many more with numbers of children standing, sitting on knees or on the floor. I stood that afternoon behind Granma who was on the front seat with Edith, Patsy and Buke, who was driving.

Beyond Tradespark he stopped to watch something going on in a field. Everyone spoke excitedly about whatever it was, but all I could do was to watch the dyke beside me rushing past our stationary car towards Nairn. It was like the illusion you get in railway stations. When a train beside you moves you think your train is moving.

I had not seen Patsy for a year and except in my fantasies had not thought about her, but at tea I loved her again for her long black hair and pale skin and the fearless way she did things that none of us were allowed to do. She took huge mouthfuls and spoke with her mouth full. She gulped tea with her mouth full and chewed with a squelching noise. She never used the butter knife but dug her jammy one in, leaving smears. She used the jam spoon either to put a dollop on her bread and butter or to scoop out a mouthful as though it was pudding and, every time, she stuck the spoon she had sucked back into the jam dish. Also she put out her tongue at anyone she did not like.

I loved her black eyelashes, especially when she shut her eyes and they made curved fringes on her cheeks. I loved the contrast between her hair and her face, bare shoulders and arms which were the colour of thick cream. She never got brown or red like us. When she came out of the sea, she found a shady place.

When the others went to the garden after tea to play croquet and tennis, Patsy asked me to go for a ride with her on the beach. Her parents had borrowed two ponies from Miss Bailey of Lochloy for the summer holidays, a Shetland called Miss Muffet and a Highland garron much larger.

—— The garron's pretty wild, she said, I can't manage him. He pulls.

I was flattered, for even at that age Patsy was an excellent rider – a few years later her skill and beauty made her the star of Rotten Row.

I stared at her, thinking does she remember how cruelly I rode her with whip and spur? For a moment I believed she had actually taken part in my fantasy. Without my spectacles I was secretly scared of riding the garron. For one thing I feared he might be a stallion. To ask her that would have shown her my fear and being unable to see between his legs I felt with one hand as I was saddling him. He had been gelded, which relieved one fear. But, still, I had to ride him without spectacles down the long, rough path to the beach. He was difficult, but all Highland horses are sure-footed and we had a joyful gallop on the sands without an accident.

Buke drove us back to Nairn and left Granma, my mother and us at Tigh-na-Rosan. He went on with my father to Newton.

It had been Granma's first visit to Sandwood House.

—— What did you think of it? said my mother in the drawing room.

—— It has no front door, said Granma, by which she meant its front door was narrow. Joan and I laughed. We remembered how she had once dismissed one of our playmates by announcing,

—— He has no mouth.

The August Farm Show was for me even more exciting than the Highland Games or the Fair, which both took place on the links. I believe the showground belonged to Uncle

Robert; it had once been part of the Newton farmland and was a lovely field opposite the main avenue gate lodge, separated from the other fields of Newton only by the Inverness road. It was bordered by tall trees and fenced with a dry-stone dyke against which wooden pens for sheep, pigs and calves were built. Each pen had a hand-written label pinned on it, which got smudged if it rained, and from these we learned the names and looks of every breed. We looked longest at animals bred in the Lowlands, in England and the Channel Islands, which were not seen in Nairnshire except on that occasion: Belted Galloway bulls and cows, Red Polls, Dexters, Devons, Friesians, Herefords, Longhorns, Shorthorns, Alderneys, Jerseys, Guernseys. We stood a long time by each of these and only glanced at the kinds we saw daily in the Nairnshire fields and moors. Lowland sheep, English sheep – Cheviots and Borders, Dorset horn, Oxford Down, Cotswold, Lonk, Hampshire Down, Shropshire, Dartmoor, Lincoln, Leicester were huge compared to the Highland Blackface we saw every day.

I don't think my sisters, except perhaps Joan, liked pigs as much as I did. They had never looked after them and got to know their ways. I loved the look of Tamworths, long and lean like pictures of medieval swine and covered all over with thick golden-red hair, and of the others different-ly, the naked, the bristly, the squat, the lanky, stumpy legged and long legged, and their names, some of which I learned not at the show but from a pig-breeding book I had discovered amongst the poetry and literature of the library my uncle Bill had bequeathed to me: Chester White, Black Essex, Angerrone, Poland-China, Périgordine, Large Black, Neapolitan, Small White, Middle White, Large White boar, like the one at Sandwood but aristocratic. From one of the labels I learned the name of the Sandwood billy goat: British Alpine. No one on the croft knew it.

Bulls, cows and horses were tethered to posts driven into the ground against the dyke, and stood as though in stalls with their hindquarters to the ring, so that when you walked round the field the nearest view you had was of udders, stones, hips, buttocks and tails, all of which aroused the unruly member, as Rabelais called it. Horses aroused mine. In a semi-conscious way I had always felt for them as I felt for Jeannie and other girls who had never spoken to me, a mixture of heartfelt love and physical desire. I longed to comb Jeannie's hair. I was allowed to comb Flossie's and although everybody on the croft took good care of her as they did of all the animals, it was only I who gave her a bath once a year with delousing liquid and warm water, who mixed molasses with her feed to make her coat shiny, who spent an hour grooming her and only half an hour on the bigger horses. She was my pride and my loved one.

If you look at a pony from behind it, as you do when driving or entering a stable, you will see how that part of its body resembles a woman's. A long tail like Flossie's was like hair flowing between rounded shoulders. A very short tail like Tweedledum's roused in me a secret and forbidden emotion which I did not understand until I was about sixteen, when a beloved girl took off her clothes and stood before me naked. A pony's hindquarters are shaped as a girl's body from the waist down is shaped when she stands facing you, plump thighs narrowing towards the knees, the calves of the legs tapering down to slim, dainty ankles. The soft bud of hair, above, which was all that the fashionable horse was allowed to keep in those days, resembled pubic hair.

Most cart and plough horses were docked to show the strength of their hindquarters which long tails hid. Horse-men in the north of Scotland had devised a more humane but ugly fashion – the tails of their Clydesdales were left on but shaved to within a few inches of the root where the remaining hair was bunched up and tied with ribbons. I liked the look of the closely docked ones best and that always worried me afterwards with guilt; it was one proof of the justice of Margery's accusation. My cruel instincts lay side by side with the kindness and generosity some people loved me for.

Clydesdales, Shires, Shetland ponies, Highland and Western Island ponies, hackneys, hunters, Holstein horses, Percherons, Punches, Palominos, Belgians,

Burgundians, Cleveland Bays, Hollandaise, thorough-
breds, Aragons, Arabs.

'And Adam gave names to all the cattle, and to the fowl of
the air, and to every beast of the field.' But at that time he
had no name himself, for Adam means in Hebrew 'the
man'. And Thomas Urquhart of Cromarty, near us, made
in his translation of Rabelais, lists of names that Rabelais
had never used.

I hid from others the sensual, often sexual pleasure
animals gave me – sight, touch, smell. I have known some
who like the smell of pigs and nanny goats which smell
faintly, like ewes. Billy goats emit a powerful smell which
disgusts most people, but is to me nostalgic and homely.
Even stroking a cat may be regarded by strict Presbyterians
as a carnal sin.

*

The pleasure or revulsion we feel at the sight or touch of
animals – the arousal of our deeply hidden instincts – may
be just what makes animal symbolism in church, religious
ritual and in myth so powerful and universal. Figures of
animals adorn doors, walls and ceilings of the Christian
Church; they are carved into ancient stone crosses. They
call forth instinctual responses and point to spiritual
insight.

Jesus Christ is the Lamb of God, his followers are sheep
and the identification between men and animals was in the
early years of Christianity as close as it had been in the
Stone Age. The Lamb is also the Good Shepherd who in the
form of a man carries his lambs, and who is, in the Book of
Revelations, portrayed as a lamb carrying a milk pail and a
crook (*Rev. 7.17*. and for carrying lambs – e.g. John 10.14).
An ox and an ass, in legend, were present at his birth. A
week before his death he rode in to Jerusalem in triumph on
an ass, and the ass, like the fool, became holy; it bore ever
after a dark cross on its back. He had foretold his sacrifice
upon the cross by saying: 'And as Moses lifted up the
serpent in the wilderness, even so must the son of man be
lifted up' (*St John III.14*).

Religion, music and literature flow through the centuries

like the waves of the sea, each wave bringing part of the wave before it on to the present shore. The gods of ancient Greece turned themselves into animals for various purposes. So did the witches of Nairn and Auldearn.

The Bull is still ritually killed in the bullring with a sword as it was by the Mithraic priests of ancient Persia. The dove, Noah's dove, which became a symbol of peace, is still sacrificed symbolically by the warmongers as it was literally sacrificed in the Old Testament days.

People believed that the sacrificed animal was redeemed by its death just as those who gave it to God hoped for redemption, and many of the creatures chosen to be offered to God were thought to stand for immortality. Most stood for fertility as well, for procreation is in a sense immortality – that is the continuance of life from father to son *ad infinitum*, the continuance of corn from seed to harvest, the eternal fire raised from last night's embers, the eternal bread from dough which had made bread for generations.

Some symbolic animals were so sacred that they could not be used for food or work, horseflesh in England, beef among Hindus are still taboo. The Kings of Israel were forbidden to breed horses in great numbers because the horse was connected with the worship of the sun. It could not be used as a beast of burden by the Israelites; it could be ridden for hunting or driven in chariots at war.

Of course I knew nothing of this at the age of twelve, but Canon Ballard's readings from the Bible and Mr Rae's telling of Greek myths and Aesop's fables had already made the animals I knew into a mythology of my own.

*

One night soon after the show I had a dream which still recurs to me. We sat in a wide circle round a large beautiful black bull which stood in the centre.

We were each given a flat disc or plate but its rim was not upturned. In the centre of the plate there was a black object in relief – a long figure with rounded ends, both ends the same and pleasing to look at. I wished to touch mine, but did not, because it seemed to me sacred, not to be touched. All round the circumference there were white saucers like seashells filled with pale seed. We held these plates in both hands steadily, not to let anything spill.

Looking down at the plates which were near but not resting on our knees, as we sat on the very green grass, we raised our faces to the live, life-sized bull which stood at the centre of the circle of which we formed the circumference. Glancing at him and down again to my plate, I knew that I held in my hands a plate which described the scene in miniature. The black relief in the centre of my plate which was not shaped like a bull stood in my mind for him, the white saucers for us who sitting below him on the grass formed a perfect circle; the grains were our offering to him. We all knew that he was about to be sacrificed. That terrible moment was near.

We saw no priests, but I knew they would enter the circle in their white robes. I was afraid and expectant. I saw in my mind a procession of monks surrounded by choirboys chanting a litany and at their head a mitred bishop with a long sword in his hand. When they stood still around the bull, choirboys and priests chanted the last rites, one deep voice singing alone one sentence at a time, the choir of men and altos singing responses.

I woke up before the High Priest plunged his sword into the neck of the bull.

I knew nothing of Mithras at the time and except for fortune-telling with Mina and Janet sought no interpretation of my dreams, but behind the little ornaments on the mantelpiece of the Tigh-na-Rosan parlour, a seldom used room joined to the drawing room by a curtained arch, there rested a faded drawing of a bull and a man which, breaking the rules, I often examined secretly. The man was either a giant or the bull a calf, for he was standing over it, pressing it down with one knee on its back and, gripping its muzzle, he had pulled its head back towards his breast, so that its mouth was open and its tongue exposed, its horns turned back towards him. With his right hand he was plunging a broad bladed sword into the bull between the neck and shoulder. A snake and a dog which may have been a fox were drinking the blood from the wound, and a creature I thought to be a lobster, but is a scorpion, was underneath its hind legs clawing its stones. The drawing was signed Patrick Chalmers, Rome, with an eighteen hundred date which I could not read. He was probably Granma's father, my great-grandfather, but generations of Chalmers were called Patrick and most of them lived part of the year if not whole years, in Italy, so it may have been his son.

I now know that the drawing was of the ancient Persian god Mithras drawn from one of the many altars which can still be seen. The mother of Mithras was a rock and, finding himself cold in the wind when she gave birth to him, he went to a fig tree, ate its fruit and clothed himself in its leaves. Some shepherds saw him, brought gifts to him and adored him. He worshipped and adored the sun. He fought and conquered the sacred bull, upon which the sun sent a raven to him – a messenger commanding him to kill the bull. Mithras did not wish to kill the bull but he obeyed and the blood of the dying bull created life on earth. The bull became immortal and the guardian of all herds of cattle and all flocks of sheep on earth. Thereafter a bull was sacrificed every year to preserve and increase fecundity, but like all animals used for sacrifice it had to be under one year old. Any man can kneel on a yearling and hold it down.

*

Kolya came that summer with his mother. I was shy when I first saw him in the Tigh-na-Rosan drawing room. In the garden we were more at ease together because his hair was matted and he asked me to cut the clogged bits out. I asked him whether he had seen Jeannie.

—— Who?

—— Your cousin.

—— I've so many of them. What does she look like?

When I had described her and her sister Chrissie and their farm in the hills beyond Auldearn he made it clear that he had never seen nor heard of them. My jealousy subsided and we became friends again. We climbed the roof of Tigh-na-Rosan and pelted the passers-by from the front wall with moss and mud as before. Granma and Margery were cross as before. We swam together sometimes with my sisters, sometimes alone, usually in the sea but on rainy days in the indoor pool, which was refilled with fresh sea water at every incoming tide. Long loose bathing dresses had gone out of fashion by then; boys and young men wore pants and girls had sleeveless tunics with short trouser-legs like combinations but neat. When they came out of the water their tunics stuck closely to their bodies. With all these bodies and the warm closeness of the air we felt desirous of each other. The baths had a lusty smell which I have never smelt elsewhere.

Over the water from deep end to shallow end hung a row of iron rings on ropes. You caught hold of the first ring with both hands, standing on the rim of the bath and pushed yourself off swinging to and fro with your feet dangling over the water till you got up enough impetus to reach the next ring with one hand; then if you were strong and your arms long enough, you could swing from ring to ring the whole length of the bath. There was one long-limbed girl of about seventeen who could swing the length and back to the deep end without a rest before letting herself into the water and Patsy's elder brother John, who always had to win, having watched her one day, did four lengths after her performance. But I, who was sitting on the rim, saw that he was too tired and out of breath to do his usual showy crawl after it. He climbed out and sat beside me for a bit, then said,

—— Let's dive off the high board, come on!

He knew I was not allowed to dive, because of the head down position; my mother, to my shame, had warned everyone to stop me if they caught me attempting it. I did jump in upright from the lower diving board but knowing John's talent for humiliating others I would not go with him at all.

I looked up at him, springing on the end of the high diving board, and saw through the wet pants which clung to him his bulging stones and the tall thick mast above them. When that happened to me in the baths, I hid it with a towel or slipped into the water where the cold brought it down, but John stayed longer than usual before diving as though he wanted everyone to see.

I thought of it in bed that night, wondering whether I would do the same when I grew up.

I never saw Jeannie at the baths, but with Patsy, Donald and John, the Lochiel boys and girls, the other Cameron girls, their cousins, our cousin Rosalind Finlay and other children we knew slightly, a cold or rainy morning turned into a party. Some parents came too. Mother swam well, but only breaststroke, and with her long hair bunched under a bathing cap looked like a stranger to me. Father, who had given up swimming after a long ago illness, came only when the weather was too bad for golf or fishing and watched from a bench – the pool was surrounded by benches – his eyes moving everywhere, not anxiously but as though he was looking out for a child in danger. He smoked his pipe all the time. In good weather we were separated from friends because each family bathed near to its own bathing machine which was hired for the season. But in spite of the smells of our bodies, the men's tobacco and the women's scent, the Nairn sea water pool did smell of the sea.

As a special treat, and only after much clamouring from us, because it was expensive, our parents had sometimes allowed us to have a seaweed bath. The seaweed bathrooms were at the other side of the building in cubicles with doors. The baths, filled with slippery brown seaweed and warm water were wide, deep and long and when we were small all four of us got into one. You did not use soap; you just rolled over and over and swished about, putting your head underneath and blowing bubbles. But this year, to my disappointment, my mother insisted on my having a bathroom to myself because I had reached the age of twelve. We had never till that day been kept apart. We had always undressed together. Joan used to shake what she called my 'tassel' in the bath as though it was a bell pull and I used to soap Barbara all over with my hands.

I refused my mother's offer. One bath cost the same, however many people climbed into it, and then I knew I would not enjoy it by myself. She had always encouraged us to bring seaweed back to Newton and have our seaweed baths there, so I told her I would go to the beach and gather enough for that.

*

There were two collieshangies at parties that summer, both caused by Kolya who usually did what no one else dared to do. The first was at Tortola, a house almost opposite Tigh-na-Rosan on the corner of Viewfield Road and the brae that sloped down to the pool. Two old maids, Rosie-and-Nora, friends of Granma, lived there with their two servants; my mother, bringing us with her, was a frequent visitor on our way back from the beach and every summer Rosie and Nora gave a lavish children's tea party. They and their cook made the cakes and scones, but bought meringues, éclairs and cream cookies from Asher's. We, perhaps fifteen of us, were talking and giggling about the best way to eat a cookie – Asher's were four inches high and you either had to eat through the plain bun till you came to the sandwiched cream or spoil the shape by breaking it in half. Suddenly Kolya stood up, placed his cream cookie on his chair and flattened it by sitting on it. Our laughter was quenched by Rosie-and-Nora's rage, for he had squashed the sticky top of the bun and the thick cream into the beautifully upholstered seat of an heirloom, an upright Chesterfield or something. Had he been sitting like most of us on a wooden dining room chair, I think they would have laughed too, but instead there was a turmoil of grown-ups with cloths and soap and a bottle of cleaning spirits. Kolya grabbed as many meringues and éclairs as he could carry and escaped to the garden, followed by the others who had seized whatever dainties they could reach. I choked, gulping a last mouthful of tea which escaped from my mouth, as I coughed, over the white tablecloth, then left the room hurriedly, not for the garden but the drawing room where I thought I should be alone.

I loved the jigsaw puzzles they kept there, enormous ones, which took them weeks to solve and covered a large card table from rim to rim. Their housemaid never touched the puzzle with a dustcloth; she flicked it with a feather duster as she flicked the precious china on the mantelpiece. Rosie-and-Nora often invited us to help them with it but the pieces were minute and the picture complex. As I sat beside it, picking up pieces and trying to fit them in, I heard the door handle turning. For a second I feared it was Kolya searching for me; he would probably have knocked the half completed puzzle to the floor and run away, leaving me to take the blame. But it was Rosie-and-Nora talking intently in whispers and not seeing me.

—— It's his foreign father and his mother's a good-for-little. No manners, no upbringing.

—— You should have pity on the boy, said Nora.

—— That won't take the stain off the chair.

They walked across to the front window, speaking in low voices. I had excellent hearing in those days, as acute as Mrs Grimmett's, who could literally hear a pin drop, as finely tuned as any blind person's.

—— It's the same with the Mazarelli girls – running wild, no discipline. Foreign ways.

—— Their father and grandfather were born in Glasgow.

—— Doubtless, said Rosie. The Gorbals. And what do they do? Away to foreign parts, desert their children and this uncle of theirs, Major Whatsit, is no fit person to tend them.

—— I know he likes his dram, Rosie, but they have a good governess.

—— A German, yes. A Bosch. A Hun.

By now I knew they were speaking of Jeannie and Chrissie in a way they would hate me to hear, but it seemed too late for me to announce my presence, and of course I longed to hear more, so I kept my head down over the puzzle and sat still.

—— Mr Mazarelli's cards had black borders, said Nora, as though the little girls' mother was dead.

—— Scarlet creature! She was as good as dead to him on the night she ran away.

When they started screaming at each other about whether Mr Mazarelli or Mrs was the first to leave the other, I called to them saying I had found a piece to fit. They came to look. It did fit. I was a clever boy but would I not like to join the others in the garden? I told them I would find one more piece before going out and they resumed their whispers by the window, more quietly than before. I could only hear the words Italy and Peru. I guessed that Jeannie's father had gone to live in Italy, her mother in Peru. But at least I had heard Jeannie's surname for the first time.

Our second collieshangie could, my father said, have killed Kolya. It happened at Lamb's Bank, a large pleasant house with a lovely garden at the corner of the High Street and Leopold Street. The ground floor was the bank. The Lamb family lived on the two upper floors of which we knew only the first, with its spacious lofty dining room and drawing room and windows which looked down on Dr Grigor's hat. They were giving a birthday party for one of their children, and had it not been rainy, Kolya would have been safe, for we would have played and danced on the lawn after tea. But instead the dining room table was pushed aside and we danced to the gramophone there. The walls of the dining room were hung with African shields, swords, assegais and daggers and after one dance Kolya seized two long daggers from their hooks and danced a war dance by himself, waving them, stabbing the air in all directions, as his arms and legs moved wildly round and round with high jumps and crouchings and yells. We all stood back to give him space. We clapped. Someone put on a Highland fling and he danced more wildly than before. He bent and plunged the daggers between his legs, raised them above his head with a jump and plunged them again repeatedly until he fell. He dropped one dagger and held both hands to the other which was sticking out of his thigh. He did not scream. He was writhing on the floor. We screamed. Some ran to the drawing room for the grown-ups, who, hearing our commotion were already on their way. My father who was the first to examine his wound thought it best not to pull the dagger out until the doctor came, to put a tourniquet above it and raise the leg on to a chair keeping Kolya flat on his back on the bloody floor. He had stabbed himself deeply on the inner side of his naked thigh just below the rim of his short shorts which might have blunted the blow.

Dr Wilson loosened the tourniquet but left the dagger in. They carried him downstairs and Mr Lamb drove him and Dr Wilson to the infirmary in his motorcar.

Later we heard that he had only just missed the main artery; tetanus and blood-poisoning were the only dangers. He recovered quickly but I did not see him again that summer.

*

The greatest blessing bestowed on me by my parents that summer of 1926, and probably the greatest of my childhood, was touch-typing. They bought me a small Corona portable typewriter and found a teacher for me in Nairn who came to Newton several times a week. I think he was a student on holiday with his parents, about eighteen. He was lithe and witty, strong with a deep voice, the kind of man boys make heroes of; but I have forgotten what he looked like. I think he had red hair and that fair skin that goes red with the sun. His forearms, which I saw most of during my lessons, and even the backs of his hands were covered with hair. The new typewriter delighted me too but I was slow to learn.

He taught me in the billiard room at the little escritoire where Granny used to write her letters, between the Oriel window and the great fireplace and just behind the armchair in which Uncle Jim so often lost his pipe 'on the ledge'. Indeed Uncle Jim was often sitting in it during our lesson respectfully silent, except for bouts of snoring which made my teacher silently amused.

By the end of the holidays I had learned to type well enough to start my first novel. My sisters took turns to read pages out to me and correct typing mistakes in ink. Unfortunately for me, but for no one else, I have lost it. The setting was the Battle of Culloden. Being unable to think of names that pleased me, I called the main characters, A, B, C, etc. My sisters thought this 'stupid' – it was certainly confusing for anyone who read the thing – but my idea was to give them proper names later on. By the time my family came back to Nairn, a year later, the book was too long for anyone on earth to read.

I returned to Tigh-na-Rosan in September after seeing them off on the night train to London. As I stood on the platform, staring at the blunt end of the guard's van until it disappeared, the station-master came to me from behind and laid a hand on my shoulder,

—— Do you feel lonesome, David?

—— A bitty lonesome. Aye.

—— But you'll go south for Christmas. You'll never heed the days passing.

—— I ken it's no long.

Except in our mimicry and light-hearted play with language, I had spoken straight English for six weeks. I reverted to Scots at that emotional moment partly as an affected protest against the affected English this kind man assumed for me and partly because lonesomeness drove me suddenly back into my old Nairn life. I was sad and at the same time relieved. If I had been freed from adults I would have bicycled from the station to the croft. The MacDonalds would have fixed up some sort of a bed for me there and I would have had salty porridge with them without fuss, Githa and Ireen teasing me, me teasing back, the men treating me as an equal.

Tigh-na-Rosan instead, Margery and Granma, Canon Ballard and Mr Rae.

Such tearing of body and soul in opposite directions inevitably led to crises.

On a Monday about a fortnight later Duncan asked me to 'help him out': he had ordered two loads of draff from Brackla Distillery near Cawdor which had to be collected on Tuesday afternoon. Other work had turned up. He could not go. I was to take the two farm carts to the distillery, driving the younger horse in front, with Bessie attached to the tailboard by a short rope. I had sometimes been with Duncan driving Bessie behind him. It was a pleasant road winding for about four miles, across the bridge over the Nairn and up to the right through woods and fields past Geddes, where the sawmill was, to which I had often travelled too. It was easy going; both horses were quiet and accustomed to motors, but on the way home with loaded carts – each held just over a ton – you had to take care about holes in the road.

Draff is the residue from malted barley, a nourishing, milk-getting winter cattle feed when mixed with linseed cake or chopped oat straw. When the cart is loaded at the still the draff is hot and wet and, sitting on it on the way home, the seat of your trousers gets soaked with warm damp.

On my way back to Tigh-na-Rosan I called at Canon Ballard's and at Mr Rae's who agreed to change my lessons to the morning; and then at dinner, urged on by pride and excitement, I told Margery all about it.

—— Two carts?

—— Do you wish to kill yourself and both the Mac-Donald's horses? Granma said.

—— Duncan will come with me on the main road. After the crossroads there's no tarmacadam all the way to Cawdor.

—— What difference does that make? said Margery.

—— The horses can't slip.

—— But the traffic . . .

—— They're used to it.

—— The Cawdor bus.

—— You just say 'Wheesh' if it comes.

—— What do you say? said Margery, smiling.

—— You don't need reins except for the police. They come in to the left at 'Wheesh' and to the right if you call 'Come high'. Never heed, Granma, I'll wun through.

—— Your language is as bad as your boots.

There was an awful silence until Granma said – I forbid it! I forbid you to go, do you understand?

After my lesson at the Manse, Dr Wilson, on his bicycle, stopped me in Thurlow Road and advised me not to drive the carts to Brackla. He was gentle. He did not give orders. When I asked him if he had ever driven a farm cart he shook his head smiling and I explained that it was not 'driving'; oldish horses, well trained and accustomed all their lives to traffic walk slowly along the edge of the road.

—— When is your birthday?

—— Next February.

—— Wait till you're thirteen.

He mounted his bicycle in his peculiar way. Leaning

forwards with both hands on the handlebars he took a few quick steps to get it moving, then placing his good foot on a short bar which stuck out from the back axle, swung his lame leg over and reached the saddle. As I watched him turn out of Thurlow Road, I thought it was not my age but my short sight that worried them and although I was hurt by disappointment, I loved Margery for going to consult him for my sake. Had he given her his approval she would have let me go, protecting me from her mother by deception.

All night my mind was in a turmoil of indecision: whether to deceive her and Granma, for which purpose I conceived several plans, or to tell Duncan early next morning what had happened and land him in a fix. Either decision, if ever I reached a decision, would be a sin in Canon Ballard's opinion. His teaching of Christian ethics and morals governed many of my actions at that time, but one of his main devotions was the care of the poor by those who live well enough to help them. The MacDonalds were poor; the loss of five hours on that Tuesday afternoon, plodding to Brackla and back, queuing at the distillery behind other carts, loading with shovels, would have cost some muckle silver pieces. But when I woke next morning, lying to Granma seemed the greater sin.

After my milk round, when I had trotted Flossie and the empty clattering cans with my bicycle roped on to the float at a dangerous fast pace up the Inverness road, I went straight in to Duncan and told him the whole story. He was mucking out the empty byre, for the cows had gone out after milking to the field. He took off his bonnet and ruffled his black hair.

—— Well. So. Davy loon. We are catched, the two of us, each one in his own snare.

—— I'll go wi' the horses, Duncan. I'll no' gae hame to my dinner.

—— Ye munna displease Mrs Finlay.

—— My bicycle might take a puncture going on for one o'clock.

He laughed and told me I must go home, saying

—— God gives and he takes away and gives again the morn. I will win through.

—— It's sin to break my promise.

—— 'Tis a sin to turn against your grandmother.

—— But I canna help ye here neither. I changed the hour o' my studies. I've to be at the Manse at ten.

—— Go. Go! And we'll see ye the morn, please God. Is Lord Finlay away south?

—— Yes.

—— And your Newton Granny?

—— Still there. He went out and came back with a dead hare, tying it to my handlebars and telling me to take it to Granny. He had shot three the day before.

I went, dejected. I gobbled down my dinner, waited looking at the mantelpiece clock till Margery and Granma had finished, then making an excuse about bringing the hare to Newton, rushed away.

Without asking for Granny I went in through the tradesmen's gate and threw the hare on to the kitchen table in front of Mrs Waddell, who, beginning to speak, broke off as though fearful of exchanging words with a madman.

Duncan had started out. I met him at the crossroads where you turn down a rough narrow lane which leads into the Cawdor Road. It was not difficult to assuage his misgivings and we swapped carts for bicycle without a minute's delay.

This Cawdor road crosses the river Nairn at the highest place I ever fished in by a long narrow bridge, then turns steeply to the right and winds uphill and down along the valley, leaving the upstream course of the river and bending downwards in places to a straight stretch by the riverbank. I loved it for its lonely beauty, the woods on either side, the rows of separate trees, the green hilly fields to the left spread with cattle and sheep, the sandy side roads, one of which leads up to Geddes where a branch of the Rose family lives very near to an ancient graveyard set round a ruined church within which the name on every tombstone is Rose. This is the Geddes graveyard, to which the farmer had brought us long ago – a graveyard in which a horsefair was once held. I still love this road but in the summertime it is no longer lonely.

The long, low, whitewashed buildings of the Brackla

distillery with their slate roofs and narrow cell like windows resembled a monastery built long ago among trees on the right-hand side of the road. There were some round conical structures with dome like but pointed roofs, and the green wooded land at the back of it which stretched to the river bank was dotted with small stone houses where the distillery men lived with their families.

There were only two carts before me. I was not late. When I jumped off mine at the weighbridge I saw the first carter with a shovel in his hands helping the distillery man to load his cart. I decided to play the gentleman and when my turn came I put on what I thought was a public school accent and stood aside to watch. It was a relief to see that they did not expect me to help. Two men loaded my carts quickly, the weighbridge again, a sheet of paper which I read on the way home, leaning back on my warm, wet couch. One ton, one stone on the gelding's cart, less than a ton on Bessie's. The figures subtracting the weight of the empty carts were written in beautiful copyhand.

Several cars passed me on the way back and of course I was seen. For some days I thought I was safe, but as everyone knows every other one in Nairn, the word reached Granma.

\*

*Fettes College*

† *Beloved Brother, jewel of Holy Russia, most learned of the Book, greetings!*

*The blood of Pan washed even the feet of the little ewe lambs to whom I send in remorse my love. I put you under cross and spells, in the good fortune which keeps you all the year round in Nairn, not to steel Catríona from me who, although she does not know it, in* sua innocentia puellarum *is betrothed to me by solemn vows. You may take all or any of the other lambs but on pain of death by the Court of the Red Hand avert thine e'en from her white fleece.*

*The Latin master here is an English stickleback, the Greek a decaying fat perch, hooked out of the Thames by James VI in 1603. The French – French* vigoureux.

> *May the blessings of God and His servant Kolya lie on your head.†*

It was the autumn of my confirmation. Mary and Joan had gone through that ordeal before me but said nothing to me of the mysterious preparatory rites, which for me were conducted by Canon Ballard in the study where I always had my lessons; but as an extra, which annoyed me because it doubled my time in that dusky room at St Columba's Manse. Canon Ballard won me to him in a spiritual sense and for a few years I was devout, unquestioning, emotional, religious in the old sense of the word: to be tied heart, soul and mind. There is, I think, a fanatical quality in my nature which has risen up to govern me on several occasions during my life. Perhaps this made the task of instruction easier for Canon Ballard. At the beginning he found me in a serious mood and by the end I was fanatical. I even wished to become a minister.

To begin with, the Catechism pleased me by its language and rhythm, its shapely question and answer design. I was quick to learn by repetition and I learned the whole, both questions and answers, by repeating it sentence by sentence as he read it out, just as I had learned some Scottish ballads and Shakespeare sonnets, bits of Milton's *Areopagitica*, the whole of Bacon's essay beginning 'What is truth, said jesting Pilate', from other people. My mind was a storehouse of such jewels in those days. My mind was a library, from which I could choose invisible books from invisible shelves and read brightness in the darkness of the night, in sorrow, gladness or physical pain.

*Question*: What is your name?
*Answer*: N. or M.
*Question*: Who gave you this Name?
*Answer*: My Godfathers and Godmothers in my Baptism; wherein I was made a member of Christ, the child of God, and an inheritor of the Kingdom of Heaven.
*Question*: What did your Godfathers and Godmothers then for you?

*Answer*:    They did promise and vow three things in my
name. First that I should renounce the devil and
all his works, the pomps and vanity of this
wicked world, and all the sinful lusts of the flesh.
Secondly, that I should believe all the Articles of
the Christian Faith. And thirdly, that I should
keep God's holy will and commandments, and
walk in the same all the days of my life.

*Question*:    Dost thou not think that thou art bound to
believe, and to do, as they have promised for
thee?

*Answer*:    Yes, verily; and by God's help so I will. And I
heartily thank our heavenly Father, that He hath
called me to this state of salvation, Through Jesus
Christ our Saviour. And I pray unto God to give
me His grace, that I may continue in the same
unto my life's end.

Then the catechist was to ask me to rehearse 'The Articles
of thy Belief' or in other words the Creed, which was easy
because I had heard it so often in church and learned it by
rote without meaning to.

*Question*:    You said, that your Godfathers and Godmothers
did promise for you, that you should keep God's
Commandments. Tell me how many there be.

*Answer*:    Ten.

*Question*:    Which be they?

These, too, I knew by heart.

Then came the secular, royalist passage against which
the Covenanters had fought. I had to promise 'to honour
and obey the King and all that are put in authority under
him'. This caused me no qualm of conscience, for the King
and government seemed more remote from my life than
characters in a fairy tale. But other promises did – 'To hurt
no body by word or deed . . . To keep my hands from
picking or stealing, my tongue from evil-speaking, lying
and slandering . . . To keep my body in temperance,
soberness, and chastity; Not to covet nor desire other men's

goods; but to learn and labour truly to get mine own living, and to do my duty in that state of life, unto which it shall please God to call me.'

*Catechist*: My good Child, know this, that thou art not able to do these things of thyself, nor to walk in the Commandments of God, and to serve him, without his special grace; which thou must learn at all times to call for by diligent prayer. Let me hear, therefore, if thou canst say the Lord's Prayer.

I knew it perfectly of course, but several times during my instruction Canon Ballard had to make me repeat it again and again. This was because, when I came to 'Thy Kingdom come', I was often distracted by the thought of Uncle Tom at morning prayers.

I learned the catechism until we came to its final passage without question or thought as most children do, just as we learned our declensions and mathematical tables, but at the end there is a passage about 'outward and visible signs of inward and spiritual grace' which did make me think because it put into words a private experience which I had never defined.

'What is the outward visible sign in Baptism?'

'Water . . .'

'What is the outward part or sign of the Lord's Supper?'

'Bread and wine, which the Lord hath commanded to be received . . .'

I had always had outward and visible signs of my most inward feelings: there was Jeannie's seashell ear, there was grass, wide stretches of it which appeared in emotional dreams and which in my imagination stood for heaven, there was the moon.

It made me think too of how we had been told earlier not to make or worship a graven image, of how the golden calf might have been to the people who offended Moses an outward visible sign of inward and spiritual grace.

My elder sisters had been confirmed in their school chapel in the south of England and had undergone instructions, delivered by a parson there, who did not mention anything to do with sex. He was, Joan tells me, secular and boring and she won her way through without the religious feeling with which Canon Ballard inspired me. As to physical instruction, she says that girls were not expected to know anything about love life. It came to them as a shock, often nasty, on the night after their church wedding.

This omission was, I believe, of recent origin and a mistake, for confirmation is intended to guide the child across the pubic bridge from infancy to maturity, a crossing more difficult for girls than for boys. The Book of Common Prayer does not attempt to part body and soul; witness the Catechism and more explicitly The Form of Solemnization of Matrimony, which dwells upon procreation and bodily touch. The man and woman join hands and loose hands three times during the service and holding the ring on the woman's finger, the man says: 'With this ring I thee wed, with my body I thee worship'.

Canon Ballard's sensitivity and kindness converted me to the faith he so sincerely held, but to the spiritual part of it only. It seems that a minister entrusted to prepare a boy for confirmation must also introduce his charge into knowledge of the physical transformation from boyhood into manhood. And this he did clumsily. At the last of our religious sessions I thought he had been struck by indigestion ten times as painful as that which usually caused the politely disguised belches which punctuated our lessons after his midday meal. To make our situation more awkward we sat not side by side at his writing table as we always had during lessons, but facing each other in armchairs – a position he had kindly chosen for its informality and to make me feel at ease.

He began by stammering. I had never heard him stammer and throughout our friendship which grew closer as I aged I never again heard him stammer. His pale, lined face turned red as he managed to utter clearly the word 'seed'. There ensued a long silence so unbearable to me that I was forced to break it by telling him I had learned a bit about it at Sandwood croft; not wheat, I told him, because they grew none, but I had learned to judge seed oats and barley by sniffing for must and by testing the grain for dryness and hardness by biting it with my front teeth.

—— The seed God gave you.

Now I knew what he meant, but said nothing, which led him to a gesture which shocked me. He raised his arm and pointed his forefinger, at a safe distance, to his flybuttons. It was I who blushed then because I had seen the gesture made by a strange man one evening to a shy girl whom I knew. This I had seen in the dusky Newton woods.

—— Do you understand? said Canon Ballard.

I nodded.

—— God gave you that seed to enable you, after marriage, blessed by our Church and subject to secular law, to produce children.

—— I understand, Canon Ballard.

—— Then consider it, my child. Let your mind dwell upon the purpose of that seed.

—— Yes, Canon Ballard.

—— You must not waste it. I hope, in God's name, that you never have wasted it and never will.

I wished to say something but confused images, appearing in my mind, kept me silent. I thought first of 'wet dreams', which gave me delights I had never known until that year. They wasted it, but how could anybody stop a thing that happened while one was asleep? Then I thought of the Ayrshire bull. The silvery stream that fell from him to the ground was certainly a waste. I guessed that Canon Ballard was warning me to stay inside my wife until I was sure that the last drop had entered her.

Of course I now know that he was telling me not to commit the act of Onan. It took me four years to find that out, to solve the puzzle he so shyly set me. I had seen very little of other boys, and it was by chance, at the age of sixteen that I first experienced that private and harmless pleasure. Had I been less ignorant in the year of my confirmation, Canon Ballard's well meant warning would certainly have taught me to experiment. The only physical pleasure I learned at my confirmation was love of alcohol. It seems to me now that the Christian Church, and especially the Scottish Churches, which preach every word in the Old and New Testaments as literal truth, twisted the words of The Book to make them fit various modes of modern morality.

For when Onan spilt his seed on to the floor it was not for his own pleasure, which would have been enhanced by Tamar, the woman who lay on the bed beside which he stood, but to obtain for himself the rights of primogeniture. When Er, his brother, died, their father Judah said 'Go in unto thy brother's wife and marry her and raise up seed to thy brother', which would by law have given to the child, and not to Onan, the inheritance.

*

Confirmation is an emasculated form of the ceremonies still practised in many countries which teach boys and girls how to take part in grown-up society. They go through an ordeal, which in most places includes physical torture but which, by the teaching of their elders, searched their souls. The intention was, and still is among many peoples, to separate the children from their parents and prepare them for adult life by symbolic forms of rebirth. Each child for example may be led blindfold through hazards to a windowless hut, stripped, whipped and left naked in the dark for several days before being led out into the adult world. To be shut up alone in darkness, there to recover from pain, is thought to be a way of opening the child's mind, of allowing the hidden part, now called the unconscious, into conscious life. It is rebirth.

In the north of Scotland, certainly in Caithness and probably in Nairnshire, but unknown to me, a pagan form of boys' initiation was still enacted while I was being politely instructed in the comfortable study of the Manse. No one could become a master horseman until he was admitted into the secret Society of the Horseman's Word, a craft guild similar to those of the carpenters, stationers and masons. The initiation ceremony was an ordeal of fear, anxiety, doubt and physical strain and if the boy could not bear it, he would be cast out and have to search for humbler work. An essential was to obey blindly and without question the commands of his instructors.

The approach to the altar was slow and hazardous. Near Thurso in Caithness, he was sent by himself in the darkness of the night to a long disused boneyard where most of the headstones were awry. He was told that if he felt under a certain fallen stone – the seventh on his left, for example – he would find a magic whip to give him power over horses. As he groped for it a hand from the grave seized his arm. One of the horsemen was hiding there. He was then blindfolded and led through 'crooks and straits', bending, circling, backing, slanting forward again like a young horse during its first spell of training which never follows a straight line. Every act in the trial was symbolic. At unexpected moments objects were put into his hand and taken away before he had time to identify them.

'Open this gate!' The gate to hell. It might be a gate or might be one bar of wood on which his instructor had placed his hand.

As he approached the altar his blindfold was removed and everything he saw was fearful for one who had been led by his parents every Sunday to the kirk to face a Christian minister and a Christian altar. This altar was a sack of grain with an upturned wooden bushel standing on it. The sacraments were bread and whisky. In the dim light behind the altar stood a tall dark man with horns on his head who seemed to the boy, as to generations of ministers, to be the Devil, high priest of witches and warlocks, but who was really a master horseman well known to the boy in daily life, who represented here at night a god of fecundity. On either side of him in greater darkness half visible men stood, whose incantations prayed for fertile fields and animals.

The ritual began with questions and answers and ended with the Horseman's Oath. The questions and the answers, repeated by the initiate, were factual but each had a spiritual, symbolic meaning.

'How high is your stable door?
How many links in a horseman's chain?
How were you made a horseman?'

The teaching which began at this hidden ceremony and continued for years in the fields and stables was intended not only to instruct the boy in the closely kept secrets of his trade, but to prepare him for the troubles every man must encounter when the troubles of childhood are supposed to have been put away. The principle troubles known to the brotherhood were in handling horses and women, between which, like Fitzherbert, four hundred years ago, they made little distinction either in love or severity. There is still a saying in the North that a man who does well with horses does well with women.

'Do not take a bath while you are handling a young horse, because any change in smell upsets him'. 'Sweat the cakes under your oxter before you feed them to the horse, and he will soon feel attached to you.'

In *Horse Power and Magic* George Ewart Evans, writing of this, mentions the young men of Bali who wiped the brow of the girl they desired with a sweaty handkerchief kept under the armpit. 'The horse has ten parts of a good woman and two of a man.'

The oath was morally the most fearful part of the ordeal: 'I swear before God and all these witnesses not to reveal secrets of horsemanry except to a true and faithful brother . . . not to give it to a fool, nor to a madman, nor to a drunkard, nor to anyone in drink, or to anyone who would abuse or bad use his own or his master's horse . . . not to a tradesman except to a blacksmith or a farrier . . . not to give it to my father, nor mother, sister nor brother, nor to any woman at all . . . not to write it or indite it, paint it nor print it, carve nor engrave it in the valleys nor on the hillside, on rock nor gravel, sand nor snow, silver nor gold, brass nor copper, iron nor steel, woollen nor silk, or anything movable or immovable under the great canopy of heaven.

'. . . if I fail in any of this . . . I to my heart wish and desire that my throat be cut from ear to ear with a horseman's knife, my body torn to pieces between two wild horses and blown by the four winds of heaven to the uttermost parts of the earth, my heart torn from my left breast and its blood wrung out and buried in the sands of the seashore, where the sea ebbs and flows thrice every twenty-four hours, that my remembrance be no more heard among true and faithful brethren. So help me God to keep this solemn obligation.'

*

Soon after my confirmation I was offered a man's job with
wages, which set my mind in a dudgeon more piquant and
distraught than the Brackla Distillery torment and, as with
all sudden and distressing events in one's life, every
happening, every thought, of that day and the succeeding
days stands out like the ticking of a clock, till then
unnoticed, on the day when someone dies.

I was pious and sentimental, seeing God in everything
about me, His hand in the blessed weather after the rainy
morning of my first communion – 'Do this in remembrance
of me', which I had done the day before for the first time.
God had sent to me on my milk round the first bright frosty
dawn of that autumn. The cockcrow from the Fishertown
backyards reminded me of waking up at Newton years
before. I had heard it every morning all those years, but
now it came to me with poignant clarity as all sounds do
when the air is still and freezing. In Park Street I stopped
the pony, just to listen to a bold old cock whose voice rose
from depth to shrillness. In Harbour Street, I pulled her up
again to watch a rat, the first live rat I had been near enough
to watch. It was crossing the road on its way to the river. It
was probably a black rat which even then were rare. It was
dark, round, fat and fearless. When it reached the safety of
the wall by the riverside of the road it sat on its haunches
and stared at us. The thatch and slates of the Fishertown
houses were white, for the first time since March, and I had
stayed too long in one of them, getting warm by the fire,
drinking tea and talking with one of the farmer's customers
and so I was afraid of Granma again, late for breakfast, but
even so I stopped to watch the rat. I had to stop again at the
top of Harbour Street to wait for the Elgin bus which was
queuing behind some horse lorries which had got jammed
on the bridge and it was on that corner, waiting to go up the
High Street brae, that my first job interview took place. I did
not step down from the float to listen to my willing
employer, whom I knew well by nods of greeting, but had
never spoken to, and who now had turned his motorvan
labelled 'Merrytown Dairy' from behind the bus, towards
me. I was looking at his van, a new Morris.

——    How d'ye like her?

—— She's just the ticket.
—— Put the pony by then and come for a wee spin. He pointed to the coal yard stables.
—— I've someone waiting on me.
—— Come the morn then. Find me out at Merrytown and I'll learn ye to drive.
—— I'm only twelve.
—— Never heed. Ye are tall.

He said he would buy me a driving licence; no need to show myself at the office. He offered me ten shillings a week to do his milk round, ten times my pocket money which had gone up on my twelfth birthday to one shilling. If I helped to milk the cows morning and evening I could live on his farm with breakfast, dinner and tea all found, and his was the largest dairy farm near Nairn, a short way from the bridge on the east bank of the river. He asked me to come and see him there next day.

It was like the temptation of Jesus in the wilderness. I knew that if I disappeared from Tigh-na-Rosan I would be forced back there within a few days, perhaps by the police, yet to lose those few days of independence and the glory of driving a motorcar seemed at one moment an act of shameful timidity and at the next of base treachery, a slight betrayal of Margery and Granma, a great betrayal of the Farmer. He was not a jealous man; it was I who feared that the Merrytown Dairy would oust him in the end.

'Count it all joy when ye fall into divers temptations, knowing this, that the trial of your faith worketh patience . . . he that wavereth is like a wave of the sea driven with the wind and tossed.'

Neither joy nor patience blessed me. Tormented by indecision for a week, I said nothing, did nothing. Whenever I made up my mind to stay, to go, or stay or go, God blew me round in circles like sand in a whirlwind. Only once did I cross the bridge to the gates of Merrytown and instead of going in I sat in a dither on my bicycle, one foot on the ground; then turned to the right uphill all the way to Geddes graveyard where I stooped to peer at the dates of the tombstones searching for a number which would tell me what to do. There was a raven walking there by the

wall, a bad omen but beautiful, and it made me waver
again; if it walked towards the church I would go back to
Tigh-na-Rosan by the Brackla Road, if it flew away I would
return to the gates of Merrytown and blanketing my eyes
go in. It did not fly nor did it walk towards the church. I
bicycled to Nairn by the Cawdor Road bridge, passing
Whinnie Knowe and the station. I had made a circle.

    At tea Margery said
——    You've got a Leith Walk.
——    No. Nothing.
——    You haven't spoken a word for a week.

                                 *

It was the typewriter that soothed me: C for Corona,
Culloden, Cumberland, B for Butcher Billy and Balblair.
But there had been long gaps between my spurts of writing
and having had no one to read it to me, my sisters being
away, I had forgotten what was in it. I thought of it often,
inventing new bits, and could not remember which bits I
had typed or which were still hovering in my head. I could
not show it to Margery because she was a writer. I feared
her experienced criticism; her satirical wit, passing quickly
like a dart that seemed to miss you, was very like my
mother's; it was only after she had left the room that you
knew it had pierced your heart. And to me the book was
secretly sacred, not to be shown to anyone except Mary and
Joan who were no more sophisticated than I was, whose
scorn when sometimes they showed it I could deal with
without shame. All I remember of my Culloden story now
is its passionate love of the Jacobites, its hatred of the
English, my love for Flora Macdonald whom I adorned
with long golden hair and of the dark girl from Inverness
who ran all the way to the Doune of Daviot, forded the
Nairn and the Findhorn all alone at night to warn Bonnie
Prince Charlie that the English soldiers knew where he was
hiding and were marching the long way by road to surprise
him. It was romantic, and I feel sure it was sentimental, for
no one in those days had taught me to despise that quality
in writing, but I remember as distinctly the practical matters
I made the soldiers speak of – how wet and cold they were,

how in their desperate hunger on the march to Culloden Moor some suggested breaking the ranks to raid a house for food.

I had acquired that class of knowledge from Mr Rae whose life-long interest in the history of Nairnshire led him into factual detail only to be found in rare manuscripts and a few old printed books. It was he who had inspired me to write about Culloden, but in spite of my persistent questions he did not even guess that I had started on it.

I knew he was the only person I could show it to; and that trial of courage, preceded by days of indecision as it was, was eased a little by my ability to type, for by then he was accustomed to reading out to me my homework at the start of every history and English lesson. I gave him my Culloden typescript at the end of a history lesson on a Friday afternoon and on the Monday he read the whole of it aloud to me. He did laugh, but only at the soldiers' lengthy conversations on the battlefield. He took my intention seriously and encouraged me.

\*

'Lochiel! Lochiel! Beware of the day.' I only knew the first line of the poem and mistook it for a warning not to fight in the daytime, a reminder of his lantern, the moon. It is called *Lochiel's Warning* but was written long after the Battle of Culloden.

It is addressed to Donald Cameron who was known until he died at about the age of fifty-three as 'The Young Lochiel'; young because his father was still living as a refugee in France. After his death he was called 'The Gentle Lochiel', a name I took to mean one who had rebelled against his ancestors' tradition of plunder and war.

He was the eldest grandson of Black Ewen, but his hair was fair and his clansmen believed in the old saying that no fair haired Lochiel could prosper. He probably believed it himself because people then took sayings and omens, dreams and prophecies as guides to the conduct of their lives. By his education abroad and years in the literate society in France he had been liberated from those myopic blinkers which made the Highlands of Scotland the only

place visible to most other clan chieftains. He was a close
friend of the Chevalier Prince Charles Edward Stuart, the
young pretender to the throne which, in the opinion of the
majority of Highlanders and of nearly half the English
aristocracy, had been usurped by the Hanoverians after the
death of the last Stuart ruler, Queen Anne. Most Jacobites,
both in England and Scotland, believed that a rebellion
backed as they thought it would be by the common people
would tumble the throne which was shaking from financial
troubles under George II's seat. They ignored a widespread
weariness of war, the strength of the Hanoverian army, the
new discipline in politics and military rule. Lochiel did not
ignore it.

In 1740 he had been one of seven chieftains who
promised Prince Charles the support of their clans, but
when the French withdrew after their defeat at Dunkirk, he
hurriedly called it off. On that occasion Charles reluctantly
agreed to remain in France but in June 1745, without
warning his Highland friends, without the fleet of French
troop-ships they were waiting for, he embarked with only
one ship in support. This was *The Elizabeth* of sixty guns
carrying soldiers from the Irish Brigade, a part of the French
regular army, with some cannon and small arms for use on
land. *The Elizabeth* was intercepted by an English ship-of-
war, also of sixty guns, and in the fight, although it escaped
capture, it was so badly damaged that it had to return to
France for repair. The frigate *Doutelle* which carried the
Prince in disguise, Sir Thomas Sutherland posing as his
father, the Duke of Athol and four other leading Jacobites
sailed on to Scotland. On the thirty-first day of the voyage,
when they came within sight of the Outer Hebrides, Athol
saw a golden eagle hovering over the ship. He called the
Prince who was below deck and said, 'Sir, I hope this is an
excellent omen, and promises good things to us. The king
of birds is come to welcome His Royal Highness upon your
arrival in Scotland.'

They landed in a storm on the tiny island of Eriskay
which is sheltered between South Uist and Barra, the most
southerly of the larger Western Isles. There the Prince's
rash venture into his homeland began, as it was to end, in
physical hardship.

When the party moved to Lochboisdale, the seaport of South Uist, messengers were sent to the mainland to proclaim the Royal presence and invite military help. Few received the news gladly. Hugh MacDonald of Morar, when told that the prince had landed in Scotland, said, 'What prince?' And, in dismay, when he heard it was Prince Charles, asked how many men had he brought along with him from France. 'Only seven.' 'What stock of money and arms . . . ?' 'A very small stock of either.' 'What generals or officers fit for commanding are with him?' 'None at all.' Hugh MacDonald was angry. 'I cannot help it,' said Kinlochmoidart, who had given him the news. 'If the matter go wrong, then I'll certainly be hanged, for I am engaged already.'

Such was the response either privately given between each other or directly to Prince Charles of most Highlanders loyal to the Jacobite cause. Lochiel was dismayed when he read the letter calling him to arms and so was his brother Dr Archibald Cameron, who was with him at the time. Lochiel said he would go that day to the Prince and persuade him to return immediately to France. Archibald told him to write and not present himself in person. He offered to take the letter himself.

'Why so?' exclaimed Lochiel.

'Simply because if you trust yourself with the Prince, he will make you adopt any course he pleases, and I am not made of such pliable materials . . . It is your heart, not your head, I distrust and that only where the Prince is concerned.'

When the Doctor reached Borodale on the west coast of Inverness-shire for his audience with the Prince he was received with courtesy and few words. The Prince did not hand him a reply to Lochiel's letter. He waited until after the Doctor set off for home and then sent MacDonald of Scothouse to Lochiel at Achnacarry commanding 'as a prince and entreating, as a friend, his immediate attendance.' Lochiel was of course unable and unwilling to ignore a royal command.

On his way to Borodale, he called at Fassifern, on his young brother John who did not know that the Prince had landed in Scotland.

'Archibald is right,' said John. 'If once the Prince sets eyes upon you, he will make you do whatever he pleases.'

'It is strange that both you and Archibald should esteem so lightly of me; you seem to think that I am no better than the thistle-down, which every gust blows about as it chooses.'

John spoke of Achilles who had only one vulnerable part in all his body, the heel; 'with you it is something less substantial – your loyalty.'

When Lochiel arrived at Borodale, he found many Highland chieftains assembled there. The Prince knew and Lochiel knew, 'that not one of the various clans would rise till Lochiel set them an example.'

The meeting was cordial, brotherly, a meeting of two long separated friends, but after Lochiel declared his belief that a rising at that time without French allies and against the power of Campbell of Argyll and those clans who took his part, would fail, Charles accused him of disloyalty which led at once to anger. Lochiel reminded him that the promise of the clans had been made in return for his promise to bring to Scotland with him men, arms and money from the French court. He advised the Prince to return to France without delay and to stay there or at his father's court in Rome until his Catholic supporters were ready to help.

'I will not return to France,' said Prince Charles Edward. 'Be the friends who adhere to their Prince few or many, with them I shall raise King James's standard, and proclaim, sword in hand, to all Britain that Charles Stuart is come to claim the throne of his ancestors. Lochiel, if he pleases, may sit at home in safety.'

It was the most hurtful thing he could have said and I suppose he intended it to be so. Feeling that the quarrel had gone on too long in public he took Lochiel into his private room where they remained for an hour. In private the Prince won. If Lochiel had held out there would have been no rising in 1745, for most of the Jacobite clans were properly afraid of it at that time.

The enterprise was not hopeless from the start. Even in the Lowlands where Presbyterians were fiercely anti-

Jacobite and where most people feared and hated High-landers, a large number of Episcopalians and Catholics joined the Prince's army. Edinburgh fell. The triumphant defeat of General Cope's Hanoverians at Prestonpans brought more recruits, for there on Gladsmuir near Prestonpans, the Highlanders, always feared for their sudden, hidden methods of attack, had surprised and destroyed Cope's army. He was sacked by the government soon after that, but had long been despised by both sides for his exceptional incompetence and laziness. A local farmer, Adam Skirving, made fun of him in a song my father used to sing to us long before we knew what it meant. It begins

'Hey, Johnnie Cope, are ye waukened yet?
Or are ye sleeping, I would wit?
Oh, haste ye, get up, for the drums do beat!
O fye, Cope, rise in the morning.'

In the first week of November the Jacobite army marched into England almost without opposition, but without the support they expected from the English. When they reached Derby the Prince, in his enthusiasm – I use the word in its old derogatory sense – was planning his entry to London; how best to put on a good show. The Highland chiefs put an end to that.

Prince Charles had become unpopular with them be-cause he did not hide his dislike of their general officer, Lord George Murray, whom they knew to be a better commander than he was, and because he tactlessly showed favour to the Irish Brigade, detachments of which had eventually managed to join the Jacobite army in Scotland.

The men of these detachments, or piquets as they were called, were French. They had Irish surnames but had been brought up in France where their families lived. They spoke French. A few knew some English but none spoke Gaelic. Their manners were French. They got on better with the men of the Scots Royal, the other French regiment which had sent a detachment to Scotland, than with the native Scotch soldiers. Their origin as one of the most valued sections in the French army derives from English policy.

Of all the mistakes English governments made in punitive action against the people of Ireland and Scotland, the recruitment of thousands of men for the army of their enemy is the most remarkable. After almost completing his conquest of Ireland at the Battle of the Boyne, William of Orange, by the Treaty of Limerick in 1691, offered ships and supplies to all the defeated soldiers who would not take the Oath of Allegiance and wished to emigrate to France, thus increasing the strength of a small Irish Brigade, founded two years earlier, to almost twenty-five thousand men. The Penal laws during the succeeding years, by creating unemployment and by the seizure of property, drove thousands of Irish and Scottish civilians to France where for lack of any other work they joined the army. The Irish Brigade became one of the most famous military units in Europe. Although the court of France had refused state assistance to the Jacobites, furlough was granted to volunteers from the French army who wished to fight in Scotland.

At Derby where Prince Charles's invasion of England was halted by Lord George Murray, the Irish were alone in supporting the Prince. Lord George knew that an advance on London would lead to absolute defeat. The chiefs agreed with him. The Prince, humiliated, had to agree to a retreat to Scotland, which began on December 6th, 1745, in good order and without any feeling of defeat among the soldiers who in the middle of the next month routed the government forces at the Battle of Falkirk. But immediately after that victory there was a similar insult to Charles's pride. He wanted to advance on Edinburgh, which the enemy had regained. His chiefs and Lord George, aware that the Duke of Cumberland was on his way there with a strong force, insisted on retiring to the Highlands where they believed they would have a better chance of winning when he reached them:

On April 16th, 1746 [old style] the Duke, reached them near Culloden House about nine miles from Nairn, a house of good omen for him because it belonged to the Lord President of the Court of Session, one Duncan Forbes, a powerful ally who had spent a fortune of his own gold not only in raising his clan for King George, but in winning over others – the Sinclairs, Mackays, Rosses and Sutherlands.

The government in London had been in a panic when they sent the Duke of Cumberland to Scotland and he had good cause to choose the long way to the Highlands, for in the mountains the Jacobites had informants everywhere amongst the people, and their expertise in surprise attack was well known. So the Duke marched his army all the way up the east coast to Aberdeen where he took up winter quarters waiting for the spring.

The ninety mile march from there to Nairn was slower and more hazardous. They had to ford the swift rivers, Spey and Findhorn, which were flooded with melting snow, but horse, foot and cannon reached Nairn within a week, having met only small detachments of Highlanders who retreated before them. The last day's march of seventeen miles from Alves, near Elgin, across the steep banks and rocky bed of the Findhorn, was the longest and wettest and the army, bit by bit, arrived and camped in no fit state for battle. Cumberland, alarmed by exaggerated news that the Jacobites were approaching Nairn from Inverness, forced the pace. When the advance guard, led by Kingston's horse, reached the river Nairn they found the bridge barricaded and manned by Lord John Drummond's regiment, which had the advantage over them until some detachments of infantry came and burst the barricade. There was a lot of musket fire but few killed. Drummond, told of the imminent approach of the rest of Cumberland's army, retreated towards Inverness.

Cumberland probably did not know that the Jacobite army had shrunk since Falkirk. Having been trained in the German tradition of disciplined troops, he could not have known that any season of the year would vary the strength of his enemy. April being seed time, many men of the Highland army had gone home to plough and sow. Others were scattered throughout the hills in search of food. A whole regiment of cavalry had been destroyed on the long march north from Stirling, all its horses having died of starvation and fatigue.

By the time they reached Nairn, Cumberland's soldiers

were in no better shape. They were exhausted; and although they had supply ships off shore in the Moray Firth, rations were meagre. Some who had seized cattle on the way ate well and sold the meat to those who could afford it, but on sixpence a day which was frequently paid much in arrears, very few could afford it. 'It was a cold, rainy morning,' wrote one in his recollection of the battle, 'and nothing to buy to comfort us. But we had the ammunition loaf, thank God, but not a dram of brandy or spirits had you given a crown for a gill; nor nothing but the loaf and water.' It was the custom, then, to give every man a good dram before battle. 'Never,' wrote another, 'were two opposed armies more ill-equipped for battle.'

But as to morale and weather-proof clothes the Jacobites were better off than the Hanoverians. Their eagerness in war had nothing to do with politics or military discipline. There is plenty of evidence to show that they were not devoted to the Prince, to the future of a Catholic Scotland nor to any cause at all. Some had been pressed into the army, it is true, but most, by far, were inspired by ancient tradition of loyalty to family and clan. That they were not fighting for Scotland, or even for the Highlands, that they would have supported their chieftain in any cause is evident by the conduct of the Campbells who fought with distinction and great courage for their chieftain the Duke of Argyll and thereby for the Hanoverian King George II. Each clan had its own meeting place for conference or war. Clansmen were summoned there by beacons on hill tops or by the fiery cross.

The chieftain lived with his people and knew most of them personally and was revered and defended against enemies by tradition. He had in the eighteenth century the status of any of the Irish medieval kings; his physical presence was enough to secure absolute loyalty; an oath of fealty was invalid unless it was given with the touch of hands. The chieftains of the Jacobite army, or their sons, were all present in April, 1746, at the army's headquarters in Inverness.

The lack of formal discipline such as that used in the Hanoverian army was in itself a boost to morale. No one was flogged for selling his stockings. No one was hanged for retreating from a lost battle. Thirty dragoons and thirty foot-soldiers had been hanged for being the first to run away after the royalist defeat at Falkirk at which the whole army fled after them in confusion, leaving baggage and guns for the triumphant Highlanders to grab. Absence from the Highland army was not counted as desertion; it was known as a necessity in time of need. Those hundreds who came late for the Battle of Culloden, ran ten or twenty miles from the mountains where they were on their fields or getting food. And more than anything else the confidence of the Highlander, his pride, was sustained by the respect shown to him by civilians. Even in Edinburgh, where he was feared, he was respected. Walter Scott and Robert Louis Stevenson, both writing much later, describe this.

A large part of Cumberland's army, much larger and more resentful than the forcibly recruited sections of the Jacobite army, had been captured by press gangs and forced to serve their king. The rest and of course the more reliable were regulars, especially those who had fought under Cumberland in Flanders. Few officers and probably no men believed in what they were fighting for. They had to fight. And they had to march and fight in uniforms unsuited to the terrain of the North of Scotland.

The only sections of Cumberland's army who were suitably dressed were the Campbells of Argyll and members of smaller clans who were opposed to the Jacobites. Like the Jacobites they wore the philibeg or kilt, which left their legs free for climbing and wading, and a cloak pinned to the shoulder which could be wrapped over the whole body when they had to sleep in the open. The uniforms of the English army at that time were designed for show, not action. Each commanding officer chose his own splendid design to out-do other regiments. There were tight trousers which hindered the freedom of legs on the march, bizarre and uncomfortable hats, chosen at whim.

Even in such constricted dress the older soldiers had won glorious victories in Flanders led by their hero, the 'Fat Boy' Prince William Augustus, Duke of Cumberland, son of

King George II, who now on his little horse rode round the camps at Nairn uttering in his squeaky voice some patronising words. When he came to his Highland regiments he summoned an interpreter to translate the words into Gaelic.

Part of his army camped on the flat land on the east bank of the river Nairn below the bridge, between the Culbin Sands and the riverside meadows which fed the Merrytown dairy cows in my day. The greater part camped at Balblair, less than a mile to the west, south of Tradespark, which was then an open moor – the Muir of Nairn – and on the way to Kilravock. To make matters worse, on the cold, wet morning of the battle most of them suffered from hangovers and the curing dram they expected was not issued. Dry bread was issued. They had drunk up all the spirits on the night before to celebrate the Duke of Cumberland's birthday – his twenty-fifth. He had ordered half an anker – more than four gallons – of brandy to be given to every battalion. Having toured the camps, the Duke retired to the Provost's house, in the High Street, the old town house of Rose of Kilravock, to dine and drink claret at a birthday party with some chosen general officers. The Tolbooth, a few doors along, had also been taken over; Bailie Sutherland's large house in the High Street, the Laird of Clava's which is now the Caledonian Hotel, John Falconer's, George Grant's and even the manse were occupied by officers and all had strong guards of private soldiers. The High Street from the bridge to the Horologe Stone was patrolled all night. The peaceful mercantile and fishing town of Nairn had suddenly become a barrack, noisy with drums, fifes, shouting and the tramp of hoofs and boots.

I tried in my book without any evidence at all to say what the people felt. I do not think I described their fear; only their anger or joy which I gauged by which side individuals took; for the people of Nairn were divided, as the whole of Scotland was, between Jacobite and Hanoverian favours. I now think that fear governed most of them. They had lived in peace for thirty years. The Jacobite rising of 1715, during which the Highlanders seized Inverness, had alarmed

them but the Jacobites did not attack Nairn. It was the
government forces sent to quell the rising who burned
down houses and abused the people. And the army of
occupation then was very small compared to Cumberland's.

Without any evidence at all I now say that the people
were terrified in April, 1746, when they were squatted
upon by a great army with foreign speech and extraordinary clothes. On the morning of the battle – for this
there is evidence – thousands lined the High Street to watch
the regiments which had camped by the river, march, led
by drummers, to join the main force at Balblair. There was
on that morning a cruel storm of sleet and icy rain.

The Jacobites assembled on Culloden Moor – or
Drummossie Muir as it was then called – were not ready for
them. They had had a wakeful, tiring, disappointed night
which had left them disheartened, with three or four hours
sleep in the open without tents early that morning.

Lord George Murray, for once agreeing with the Prince,
Lord John Drummond, the Duke of Perth, and Lochiel had
led a night march towards Nairn expecting the rest of their
army to follow them. One part was to ford the river a couple
of miles above Nairn bridge and surprise the Merrytown
camp from the rear; the main body at the same moment
would attack the Balblair camp. Having news of the
birthday celebration, they rightly guessed that the enemy
would be asleep and drunk, and they knew they could
surround them at dead of night. But 'before the van had
gone a mile, which was as slow as could be to give time to
the line to follow, there was express after express sent to
stop them, for that the rear was far behind [An express was
a dispatch rider who usually rode his horse at a dangerous
gallop.] . . . and of these messages I am assured there came
near an hundred before the front got near Culraick
[Kilravock], which retarded them to such a degree that the
night was far spent . . . and they still had four long miles to
Nairn . . . There was a stop accordingly. Lochiel had been
mostly in the van all night, and his men were next to the
Athol men, who were in the front . . . Mr O'Sullivan [of the
Irish piquet] . . . had then just come from the Prince, who

was very desirous the attack should be made . . . Lord George Murray desired the rest of the gentlemen to give their opinions . . . It was agreed upon all hands that it must be sunrise before the army could reach Nairn and form . . . Lochiel and his brother [Dr Archibald] said they had been as much for the night attack as anybody could be, and it was not their fault that it had not been done; but blamed those in the rear that had marched so slow, and retarded the rest of the army. Lord George Murray was of the same way of thinking.'

John Hay of Restalrig rushed up to tell them to advance. 'He began to argue upon the point, but nobody minded him.' The army marched back to Culloden and got there 'pretty early, so that the men had three or four hours rest.' It was daylight by then and the enemy's march from Nairn had begun; but slowly. When Cumberland at the head of one force reached the gates of Kilravock Castle, about 9 o'clock, Rose of Kilravock was there to greet him. 'So I understand,' said the Duke, 'you had my cousin Charles here yesterday?' 'Yes, please your Royal Highness, not having an armed force, I could not prevent him.' 'You did perfectly right,' said the Duke, 'and I entirely approve of your conduct.'

Kilravock, perhaps from fear, had told a half lie. Although he was outwardly on the Duke's side, he had welcomed the Prince to dinner at three o'clock in the afternoon of the day before, as if obeying a royal command. For the Prince had sent an officer to announce in the royal manner that he would dine with him that day. He arrived with his constant companion, Hay, and forty soldiers. The Laird and Lady Rose were delighted by his charming manner. He asked to see their children, kissed them and admired their beauty and seeing a violin asked the Laird to play a tune. The Laird played an Italian minuet, saying that he knew it to be 'a favourite of Your Royal Highness', and when the Prince asked how he possibly could have known said, '. . . whatever people of your rank may do or say is sure to be remarked.' The forty soldiers had been sent to dine in the servants' hall, but two officers with drawn swords stood near the Prince while he ate with his hosts. When the

tablecloth was removed, Kilravock suggested they should
be allowed to go to dinner: 'Your Royal Highness may be
satisfied that you are perfectly safe in this house.' They left
the room. Hay then made them laugh by admiring with
subsequious hyperbole a china bowl made to hold sixteen
bottles of liquor. They filled it with whisky punch. The
Prince said Hay should stay and drink his share till they
could see the bottom. Hay took only one glass and at last in
anxiety dragged the Prince away.

'Lochiel! Lochiel! beware of the day' and beware of
fighting on the open moor. Having failed that night, he did
all he could in the morning to persuade the Prince to
abandon the moor and move the whole army, while there
was yet time, across the Nairn and take up battle position
on top of the precipitous far bank, easily scaled by
Highlanders but forbidding to a regular army, inaccessible
to cavalry and out of range of cannon. The Jacobite cannon
and cavalry could have been brought across the river nearer
to its source at a place where the banks were flatter and then
come up a slope at the back of the hill to support the foot
soldiers at the top. There was little time. Cumberland's
army had already left Nairn. But if the decision had been
made at once, there would have been plenty of time. Lord
George Murray, Lochiel and most of the chiefs, knowing
how difficult it was for Highlanders to fight on flat land,
how unaccustomed they were to cannonades, entreated
the Prince to change the site of the battle. They could not
move him and with the help of the Irish officers and some
Scots such as John Hay he won that verbal battle and
arranged his army on the moor. His reasons seemed good
to some. He said that if they left the moor undefended, the
enemy would march on to Inverness and seize their
headquarters with baggage, supplies and armaments left
there in reserve. It seems that it never occurred to him, in
his enthusiasm, that he might be defeated on the moor and
that if that happened Inverness would anyway be lost.

The officers and troops in Inverness were waiting
anxiously that morning for troops to come to them from
Sutherland and from the Highlands south of Loch Ness. No
one was in a good mood, and when Captain Fraser of

Inchberry, in command of that clan which was stationed in a granary near the river Ness, choked on a fishbone almost to death at his hurried breakfast, he, believing the accident a fatal omen, made the mistake of telling his troops what had happened. He said it meant that he would be the first to fall in the battle and told them to fight on when he fell. Word of this portent spread through all the Jacobite soldiers stationed at Inverness and when they marched towards Culloden it was in the face of a storm of sleet, another bad omen.

The wind for once was from the east that day. It blew the sleet on to the necks of Cumberland's soldiers who were, it seems, shivering with cold, hunger and fear. Only a small section could march on the narrow road. The rest struggled knee-deep through marsh, dew-sodden grass, high heather black and dripping, clumps of wet whins as high as their chests. There were not enough Campbells, enough Highland scouts, to guide them all and many, including some gun teams, sank in the peat mosses which look to a stranger exactly like the firm land which surrounds them. Horses, belly deep, were unharnessed and helped out, their gun-carriages hauled up by rope with thirty or forty men to each.

The parts of my book Mr Rae liked best were those describing weather and landscape, the only parts founded on personal experience; and they in places like Nairnshire are eternal. He liked especially my description of the black waters of the Nairn and Findhorn freckled with foam, plunging or placid, fearful or calm, and in these I had, as every child has, a strong mixture of love and fear of the supernatural. The witches had been real to me and my sisters when we were small in the Newton woods where we hid watching fishwives gathering fir cones. Sometimes, fishing alone on the Nairn, I had been terrified by the bubbling of water and cawing of crows – no human sound to reassure me. Climbing the rocky side of the Findhorn I had once looked down on a water-kelpie, a white horse drinking at a shallow place below me, and although I knew it was a real horse I ran away. The power of lonely water, wild deserted land filled with Mina's stories, overcame me.

The witches in the woods had only to glance at you with an evil eye and you would be dead next day from scarlet fever. The kelpie taking the shape of a white horse would come to you as you stood by the flooded ford gathering courage to swim over, invite you to mount him promising to carry you safe and dry across and then in the middle of the river plunge down and eat you.

It is not only children who have such terrors in strange and lonely country and in the eighteenth century, as is clear from travellers' books, everybody had them and spoke of them as real. I know from my own experience of exploring Nairnshire and the nearby Grampians what soldiers from the south felt when they were rushed there in awful circumstances. I believe that among the people who lined the High Street there were witches casting the evil eye. For Nairn and Auldearn were as famous for witchcraft as Essex; the last trials had happened within living memory; but if you marched through Essex the landscape was English and homely and you knew that its people were on your side. The sky, too, was ominous, a sky that had often frightened me on the carse of Delnies and even on the lonely road to Kilravock which they took. Before sleet, as before thunder, there is no smooth sky such as the unbroken grey, not threatening, that goes with snow. Black pillows of cloud fringed with grey and white move above you, showing gaps of pale blue sky which they cover as they join each other in the wind. I have seen at sunrise on a sleety morning, and Cumberland's army started the march at sunrise, a dark red furnace glowing on the Moray Firth like the gates of hell, a fiery mouth in a black face. On such days the mountains to the south are indigo with snowy tops, but between the dark and light, mist flows swiftly like a ragged scarf. The Black Isle is black across the firth to the north and the white horses stirred by a savage wind race each other, submerge each other, along towards Fort George and Inverness. Walking is painful. Marching was painful. And as for dreams of home and faraway girls, I knew those too.

In the eighteenth century few people outside the intellectual society of the Age of Reason drew a line between legend and what we now call fact. The legend of the invincibility of savage Highlanders in their wild dress with their primitive weapons and the gruesome cries they uttered was so deeply impressed on soldiers of other nations that the Hanoverian command had to issue an army order intended as reassurance. The rout of the Williamite forces at Killiecrankie in 1689 had not been forgotten; the crushing defeats at Prestonpans and Falkirk in which many of the men marching to Culloden had suffered were only a few months away.

'All kinds of fire-arms,' wrote Johnstone in his memoirs, 'are directly at variance with the natural disposition of the Highlander, who are quick, ardent, and impetuous in their attack . . . Their manner of fighting is adapted for brave, but undisciplined men. They advance with rapidity, discharge their pieces when within musket-length of the enemy, and then, throwing them down, draw their swords, and holding a dirk in their left hand with their target, they dart with fury on the enemy, through the smoke of their fire. When within reach of the enemy's bayonets, bending their left knee they . . . cover their bodies with their targets, that receive the thrusts of the bayonets . . . while at the same time they raise their sword-arm and strike their adversary . . . the fate of the battle is decided in an instant, and the carnage follows; the Highlanders bringing down two men at a time, one with their dirk in the left hand, and another with the sword . . . They proved that bravery may supply the place of discipline at times, as discipline supplies the place of bravery. Their attack is so terrible, that the best troops in Europe would with difficulty sustain the first shock of it; and if the swords of the Highlanders once come in contact with them, their defeat is inevitable.'

This was true of Killiecrankie where the sudden charge downhill broke the Williamite army to pieces within a few minutes. At Prestonpans they had surprised and destroyed Cope's army. At Falkirk, descending from the heights and across a ravine, they had thrashed and humiliated the army of General Hawley, a much stronger commander than Cope. On the Moor of Drummossie by Culloden they were formed into lines facing the enemy's lines as though on a flat field in Flanders. What was worse, they were kept waiting. Both armies spent half an hour manoeuvring for better positions before the fight began; and it was said at the time that Highlanders at war are of 'a stirring hasty nature, ill used to pause.' They liked to be led into a quick charge at first sight of the enemy, and when faced by musket fire they usually gave him no time to reload. At Culloden, while waiting, their whole centre was broken by Cumberland's skilled and powerful cannonade which went on from 1 pm till almost two o'clock. Their own artillery was 'ill-served and ill-pointed'. During the cannonade, 'the Highlanders in the first line impatient of suffering without doing any harm to their enemies, grew clamorous to be led on to the attack. A message was sent to Lochiel . . . desiring that he would represent to Lord George Murray the necessity of attacking immediately.' Lord George knew it. It was the Commander-in-chief, Prince Charles, who kept them standing as though they were on a battlefield in Flanders.

While Lochiel was speaking to Lord George the clan Mackintosh broke out of the line and charged sword in hand, followed soon by the Maclachlans and Macleans, the Frasers, the Stuarts and the Camerons. Major Fraser, of the fishbone mishap, was the first to fall dead; almost all the chieftains and officers leading their men in that un-organised charge fell dead with hundreds of dead and wounded men about them. Donald Cameron, the Gentle Lochiel, who had been wounded at Falkirk, rode close enough to Burrel's English regiment to fire his pistol at their officer 'and was drawing his sword when he fell, wounded with grapeshot in both ankles'. It is said that he asked to be lifted back on to his horse and rejoin his clansmen in their lost fight, but Dr Archibald and other brothers of his carried him away. The clans, although they were scattered and pursued that afternoon, were respected in the memories of their enemy for their courage and the damage they did against a greater number of men equipped with modern armaments. Of Burrel's grand regiment which was directly opposed to the Camerons' sword charge only two men were left standing on their feet.

But the English army, in that battle, conquered the whole

of Scotland and subdued the country forever. Lochiel from
then on, though lame from ankles slow to heal, followed
the Prince and helped to protect him wherever he was
hiding.

Most of the Highlanders were shocked by the way the
Prince ran away at the end; they may have known they
were defeated; in the confusion of battle they may not have
known. But it is known that the survivors wished to fight
on and expected the Prince to lead them.

His most loyal and friendly officers said he had been
forced against his will to leave the field before the fighting
stopped, led away by men with their hands on his horse's
bridle who believed that the royal person, heir to the throne
of Scotland by divine right, must be saved at any cost. But
most of the chieftains and, I think, all the soldiers thought
he had deserted them in cowardice.

Lord Elcho, who with Lochiel and Lord George Murray
had been his wiser advisors, often in disagreement, went to
search for him and found him in a cabin, beside the river
Nairn, 'surrounded by Irish, and without a single Scotsman
near him, in a state of complete dejection. Lord Elcho
represented to him that this check was nothing, as was
really the case; and exerted himself to the utmost to
persuade him to think only of rallying his army . . . but he
was insensible of all that his lordship could suggest and
utterly disregarded his advice.'

James, Chevalier de Johnstone, *aide-de-camp* to the
Prince, went on to describe how he and Lord George's
*aide-de-camp* with a large force of men who had escaped the
slaughter of fugitives and prostrate wounded 'passed the
19th at Ruthven without any news from the Prince'. All the
Highlanders were cheerful and full of spirits, to a degree
perhaps never before witnessed in an army so recently
beaten, expecting with impatience every moment the
arrival of the Prince. Mr Macleod, Lord George's *aide-de-camp*, who had been sent to him, returned with this laconic
answer: 'Let every man seek his safety in the best way he
can' – an inconsiderate answer to the brave men who had
sacrificed themselves for him. 'We were masters of the
passes between Ruthven and Inverness . . . the Clan of

Macpherson of Clunie . . . besides many other Highlanders, who had not been able to reach Inverness before
the battle, joined us at Ruthven; so that our numbers
increased every moment, and I am thoroughly convinced
that in the course of eight days, we should have had a more
powerful army than ever . . . But the Prince was inexorable
and immovable in his resolution of abandoning his enterprise, and terminating in this inglorious manner an
expedition, the rapid progress of which had fixed the
attention of all Europe . . . The Highlanders gave vent to
wild howlings and lamentations; the tears flowed down
their cheeks when they thought that their country was now
at the discretion of the Duke of Cumberland, and on the
point of being plundered; whilst they and their children
would be reduced to slavery, and plunged, without re-
source, into a state of remediless distress.'

The Prince did seek his own safety in the best way he
could, in hardship and constant fear of capture for months
at the end of which he was rescued by a French ship. If he
had been captured he would have been hanged, drawn and
quartered as a traitor. The government offered £30,000 for
information leading to his capture. Yet, during his long
flight from mountain cave to cave, from hidden shieling to
crofter's lonely house, to the island of South Uist, where his
adventure had begun, from there to Skye, disguised as a
woman whose long manly strides alarmed other women,
conducted by Flora Macdonald, who risked her life to
protect him, and back to hiding places on the mainland, no
one betrayed him. They knew where he was. In the
Highlands everybody knows where anyone is. His courage
in flight, his kindness and good humour in cold, rain and
hunger, was better than his courage in battle.

Lochiel was hunted too, of course, as a prize more
valuable to the English than the Prince's body, not in
money but as a safeguard against renewal of the war, for
Lochiel surprised everyone, his initial reluctance to fight
being well known, by attempting to rally the other clans
and start a new campaign. The Prince was by then not to be
feared. Lochiel's devotion to him all through the three
months his wounds took to heal was so firm that even

when a chance came to escape to France on a French ship he refused it. He would stay in the Highlands so long as the Prince was hiding there.

His brothers and followers had managed to bring him, bound to a horse, safely home to Achnacarry, which seems stupid of them, it being the first place to be searched, and as he could not walk or even ride properly he was almost captured as they left Lochaber with him after hearing that Cumberland's troops were marching towards them by Loch Ness. They brought him into Badenoch, probably the wildest, most inaccessible part of the Highlands, but they got safely there only because his pursuers were delayed by a bad portrait which their commanding officer had given them to help them to recognise him. The pursuers arrested Macpherson of Urie, an ally of theirs, telling him 'that he was Lochiel and a damned rebel'. They took him triumphantly to the Duke of Cumberland at Fort Augustus. The Duke recognised him and he was released. But the comic episode had taken several days, during which Lochiel and his companions found a good hiding place near the top of Ben Aulder, where his cousin-germaine Cluny Macpherson, another wanted outlaw, had gone. It was that place so vividly described by Robert Louis Stevenson in *Kidnapped*, where Cluny, dressed like a beggar, behaved and was served like a king. Lochiel lived there for three months.

When they heard that the Prince had returned to the mainland from the Western Isles they sent messengers to tell him to come to them which he, after days of difficulty, did. Lochiel limped out to welcome him and tried to kneel at his feet. 'No, no, my dear Lochiel; we cannot tell who may be looking upon us from yonder hills, and if they see any such motions they will conclude I am here.'

In September the ships *L'Heureux* and *La Princesse de Conti* from St Malo moored off the coast of Inverness-shire and rescued some remnants of the Jacobite army including the Prince, who embarked at Borodale, the village at which he had landed after Eriskay and South Uist. Dr Archibald Cameron went with them. Lochiel refused to go. By a good chance of fog they were able to escape an English naval squadron, backed by two ships of war; and they reached France safely. The Prince persuaded Louis XV to offer Lochiel the colonelcy of a regiment. Lochiel declined that for a long time, saying that he wished to go on in Scotland with war for his exiled king. The Prince overruled him by royal command and, with his young wife who had left home to be with him when he was hiding, and a baby girl named Donalda, he escaped on another French ship and joined the French army.

Meanwhile the people of his clan had been massacred, their houses burnt down, their cattle stolen, their ploughs smashed with axes. Achnacarry, the ancient castle of his family, was ruined by the soldiers.

The Duke of Cumberland is remembered to this day in Nairn and Inverness and, I suppose, all through the Highlands, as The Butcher. Long before the cruel exploitation of his victory he had won hatred among the English soldiers under his command. Discipline, incredibly harsh as it was before he took command of the army in Scotland, became by his Orderly Book, long before fighting began, petty, malicious and bestial. Men were flogged not only for slight offences such as selling scraps of their clothing in exchange for food, but for consorting with women. It had always been the custom for a wife or sweetheart to march with her man, foraging for him when they could, carrying his musket, which weighed eleven pounds, when he with the rest of the heavy accoutrements on his back, was tired. Cumberland forbade this, ordered those women and their men to be flogged. He promoted the old penalty of hanging to an absurd degree. He loved to watch it, and thereby increased fatal casualties before a battle began. On his birthday a boy of seventeen, falsely accused of spying, was hanged in Nairn. The minister of the Kirk, one of the loyal Rose family, rushed to the Duke to plead mercy. The Duke, on his birthday, said 'Yes', and the boy was cut down after ten minutes choking. He recovered sufficiently to march and fight.

The custom of giving no quarter, taking no prisoners, killing defeated fugitives, was usual among Highlanders and was one of the reasons they were so much feared, so they had no reason to revile the Duke on that account. Yet the atrocities committed on Cumberland's orders were condemned by contemporary writers on both sides. To kill all the wounded on the field where they lay, to shoot prisoners in batches, burn to death wounded men in a sheep bothy on Culloden Moor, to slash down with swords and bayonets women and children who had come out from Inverness to watch the battle, to chase for months afterwards men who had gone back to the mountains to farm and live in peace, barricade them in to their little 'black houses' and burn them alive with their wives and children, was something that had not happened in an organised manner since Cromwell's campaigns in Ireland and was not to happen again until the wars of the twentieth century.

Twelve wounded soldiers who had taken refuge in the house of William Rose, grieve to Lord President Forbes of Culloden House, were brought out with a promise that surgeons would attend to their wounds. They were shot and pitched into one of the mass graves, which every holiday maker can still see. Near the graves there is an ancient well known as the Well of the Dead. Those of the wounded who could walk went there to drink and many died beside it. MacGillivray of Dunmaglas crawled to it. He was the chieftain whose ancester had, in the legend, rescued the Lady of Daviot from the fairies with a magic candle. The people found his body before Cumberland's soldiers came to throw the corpses into the grave, and bore it, keening all the way to the kirkyard of Petty where they buried him decently.

Perhaps – but I have read nothing to that effect – Cumberland had orders from the government to destroy Highland society for ever. This he almost did and in the long, ferocious process the destruction of Lowland culture, of most Scottish customs and institutions, which had started with the hated Act of Union in 1707 was completed too.

In 1746 the people of Inverness were physically punished by their conquerors. The people of Nairn were punished by cess beyond their means, billeting far beyond the capacity of their houses, commotion, rapine and yellow fever.

*

I never finished my Culloden novel; perhaps the excitement flagged naturally, as it so often did when I was young, in the middle of books that had started passionately. But after my thirteenth birthday I was distracted by a new kind of emotional disorder caused by religious fervour, changes at Sandwood croft, my parsimony of spirit, and Jeannie.

One Sunday in Lent, soon after my birthday, Jeannie spoke to me for the first time in our lives as we were leaving church. She even touched my fingers as though to invite me into the churchyard. She smiled as though she liked me a bit but I was too shy to speak. I let her go away. I took a bad fit of the heebie-jeebies which lasted for weeks. Kolya had told me how angry I looked when I was shy. Jeannie avoided me after church thereon.

In retrospect, I value the ardour and doubt, the occasional visions I had of pillars of cloud, chariots of fire, crucifixion, walking on the water, betrayal in the garden where Jesus was walking on the ground, but at the time they and the puzzling parts of the liturgy which after my confirmation I attended to and listened carefully to for the first time, disturbed me and distracted my mind from ordinary events which had been mostly pleasurable before. Granma was pleased and Margery surprised by my constant and punctual attendance at Holy Communion early on Sunday mornings. We were not allowed to take anything before it, not even a cup of tea, which enhanced, I suppose, the effect of the little sip of wine we had kneeling before the altar. I had never tasted any alcohol before. I loved it. It gave me not only physical pleasure. It inspired me to think of Jesus Christ.

Canon Ballard whispered as he tipped the large silver chalice on to my lips, 'The Blood of our Lord Jesus Christ, which was shed for thee, preserve thy body and soul into everlasting life. Drink this in remembrance that Christ's Blood was shed for thee, and be thankful. The body of our Lord Jesus Christ, which was given for thee . . . Take and Eat this in remembrance that Christ died for thee and feed on him in thy heart by faith and thanksgiving.'

As he said that he put a bit of bread on to my tongue, a very small square of bread, which I recognised as Asher's, shaped very much like the pieces cut from our breakfast loaf and thrown by Granma on to the snowy lawn for the birds. It too was holy. Canon Ballard had blessed it. I used to walk humbly out of church at the end of the Communion service, troubled in my heart, aware of none of the people I knew except Granma from whom I escaped as quickly as I could, grabbing my bicycle and leaving her to walk home by herself. After matins I walked out of church, held up by the crowd, without love of God, not heeding Christ's words to the troubled young men who questioned him at a place on the coast of Judaea – 'Thou shalt love thy neighbour as thyself.' I hated all those people shuffling down the aisle except Jeannie and Chrissie, who squeezed rudely through and were the first to be free. I did not honour my father or my mother at that time, neither did I love myself but I saw the mote in Granma's eye and not the beam in mine.

It may have been because my mood made me more aware of ill-happenings than I had been or it may have been because the poor of Nairn were poorer and less happy than before, but it is true that I heard more angry words and saw more fighting in the closes off the High Street, outside pubs and in the Fishertown than ever before. I knew nothing of politics. If anyone had asked me I would have said I was a conservative because my father voted on that side, but as I discovered a few years later he had no ideal belief. When mine, which he thought bolshie, developed and I asked him why he voted conservative, he said, 'Because they keep the income tax low.' I was aware that many people in Nairn could find no work, had not enough to eat while we had plenty, but never imagined that that arrangement could be changed. Except for the stoppage of railways which badly affected the fishwives and their men, the General Strike that year had slight effect on the people of Nairn, there being no large industry there, but even a boy as ignorant as I was could not go one day without hearing the words 'Depression' and 'Emigration'. The *Nairnshire Telegraph* was published as usual during the strike. I have looked at it since. It has articles fiercely condemning the strikers. On 18 May it says that the presence of seals in the firth shows that salmon are plentiful. The fishermen's catches prove it. On 1 June it describes the distress caused by lack of coal for fishing ships; part-owners are not eligible for dole. On 15 June under the headline 'Miners, Farmers and Domestics Bound for Canada', it implies that emigration, which had by then increased enormously, is desirable. On 10 August there are two bits of news side by side: 'Viscount Finlay is at present in residence at Newton' and the 'Bride Ship *Metagama* continues her good work of ferrying across the Atlantic Scottish brides for young Scotsmen in Canada and the USA, seven brides sailing in the *Metagama* from the Tail of the Bank to Canada on Saturday. It is interesting to note that the *Metagama* during the last four years has carried over one thousand brides to Canada. Sir Malcolm Campbell of Glasgow presents each bride with a beautiful bouquet. This he has done for some years and his courtesy is much appreciated by all concerned. Also on board were a party of twenty domestics selected by the women's branch of the Canadian Pacific. More Scots domestics have gone this year due to improved conditions and the demand by Canadian ladies for Scottish girls. Included in the passenger list were miners for the West, also three septuagenarians, a large number of farmworkers and some families for settlement on the land.'

Fred, the youngest of the Farmer's sons left Sandwood for Canada with a little knapsack slung over his shoulder. I saw him go one day after dinner, but he always had that knapsack with tools and oddments in it and I thought he was going back to work as usual. He had without formal training made himself into a skilled motor mechanic and been sought after by firms in Forres, Inverness and Nairn. He was then working for Knowles and Cummings by the bridge of Nairn where Uncle Robert's hired Daimler was housed. They could no longer afford to employ him. He had only worked at Sandwood on some summer evenings and at every spare moment during harvest and threshing, but his energy and bright wit enlivened the croft and his departure was one of several which by almost imperceptible motions diminished the rich quality of life there.

While people in the Fishertown and the closes off the

High Street were living on credit barely, selecting unsale-
able fish for their families, boiling scrag-end of mutton as an
occasional treat, and all the time helping poorer neighbours
out with pieces; while generous shopkeepers, of which
Rose Brothers is remembered as one, were allowing people
food on promises they knew could never be kept, I went on
hunger strike at Tigh-na-Rosan in a fit of sulks. I seldom
attended meals and when I did I picked at the food and
shoved my plate rudely away. That was why I was eating
my fill at Sandwood on the afternoon Fred went away. He
did not say goodbye to his father or brothers and sisters. He
looked at the clock on the mantelpiece, got up and walked
out of the house with the usual nod that everyone gave
after a meal. We watched him from the little window
disappear on his motorbike as he did every day on his way
back to work. They all knew they would not see him again.
Duncan explained to me afterwards that it was unlucky to
say goodbye.

Githa left the croft to be trained as a nurse. Duncan, the
eldest of the sons at home, got married and obtained a
farm, on feu, high on the hills above Cawdor where his life
was hard but happier because his wife Carrie, whom Joan
and I later knew and loved, was happy by nature. She
worked as hard as he did on that difficult land, where the
steading and house were fenced against snowdrifts by a
high barricade built of railway sleepers. Then Bob got
married to Dolly, a fat young motherly woman whom I
occasionally liked. The Farmer spoke of going to Canada
and the United States to visit his older children who had
emigrated years before. Bob became like a self-willed grieve
who ignores the old-fashioned ways of the farmer he
works for and does not consult him. He had always worked
hard but was now like one possessed by demons. He
restored the failing fortune of the croft.

The changes affected me gradually. I guess they affected
the Farmer in a similar way, for although he was over
sixty-five and I in my fourteenth and fifteenth years, we
shared an acceptance or even love for what had gone on
before. I certainly liked routine and hated change.

One morning early in the summer when I ran out from

Tigh-na-Rosan as usual towards the sound of Flossie's hooves, I saw Bob on the milk float. He was friendly and cheerful. I was hesitant, surprised.

——   Jump on!

I jumped on.

——   Is your father ill?

——   Na, na. I just took the notion in my head.

I put bottles on familiar doorsteps as before while he put his, but however much I hurried he was back on the float before me, driving off at a quick trot as I leapt on, laughing, telling stories about the people in some of the grand houses – how Mrs This never paid, and his father never asked her to pay, how Lady That on an afternoon drive had been sick into her shoe, called the chauffeur through the speaking-tube and told him to empty it out on to the heather. I liked it all. It was funny. But it was rushed. He never gave me the reins and when we had finished with the West End and charged up the Seabank Road towards the Parish Church, I nearly said 'Do you want to make butter?'

At the Parish Church he stopped.

——   Ye'll be wanting home to your breakfast now.

I was dismissed, but in a friendly way.

He told me later that he did the milk round in half the time his father took. He did not stop for a crack and cups of tea. At the croft he did want me, especially at the dung spreading and at seed time. He was by nature kind and good humoured and we got on well together. His father worked as hard as he did, but like me was much slower.

I went to Sandwood every day, even when there was little I could do. I went for company, to groom the horses, polish their harness, muck out the stables and escape from Tigh-na-Rosan. One afternoon in May, after my lessons, I heard a loud squawking as I propped my bicycle against the dairy wall and as I walked round the corner into the yard of the steading saw Bob wringing the neck of an old cluckit hen. It was warm and sunny. It had been quiet and peaceful. I was not, at that age, distressed by the killing of poultry. Githa had sometimes asked me to do it for her; she did not like it. But Bob's face frightened me. I drew back towards the door of the byre, but he came after me, gripping the squawking hen by the neck in one hand, catching me by the shoulder with the other. As he gave the final twist to the hen's throat, he held it against my face, battering me with its bony, dusty wings. Then, holding me to him he pushed it onto the back of my neck where it fluttered and banged me again.

When he left me, I was literally quivering with rage. I wanted passionately to damage Bob. I was determined not to go home without revenge. I could not fight him. I had the sense not to. I could not, or thought I could not, humiliate him with words. I could have punctured his bicycle but that seemed feeble. I could have slashed his best bonnet which was hanging on a peg in the byre. I could have tripped him up as he came in to milk.

Instead I devised the most stupid act of revenge – to dribble water down his neck. I filled an empty milk bottle and climbed up into the loft above the byre at milking time; hid there, waited long and much pent up. He had five cows to milk – someone else was doing the other five – and it took him about half an hour to reach the cow below me. The floor of the loft ended there, just above that cow's place. I lay down and peeped.

Bending as he was on his milking stool, his head pressed against the cow's flank, his bare neck below me was an easy target. I emptied the bottle of water on to it. He got up with the milk bucket in his hand and looked to the loft. I thought I had retreated in time but it was not so. He caught me outside the dairy where my bike was. It was awful to see his face above mine.

——  It went in the milk, he said.

——  I didn't mean that.

——  Did ye no, then! Well, I mean this.

He caught me by the neck, the easiest part of a boy to get hold of. He tried to force my head down. I butted him and belaboured him with my fists, kicked his shins; but his stomach was hard and unluckily I was wearing sandshoes. We wrestled in the doorway of the dairy, one moment inside it, next moment out. I managed to bite his thumb. Wrenching it away, squeezing my neck painfully with his right hand which held it, he grabbed from a shelf a bunch of sausages that had been laid there to keep cool and rubbed them into my face, greasy, flabby, cold. Then he let me go and went back to the milking without another word.

\*

From shame and from fear of what Bob would say to me if ever we met again I shunned Sandwood for all those lovely weeks from the middle of May to the middle of June, the time I still treasure in my memory as the happiest of all seasons on a farm and the most hopeful, the cows being out on pasture for the first time in the year, the meadows thick with grass which would soon be mown for hay, the oat fields that had been brown since ploughing time now covered in delicate green, the ewes and lambs; hawthorn and blackthorn green again, the beech hedge by Patsy's house at Sandwood which had been pale brown all winter now palely and beautifully green.

For the first time at Nairn I did not know what to do. The early mornings, with no milk round, were desolate; I went for long walks with the dogs on the golf course, always to the west away from anyone who knew me, sometimes to the end of the carse, and even the carse lost its magic. The hours between breakfast and lessons were difficult because I pretended I was at Sandwood as usual and had to devise other ways of spending the time. Anywhere off the Inverness Road was out of bounds; I might be seen by one of the MacDonalds. On the golf course I was exposed to Newton people; in the town to Granma, Margery and their shopping friends. I called sometimes on Michie and when he could, he came fishing with me high up the river towards Brackla. Those were the best days. I loved his serious manner as he taught me about the water and the sky. When no fish were rising we would sit on the grass and he would light his pipe, take off his bonnet and out of the many flies he carried on it unhook the most hopeful ones for the day. Then he would point to the others saying which would draw which breed of fish, which suited cloudy skies, dark shaded water on a bright day, flickering windy shadows in the sun, low pale water, brown full water, the swirling mud of the river in spate when one could try a white fly but the best thing was a worm.

—— Your father wouldna like to see ye fishing wi' a worm.

—— Where can I buy flies like yours? Tell me, Michie.

—— I'll make them for ye. Ye canna buy them.

He asked me to come fishing with him on the Findhorn at night with white maggots. We would take the evening bus to Forres and walk the bank. I could not.

Janet was astute enough to know that my hunger strike was caused by sulks and seldom practised outside Tigh-na-Rosan. She always kept something for me in the kitchen, even when I did not appear, and during that time she fed me when she could without reproof. If she saw me in the garden or the drawing room alone she would beckon to me silently and I would go. She would take a large plate of meat and vegetables from the oven and lay it before me on the kitchen table. She said,

—— A loon your age is always hungry, and you are muckle, like a horse.

Margery came in with her hat and coat on. Perhaps she knew I was there. Perhaps she only wanted to ask Janet what messages were needed from the High Street, but after speaking about that she told me that the Farmer, whom she called Old Duncan, had been that morning to seek me. He had told her something vague about my quarrel with Bob and said I would be welcome back, that they missed me.

—— Then where have you been all these mornings?

—— On my bike.

In Nairn one could hide nothing. Nothing at all.

\*

*Nones*                                    *Fettes College,*
                                          *H.Q. His Majesty's*
                                          *Colony of Scotland*

*Dear Thomson,*

*Has your Corona machine broken down? Macrae and Dick and Knowles and Cummings will join hands and heal it. If both your arms ditto and head ditto call at the infirmary which healed the noble Kolya, or upon his Pater, cunning*

*chirurgeon and physician, in Besserabia or Ukrainia or wherever he may now be, for that is unknown, all the geese in Russia having flown away with his quill pens.*

*I am deserted. I am imprisoned in Collegium Fettes – dry as dust. And you, my friend, send neither epistola, ignis nor aqua, those essentials with which the jailor is required by law to provide the most heinous criminal.*

*And there you are, David, in Freedom, in Nairn, with girls all about you. Alive.*

*I dream of lambs. And what dost thou dream of, my brother in God, in thy bliss?*

*Amantium irae amoris intergratio est, or may I say, in deference to your shaky knowledge of the fount of wisdom – 'the quarrels of lovers are the renewel of love', an optimistic saying which I have this evening quoted in my dissertation on the copulative verb, which the Fat Perch requires of me for tomorrow's Latin. What would you say if I became a lawyer? It was the said Perch, not you or your typewriter, who drew my attention to a slim volume about the importance of the classics in education. In fact he forced it on us all and I thought it would be a bore but it wasn't. Then he took it away. If you've got a copy, lend it to me. It was published a couple of years ago, at about the same time as your last letter to me, and I'm sure the author gave you one – he being your great-uncle Robert, the Most Reverend Lord Finnan Haddock, one time Minister of Breakfast Prayers, the Right Hon. Viscount Finlay of that Ilk whose portrait adorns the Fisherman's Hall in Nairn, some time Liberal MP for the Inverness Burghs, another time independent MP for the Universities of St Andrews and Edinburgh, sometime Lord Chancellor of that rascal kingdom of England, old pupil of the Edinburgh Academy, Supreme Mareschal of the Nairn Golf Course and later translated to the International Court at the Hague, from which Tower of Babel, communicating with the other judges in Latin, he delivers judgement upon the nations of the world.*

*Me absentia, Kolya.*

I wrote to him, and annoyed him, I suppose, by saying I would prefer the Fettes Prison to the little one of Tigh-na-

Rosan, to which, because of the shortage of warders, the old High Street Tolbooth had been moved. I told him about the Battle of the Hen. I asked how much the fare to Russia would be. Would he go there with me? I said the only 'girls' about me were old fat fishwives and schoolgirls I saw playing on the links. Patsy was at school in England, Githa away nursing. Ireen too busy to speak to anyone.

A few days after the Farmer's message I set out for Sandwood but just as my courage was shrinking I saw two magpies in a field. Any excuse would have served. I was looking for omens as one does in doubt or fear – 'If the bus passes me before I reach Trades Park, I'll turn back. If I see one magpie, I'll go on.'

> Ane's for joy,
> Twa's grief,
> Three's a wedding,
> Fower's deith.

Twa was what I was hoping for and there they were, a pair of them, stalking near me on the grass beyond the dyke to my left. My left! I turned right at Trades Park towards the beach.

But a few days later I met the Farmer in the post office and we went out together and sat on a bench. He said he was sorrowful. He looked at me not with the eye that saw but with the crumpled one. He said if there had been a colliebuction Bob had forgotten it next day.

—— Do ye despite him yet?

—— I despite myself.

—— Did he doossil you?

—— What?

—— Thump you?

—— No. I put water in the milk.

The Farmer laughed. We bicycled out to Sandwood together.

There Bob treated me with his usual good humour and there the spring and summer passed with the usual happenings but less joy. I had grown harder in my response to other people, less tender towards animals,

more self contained than I had been, and when my parents
and sisters arrived for the summer holidays I was split in
two. Joan came to Sandwood with me every day. Barbara
and Mary occasionally. The Macdonalds had always
hidden from them the harsh aspects of farm life – slaughter,
castration and so on – and now I feared that one of them
would casually mention how useful I had been in such
work. I don't think I would have volunteered to pierce pigs'
nostrils and put the rings in, but I was not considered
strong enough to hold the pig and that was the job they
gave me. It was I who tightened the twitch on horses'
lips when anything was done to them; the pain kept them
still. I gutted and skinned rabbits, killed and plucked
poultry. I did not want my sisters to know I did such things.
I did not want the MacDonalds to think I had turned
girlish.

The summer holidays at Newton, where I was as usual
from late July to early September with all the great-uncles
and grouse-shooting guests, merge in my memory with
other summers except for one short dreadful experience,
which I typed out later.

My mother told me that I sometimes used to walk in my
sleep when I was unwell and feverish. I do not think I was
asleep. I remember having a cold and being sleepless,
going downstairs to the billiard room early one morning
and hearing the thumping of wood against wood outside
which alarmed me, for I knew none of the servants or
gardeners would work noisily near the house at that hour. I
ran to the oriel window and saw a furniture van with its
doors wide open backed up to the gateway of the kitchen
yard which was too narrow to receive it. Two men in
striped shirt-sleeves and green baize aprons were unload-
ing boxes from it. A third was inside the van pushing each
box on to the tailboard, and others who were standing near
came forward to help with the lifting and carrying. They
were all dressed alike though some wore bowler hats, and
they were all townsmen, pale as invalids. I saw goose-egg
heads, and some bowler hats hanging on the gate. The
boxes were heavy. They hoisted them on to their
shoulders, three on each side of a box, and carried them

slowly out of sight, below the window, where the thump of wood began again as though they were stacking them and changing the positions of those they had brought in earlier.

I heard the sound of other motors, not one but many engines, starting with a roar and saw another furniture van emerge from behind the rhododendrons, turn in the avenue and back towards me. The first one, now empty, made way for it. Then the huge clumps of rhododendrons began to move down the avenue, towards the gate lodge, exposing the black roofs of a long queue of furniture vans which were waiting to come up to the house. I ran to the garden door but found it locked, down the long corridor to the front, but that was locked. I felt ill and lay on the drawing room sofa where I suppose I slept.

When I went back to the billiard room I found it dusky. The sun, always full in the morning room at that hour, should have been brightly slanting on the billiard table but was only shining on one wall near the ceiling. The lower part of the window was obscured by those long boxes, which the baize-frocked men continued to stack. I saw ropes dangling above and, standing on the window seat, saw pulleys and men on ladders pushing the boxes into place as they were hauled up. And only now that they were near enough for me to see their shape did I know they were not rectangular; one end had sides slanting inwards to a narrow butt. They were coffins. Each had a corpse in it. That was obvious from the weight.

Within a few minutes the wide oriel window was covered and the whole billiard room as dark as night.

*

Kolya did not come to Newton that summer but wrote to me there from Brechin where he was staying with his mother.

> *David. You wrote, You said nothing. But I thank God for small mercies, and I am glad in my heart as I think of you in the heart of your family, your bonny sisters, amid ten-thousand uncles and aunts, gorging themselves on grouse and venison at this bounteous season of the year.*

*A propos the blessed Lamb Catrìona, I have today received an express from the Metropolitan, Patriarch of all the Russias, granting a dispensation for you. You may glance at her ankles, raise your eyes to her eyes and speak. You may ask her whether she has received one or one thousand missives from the Patriarch's Scottish emmisary. Looking upon her serene and beautiful visage, you will silently judge whether she is sane, and if sane whether she be governed by God, Satan or a man less worthy of her love than your melancholy cousin Kolya.*

*If you love me no more, end your life in the Moray Firth. Splash!*

*If she of the white fleece who never did love me loves me no more I shall end mine in the Firth of Forth, for the waste-paper baskets of Lamb's bank are filled with the shreds of my soul. The people of Nairn are dying as it might be by sandstorm or flood, smothered in scraps of my letters casually torn up. The High Street is choked.*

> *' "If seven maids with seven mops*
> *Swept it for half a year*
> *Do you suppose," the Walrus said,*
> *"That they would get it clear?"*
> *"I doubt it," said the Carpenter*
> *And shed a bitter tear.'*

*Adieu, good David. Do not write to me unless you have something to say.*

*Your companion and brother in faith,*

*Kol.*

*Post Scriptum: Ask your friend the piper – Michie is it? – to play a lament for me, one of those ones that never ends. My music master to whom I must soon return is a suet pudding with sugary coat – prefers Elgar to Tchaikovski. Hobbies: jolly folksongs. K.*

\*

That year I was entirely sorrowful when the school holidays came to an end. For the first time, I had no split emotions when my family left for London. I wanted to go with them. But gradually routine took over. It is a blessed thing, and meals are part of it.

I had given up my hunger strike when I moved to Newton and now at Tigh-na-Rosan I sat down punctually to every meal, my hands washed, my fingernails like pearls. As I became kinder to Granma, she became interested in me. I told her details of the Battle of Culloden and its aftermath which astonished her. She knew a bit about the Moray Floods but not so much as Michie and Mr Rae had told me. Granma began to listen to me and ask me questions, as though I was no longer a boy she had to put up with.

Mr Rae, observing, I suppose, my despondency that autumn, advised me to go on with the Culloden book.

—— You are prejudiced. So was Lord Clarendon in his History of the Rebellion. So was Macaulay throughout his works. You are absurdly patriotic – is there no country but Scotland? You are enthusiastic. Was Flora Macdonald beautiful? Was she the only one to risk her life to save Prince Charles? It does not matter, Thomson. Facts are the dried up skeletons of history. You have put flesh on them. But finish it with fact.

He meant that I should write about the results of the battle which he thought more decisive than those of Marston Moor. He said I was wrong in thinking that the Forty-Five was a war between England and Scotland; it was a civil war with Scots on both sides, in some way to be likened to Cromwell's civil war. But it affected Scottish culture permanently, mostly by destroying it but partly by reforming the old-established legal practices and diminishing rapine, cattle and horse reiving, clan warfare and the hereditary right of landowners to sit in judgment.

Having long grown out of my fear of him, my acceptance of his every word, I answered that even if it was a civil war, the cruelties after it and the destruction of what he called Scottish culture were ordered by Englishmen in their London parliament.

—— Yes. Write that then. Shall I read to you now?

—— Read something about it.

He read bits and spoke of them describing acts of parliament that were welcomed even by the Jacobite clansmen, though not by their chiefs, the most important of which was the act abolishing heritable justice, a right of summary justice possessed by many lairds and chieftains – the right of pit and gallows (dungeon or hanging) and the right of the Red Hand, which meant that anyone caught red-handed in a crime could be punished at will. These rights were an ancient gift of the Crown, under Scots law.

Some abused these rights so savagely that no court was ever held without a hanging afterwards, which gave rise to the Gaelic proverb: 'It is not every day that the Mackintosh holds a court' – which meant that if he sat in judgment every day, there would be no people left alive.

The gift from the Crown being hereditary came to an eldest son, even if he was a born idiot, and those who possessed it were themselves lawless. Some say that, even in the later years of the eighteenth century, they disregarded central government and acted as independent rulers just as the medieval barons of England had acted long before. They stole horses and cattle from their neighbours. They encouraged smuggling and sent their servants to fight the customs and excise men in battles that often resulted in death. This form of lawbreaking was popular. People living near the coast went, without orders from the lairds, to help the smugglers. They wanted tea, and malt for their home brewed ale. The lairds wanted gallons of claret to drink with their hundreds of guests, silks and cambrics for their ladies, brandy, Holland schnapps, and of course tea like everyone else. All these necessities were subject to excessive taxes, and were brought to Scotland tax free in fast ships which could usually outsail the government patrol boats. There were some privateers, but most of the traffic was done by armed ships owned by large smuggling companies in which some of the lairds had shares. Poor and rich, bailies, burghers, even provosts and sheriffs did all they could to protect the trade.

The Burgh of Inverness, which was, I believe, the only public body to possess the right of the Red Hand and three of its bailies (magistrates) got into serious trouble when they used it against an excise man and two soldiers in 1723. They, like the rest of the inhabitants, hated the customs and relied on smuggled goods. The three were summoned to appear before the Lord Advocate at Edinburgh and together with the Provost, Dean of Guild and other bailies sent a petition against the summons in which they pleaded that they did not hang the murderers, according to their right, but only had them whipped. They said that 'on the 11th June James Millar, tide-waiter [customs man], and Richard Barlow and Francis Powell, soldiers, before it was daylight in the morning, having called to a boat which was rowing about a hundred yards' distance from them on the river to come to the shore, and the boat not having readily answered, the tidesman ordered the soldiers to fire and three shots were fired, whereof one pierced the boat and another killed one of the boatmen.'

The people were enraged. A number who witnessed the shooting took the tidesman and soldiers prisoner and soon a great multitude assembled and carried them before the magistrates, crying for justice and demanding the extreme penalty for all three, but the magistrates 'to prevent the people becoming insolent and the officers being discouraged' avoided the capital penalty. The tide-waiter alone, in addition to his whipping, was ordered to pay £33 6s. 8d. sterling as assythment or reparation to the widow and children of the deceased.

The powerful men of Scotland, and especially those of the Highlands, continued to ignore central government, did what they wanted to do and when confronted by the law, which seldom happened because their lawlessness was uncontrollable, they faced the court as they would face a victor after a battle. The rape of land, horses, cattle, sometimes of women captured for brides, usually escaped the law.

I used to assume that most of the stouthreif (forceful theft) of animals was done by brigands or poor men who had no other means of livelihood, but it is not so. Most was done by great lairds, chieftains and noblemen and the usual reasons for it were two – to take revenge on powerful neighbours in a quarrel or to find tocher (dowry) for a daughter's wedding. It happened all over the Highlands and the North East and led to an élite profession – the hoofmark men.

Well as I knew each of the ten Sandwood cows by sight and touch, by horns, eyes, muzzles, udders – I could have been led blindfold into the byre and known by the feel and shape of the teats which cow I was milking – I could never have told which was which by looking at their hoofmarks in mud or dust. And yet for hundreds of years, farmers and landowners employed experts whose skill was to recognise by hoofmarks any strange cattle or horses that passed through their land. If the marks could be traced into the land beyond his territory, the landowner was proved free of guilt.

The most notorious robbery Mr Rae told me of happened near Nairn in 1716, when Simon Fraser, Lord Lovat, plundered the stables of Mr Dunbar, gentleman of Thundertown in the county of Moray. In the course of an old quarrel about land and money, Lord Lovat sent six men, one of whom was a customs officer from as far away as Cromarty, to break open Dunbar's stable doors at night. They took nine horses: a light bay horse worth £8 12s. sterling; a large white gelding, worth £16 10s.; a sorrel horse, worth £10 15s.; a grey horse, worth £12 sterling; a bay Galloway or pony, worth £4 16s.; a large, fine bay gelding, worth £21 10s.; a fine large mare, worth £16 sterling; a fine large grey gelding, worth £27 sterling; a strong grey horse, worth £15 sterling; and a strong stoned work-horse, worth £4 sterling; and a mare with foal, worth £3 sterling.

After a court order, three of the nine horses were given back, but Lord Lovat held on to the others because he wanted to make a fine appearance with them at Lord Cawdor's funeral. He was executed for his treacherous part in the '45, when he pretended to support the Hanoverians and at the same time sent his son to fight against them at Culloden; but the litigation between his family and the Dunbars went on for fifty years until both families were impoverished by it.

Mr Rae delighted in all such scraps of history and whatever he said or read to me, he expressed with amusement or serious vigour. He kept on going back to the Forty-five, as a turning point in Scottish history.

He read passages from Lord Elcho who fought at

Culloden and from Charles Terry's anthology of contemporary reports and during the next six weeks or so he
read to me the whole of *Waverley* which he said 'fleshed
the skeleton' of the Forty-Five better than any man who set
out to write history. He said Walter Scott, who liked writing
novels, was a great historian by nature, that he had started
the fashion in Europe where, after *Waverley* was published, many writers took to historical novels.
—— You can follow his footsteps.

I never did. I never even took his advice. My Culloden
book remained unfinished. But Mr Rae sowed seeds in my
mind about the history of Scotland and Ireland which grew
into green stalks if not flowers when I went to read history
at Oxford.

I now believe what the Gentle Lochiel believed at the
time, that the Jacobites should have lain low. Scotland
might then have retained its individuality within the
nominal and superficial English rule which had existed
since the so-called Union of 1707. Clan warfare, cattle
thieving and other evils of the old society would, I think,
have died out without forceful laws. Lochiel, the chief of
that feared and strong clan Cameron, had begun that
reform before 1745. His example might have been followed
by the many chiefs who waited for his word before they
took part in the rising.

All conquerors impose dictatorial rules on their victims,
the idea being that if the conquered give up their native
ways they will gradually become indistinguishable from
their conquerors. As among schoolchildren discipline is
more easily enforced by insisting on uniformity of dress,
speech and social custom.

When I heard of the law forbidding the wearing of the kilt
(the *feile-beag* or small fold), the plaid or any garment made
of parti-coloured stuff, I imagined Granma being forced to
take off her long black dress and walk down the High Street
in my shorts. I remembered my own shame and discomfort
when at the age of eight I was dolled up in school uniform.
But Granma, had the law required it, could have bought a
pair of grey flannel shorts at Burnett and Forbes. The
Highlanders owned no clothes except the traditional ones

made at home and even if they had the money to buy breeks there were no shops. Besides, one of the results of the burning of houses, sequestration of cattle and destruction of crops which followed their defeat was famine in some places, and near famine in others. Granma, if seen in her traditional long dress, would have been sentenced to six months' imprisonment – no bail allowed – and on her second offence to 'transportation to any of His Majesty's plantations beyond the sea for seven years.'

Some men took large safety pins or the shoulder brooch that once had held the plaid, and pinned their kilts between their knees to look like short trousers. Several lairds and noblemen of the Hanoverian persuasion protested to the government. The Lord President Duncan Forbes of Culloden House wrote to explain that the kilt, being loose, was best suited to mountain life, for wading rivers and climbing rocks, for protection in bad weather, 'which men dressed in Low Country garb could not possibly endure'. The absentee Thane of Cawdor, then spelt Calder, wrote from his estate in Wales to his Cawdor factor, 'I have thought that the poor Highlanders who are distressed by wearing breeches might be very agreeably accommodated by wearing wide trousers, like seamen, made of canvas or the like. Nankeen might be for the more genteel. But I would have the cut as short as the philibeg, and then they would almost be as good and yet be lawful.'

But who could afford to buy canvas, or could even the 'genteel' buy nankeen? Also Cawdor misunderstood the distress. It was not inconvenience. It was shame.

Cawdor was not punished for his plea to the Government. The Lord President was disgraced and made bankrupt for his. Sir Walter Scott, in a review of the Culloden Papers, wrote of Forbes:

'. . . we suspect that the memory of his services was cancelled by the zeal with which, after the victory, he pressed the cause of clemency . . . When the venerable judge, as well became his station, mentioned the laws of the country he was answered . . . What laws? By God, I'll make a brigade give laws to the land! . . .

his repeated intercessions in favour of those who for prejudice of education, or a false sense of honour, had joined the Chevalier, were taken in bad part and his desire to preserve to the Highlanders a dress fitted to their occupations, was almost construed into disaffection.'

Scott said that Forbes died broken in spirit and impoverished in estate 'by the want of that very money which he had, in the hour of need, frankly advanced to buy troops for the service of the Government'. By a sort of posthumous ingratitude, the privilege of distilling, without payment of duty, which had been given to his son as compensation for his father's losses 'was wrenched from the family by Government in 1785'. Burns called this privilege 'Lord Forbes' Chartered Boast'.

The Disarming Acts, the Acts of Attainder 'against notable rebels, chiefs, lairds, tacksmen and lords' were cruelly and usually unjustly enforced. A proposal to evict the common people by law and plant the Highlands with Englishmen and Lowland Scots, as Ulster had been planted, was cast out. But soon that was to happen without an Act of Parliament.

Most of Nairnshire, like the rest of the Highland regions, had been poverty-stricken for years before the Forty-five. The punitive measures enacted by the Hanoverians made the people not only poorer but homeless, and many of the better off could not escape that fate which led, as financial distress often does, to corruption in local government.

In 1751 George Irvine, owner of Newton and son of the agent for the Royal Burghs, a man of power in Nairn, started proceedings against the council of the Royal Burgh of Nairn for arrears of missive dues. He said that the money in the burgh coffers 'will scarce amount to £50 Scots, which is not sufficient to pay the town's servants, support the windows of the court house, and defray the charge of coal and candle to the military . . . who in the winter are constantly quartered here, and are daily passing and re-passing.'

George Irvine, in his memorial, states that 'several of the

treasurers of this burgh have broke and gone off with the town's revenue, small as it is, without accounting for several years, . . . the King's House, public streets and harbour are all decayed and in a ruinous state.'

The Hanoverian military were a nuisance in Nairn, noisy, diseased and disturbing. The first troopships from England arrived just too late for the Battle of Culloden and the soldiers squatted in people's houses all over the town. Some of them had yellow fever, which killed their fellow soldiers and killed many of the Nairn townspeople.

The government at Westminster had the cunning of the Roman Emperors – divide and rule, and make the conquered work for the conquerors. The clans who until the middle of the eighteenth century had fought only in Scotland were organised into a force that fought for a British Empire. In Nairn the process began in the 1750s.

It was not difficult to raise that force. Starving and homeless people make willing recruits.

The Fraser Highlanders, one of the earliest of the new regiments, was established with remarkable cunning. The Hon. Simon Fraser, son of the treacherous Lord Lovat, was appointed to raise a battalion on the forfeited estates of the family. With no trouble at all he raised seven hundred of his clansmen and quartered them in Nairn while recruiting of others went on. Recruiting by some of the gentlemen and ladies became a maniacal hobby. The ladies were inspired by enthusiasm like that which possessed the white feather ladies during the 1914 war. A Nairnshire lady wrote to a friend in the year 1757, 'I have made out my man!', meaning that she had persuaded someone to join a Highland Regiment. The headquarters of the new levies was Fort George which is about ten miles from Nairn. Most of the regiments were named after the clan from which they were recruited. Only one – the Black Watch – was composed of renegades and desperadoes without a homeland of their own. It had been founded in 1729 as a police force or 'watch' mainly to enforce the Disarming Acts after the rising of 1715, but was greatly reinforced after 1745 and it rapidly became as useful to the Government and as hated by the people as the Black and Tans were to be during the Irish War of Independence. Both the Black Watch and the Black and Tans were so named by the people after the colour of their uniforms. Companies of the Black Watch, the Frasers, and the Seaforths were stationed in Nairn for many years.

The historian William Ferguson wrote in 1968: 'Much more than Jacobitism died at Culloden.' He was referring to the disintegration of Highland society. In burghs such as Nairn local government fell to pieces too and was not repaired until the reform acts of 1833. In the mountains the Jacobite chieftains were displaced. In the towns the local councillors were replaced by officials who lived elsewhere. By 1783 only three of the seventeen members of the Nairn Burgh Council belonged to Nairnshire. Even the Provost was an absentee. The people protested, firstly to their magistrates and secondly to the House of Lords, but in vain. Two years later, in 1785, they made another petition but at the election of that year only one Nairn man out of the seventeen was chosen as a burgh councillor. It was this that caused the Nairn Riot in which many people were wounded and many houses wrecked. The case against the rioters was brought before James Brodie of Brodie, JP, who said that the rioters were subversive of all government and good order, and destructive of the peace and freedom of the community. The House of Lords decided, in the Nairn case, that it was not necessary that the Provost should be resident. Their decision, trivial as it now seems, local and unimportant if you think of Scotland as a whole, may be taken as a microcosm of government by foreign and remote control.

It was remote control that depeopled the Highlands at an expense of lives and happiness which in the end was of no benefit at all to the new 'British' Government. Scotland was represented both in the Commons and Lords but was subject to a large majority of foreigners.

The 'Vesting Act' of 1747 handed over to the Crown the titles of the Jacobites' lands. The 'Annexing Act' of 1752 replaced the chieftains by factors and officials chosen by the Government as rent collectors and resident administrators.

Rents and profits were to be used 'for the better civilising and improving of the Highlands' and for 'preventing disorders there for the future'. The rents of fourteen specially named estates were to be used 'to promote the Protestant faith, good government, industry, manufactures, and loyalty to the King.' Amongst these fourteen were the huge estates of Lochiel, Lovat, Cromarty and Keppoch.

The Commissioners appointed to administer these laws were mostly Scotsmen. They had little success because the clansmen sent their rent, in kind or money, to their outlawed chieftains and had nothing when the official rent collector came. Alan Breck Stewart, alias Thomson, renowned by Robert Louis Stevenson in *Kidnapped*, was thought to have killed a government factor, who was trying to collect rents, or serve eviction orders. Breck fled. His relative James Stewart was caught and hanged, but no one knows who did it because the people were united in silence and at the trial, eleven of the fifteen jurymen belonged to their hated Clan Campbell. The Presiding Judge was their most powerful enemy, the Hanoverian Archibald Campbell, Duke of Argyll.

On Lochiel's estate in Lochaber rents doubled between 1755 and 1788 without any investment in improvement being made. The case was not exceptional. It soon became evident that rents, however high, would bring no profit to a landlord from the over-populated lands; the only way was to clear the people out and put sheep in: a cruel process which began in the eighteenth century and went on in place after place for about a hundred years.

The government did not, so far as I can judge, intend this to happen. In 1784 Pitt the younger, with his Home Secretary Henry Dundas and the Lord Advocate of Scotland, Robert Dundas, Henry's nephew, restored the Jacobite estates 'at a fair price' to their heirs of the old owners. But the heirs, so long in exile or hiding in humiliation, were not at all like their fathers. Many of them had acquired in Edinburgh, Paris or Rome, a taste for luxury, for Society Balls and drawing room entertainments; many had married Lowland ladies and like those ladies could not bear the isolation, the old-fashioned simplicity of living in the cold, rough castles of their forefathers. They needed Society; no one can keep a place in society without plenty of money. Wool, exported to England and the Lowlands, made plenty of quick money. This they learned in the Border country where sheep farming flourished.

The Brahan seer said that 'the clans will become so effeminate as to flee from their native country before an army of sheep' and another time he said that 'the day will come when the Big Sheep will overrun the country until they strike the northern sea.' By which he meant Pentland Firth and the open sea north of Cape Wrath. Gaelic readers say that the word translated as Big Sheep may mean deer, but if it does the prophecy also was fulfilled, for when the sheep had taken the place of people and done their money making work, the deserted Highlands were turned into deer forests for sport, for after 1850 the quiet beauty of the empty mountains, enhanced by romantic literature, became known to wealthy merchants, lawyers and politicians, most of whom were English, who in their enthusiasm turned the country into a holiday playground and were more profitable to the younger chieftains than sheep had been.

'Since you have preferred sheep to men let sheep defend you,' said one clansman to his chief.

When the first evictions took place, emigration to America was orderly and obedient in spite of broken hearts, and the greatest protest, which became known as the 'Drive of the Big Sheep', was absolutely peaceful in its aims.

It seems, but is not, truly difficult to come close to the emotions of people who lived two hundred years ago. You have only to consider what is happening in your own time: for example what is happening to printers, journalists and writers of books. Printers who have worked all their lifetime, and many have inherited the skill from their fathers, are evicted, cleared from their traditional place in society and work, by a new moneyed landlord, perhaps from a foreign country like Australia, a landlord who regards money as more important than the welfare of his people. Writers who once belonged to a small family publisher are like serfs in medieval England, who whether they loved or hated their baron had a personal relationship with him. When he lost a war against a richer and bigger baron they were ruled by a stranger. So it is when a small and literate publisher is 'taken over' by a large, illiterate, greedy for money one.

The Drive of the Big Sheep began in Ross-shire, during the French Revolution, news of which had a strong effect on the common people of Scotland.

It began like the rallying of friendly clans to war but without fiery beacons or fiery cross. Men in taverns and at church doors spread the news. Runners were sent all over Ross, Cromarty and Sutherland to tell the people to gather the foreign sheep. They were good and quick at that; it was their way of gathering deer and wild horses from scattered herds on the hills. The new shepherds and even their dogs who had been brought from the Lowlands to tend the Lowland sheep were helpless. Some of the shepherds were so frightened that they helped the Highlanders to drive the flocks of sheep away.

John Prebble, in his vivid description of the scene, tells how the hills were covered with bleating, drifting animals and how men and women 'came to their doors to watch them pass, to offer water and encouragement to the drovers.' He quotes David Stewart of the 42nd regiment – the Black Watch – who wrote:

No act of violence or outrage occurred, nor did the sheep suffer in the smallest degree beyond what resulted from the fatigues of the journey and the temporary loss of their pasture. Though pressed with hunger, those conscientious peasants did not take a single animal for their own use contenting themselves with the occasional supplies of meal or victuals which they obtained in the course of their journey.

The plan was to herd all the immigrant sheep from the north as far as Inverness in the hope that men from there would drive them southwards and that relays of men would send them on to the Lowlands where they had come from.

It did not happen. Sheep walk slowly and it took several days to reach Strath Rusdale near Dingwall, on the northern side of the Cromarty Firth which divides that part of Ross-shire from the Black Isle. In this valley, nearly twenty miles from Inverness, thousands of sheep and hundreds of clansmen rested in the open air for the night.

The gentlemen owners of these men and sheep – it is inaccurate to call them lairds or chieftains because, although most of them were blood relatives of the drovers, they had become landlords in the English sense – had sent servants to spy the drovers out. They had also summoned some companies of the Black Watch from Fort George. The drovers did not need spies; people from miles away came to warn them that the soldiers were marching and they went home, leaving only the sheep for the soldiers to arrest. The sheep were divided with great difficulty and herded back in small flocks to the lands of their owners, some of which were fifty or a hundred miles apart.

The men who had made this peaceful protest were hard to find, because they came from all over the northern lands and had places to hide in when warning came. Only five were surprised and caught. They were brought before the Circuit Court at Inverness as ringleaders of sedition, etcetera. In fact there were no ringleaders. The protest had been spontaneous amongst all the people and encouraged by a majority who took no part in it.

The prosecution asked for the death penalty but the court imposed milder sentences. One of the accused was to be transported to Botany Bay for seven years, one to be fined £50 and imprisoned until he paid up, two were to be banished from Scotland for life and one was to be jailed for three months.

All five were imprisoned at Inverness to await the execution of these sentences. But somehow – no one knew how it happened – the prison gates were opened one night and all of them escaped. £5 reward was offered to anyone who found them. They were never informed upon, never found.

Money wins as it always does. And now the herding of the people from their land, which had begun before the herding of the sheep, increased tenfold. The Clearances in the Highlands, though probably less known to English people than the notorious evictions in Ireland, were done in the same way. The cause was different, the methods alike – burning of houses, sometimes with sleeping people in them, seizure of farm animals, destruction of growing crops, deaths of old people from heart attacks and fear, miscarriages of pregnant young women, starvation, homeless wandering, massive emigration. The Highlands of Scotland like the Highlands and Lowlands of Ireland were quickly depeopled and became the lonely, beautiful wastes we now enjoy.

*

Reports of these happenings are easily found in contemporary newspapers and books and more easily in the works of twentieth century writers, who have quoted the evidence and considered it untroubled by the emotions of the time. But the known and printed evidence comes only from parts of the Highlands and Western Islands which have little winter snow, those parts where the big and comparatively delicate Lowland sheep, such as Cheviots, could survive the whole year round. I am sure that clearances were made in Nairnshire, Moray and the Cairn Gorms, but I, for one, have never read about them and can only guess by what I see as I travel about. There are now few houses on the grouse-shooting moors or the deer-stalking hills of the Cairn Gorms. The large number of smoking 'black houses' which Walter Thom saw on his way from Nairn through Tradespark and Delnies to Fort George, in 1811, are all gone.

*

During the summer of 1928, my last year of living with Granma at Tigh-na-Rosan, somebody got married. I do not know who got married. But there was a great to-do at Newton before and after the wedding. All uncles and aunts and cousins and lovers went away in motorcars and stayed away all day. Some uncles and one aunt were drunkish when they came home and the aunt said,

—— It distresses me to think of all that money running away in one day.

—— Did you not enjoy it then?

—— I am not speaking of the wedding breakfast but of the wedding dress.

—— It was a lovely dress! a younger woman said.

—— Take a little bit of bread and no cheese! said the yellow-hammer through the open drawing-room window.

—— The dress was magnificent and she suited it. But the price. And then it will hang in her wardrobe until the day of her death. A simple taffeta with some muslin and lace would look as well.

—— The cheapest would be no clothes at all.

—— Tom!

—— How much will it have cost her parents, then? said Uncle Jim.

—— Two hundred pounds or more.

—— A peppercorn, said Uncle Tom. The Thane of Cawdor spent two thousand or more on his daughter.

—— Must we believe it?

—— *Cui bono*?

—— I'll show you. I'll show the bill. Are the Spalding Club books in your room, Robert?

—— You know very well where they are, said the Great Panjandrum.

—— Tak' two coos, Taffy, said a cushie doo, softly from far away in the woods and another answered 'Tak' care noo, hinny. Tak'.

—— Is she anything to Cawdor – the bride?

—— No, no.

—— She is second cousin twice removed to Rothie-murchus.

—— The Spey. The Spey Grants. The Spey.

—— Bite, bite, bite, said a sea bird. Go-back, go-back, go-back! said the grouse. And the more melodious birds, mavis, merle, the garden warbler sang evensong in the bushes near the window.

—— Did you bring dreaming bread, Aunt Jessie?

—— They gave us all a piece, said Granny. The wedding cake was like a cartwheel with smaller and smaller wheels going up to a tower on top.

—— I don't like the marzipan part.

—— Why do you wish for dreaming bread? said Granny, pretending not to smile.

The girl blushed.

—— Here is a ju-jube, although it is wrong to eat sweets before a meal. The dreaming bread at bedtime. Then you'll see your intended in the night.

Uncle Tom came back with one of those huge Spalding books, leather bound, with gilt titles, which I had never opened because they looked boring, and read bits from a long bill for paraphernalia supplied for the wedding of 'Mistress Jeane Campbell, daughter to the Laird of Calder [Cawdor], who was wedded to the Master of Forbes in anno domini 1646: silk and worsted stuffe, silver and gold lace, a large crowned love hood, a banded tafetie hood, Isabella (pale yellow) and red ribbons, shivernanes (gloves), limond stockings, a black English domed hat, a silver and gold handle, Spanish gloves, Spanish tafetie, French poudesay, rose-coloured moyhair, orange tafetie, silver pearling. Seven pepper of pins at £2 3s. Six pair of stockings two at 8 merk and four pair at £4 the pair. Two coffers at £9 10s. the piece, and a little red coffer at 5 merk. An embroidered woman's saddle and all furniture (for riding to the wedding on her palfrey) at £12 sterling.

The whole outfit amounts to the sum of £2093 6s. 8d. It is thus subscribed by the bride in a pretty hand.'

Uncle Tom always commanded attention when he read aloud. He read this like a prayer without expression. At some things in it people laughed and even Uncle Robert laughed. He said, as Tom closed the book,

—— It is delightful. And in all the years it has stood on my shelf I have never looked at those accounts near the end. Would you hand the volume to me, please, Tom?

—— When's supper?

—— What's for supper?

—— Oh, look, look! A hare on the lawn.

—— Very soon. You are so impatient. Charlotte will be here to call you soon.

—— Now, Tom, said Robert after turning many pages, this passage may touch you very near. You will remember that in the year of our Lord seventeen hundred ought four, Sir Hugh Campbell of Cawdor published his Essay on the Lord's Prayer with the intention of introducing it into our church service and how many ministers attempted to confute it.

Uncle Tom muttered something inaudible.

—— But many supported him, of whom the Countess of Moray was one. She wrote to him an encouraging letter which is printed here: 'I hear some of the ministers in the country begin to say the Lord's Prayer. I hear Cuming is on who lives near Edinburgh; also upon Sunday last Mr Carstairs who preached in the Abbey to the Commissioner said the words with a paraphrase upon every sentence. I hear Balnagoun has brought a little book to confute yours.'

—— There may be little objection when a paraphrase is given, said Uncle Tom, for then it becomes a quotation with glossary. It is not so much the prayer itself that we take exception to; it is that we are required to kneel in the Popish and English fashion when it is recited. And you cannot deny, Robert, that it is a set form of prayer which may be recited without thought or faith. A tincture of Anglicanism had by then infected Cawdor and the Countess of Moray.

There was silence for a moment, then whispers and giggles from the children by the window:

—— The Countess of Moray
She was in a hurry
And got covered in mud
Before the Flood.

—— And the bonny Earl o'Moray
O, he was the Queen's Love.

—— They ha'e slain the Earl o'Moray
And they laid him on the Green . . .

Barbara ran into the drawing-room and whispered
—— Kuti's left her card in the hall!
—— Help.
—— Get a cloth quick before Granny sees.
—— It wasn't her fault. Someone shut the front door.

We and our parents used the phrase 'leaving his or her card' about dogs pissing because they often do it, not from need, but to show other dog. that they have been visiting a certain tree or rock. Wolves do the same and the chosen tree becomes a gathering place for a tribe at which, by the individual smell, they can recognise each other or, if no other wolf is there, leave a message. In Nairn, in my boyhood, when very few people had telephones the gentry left their visiting cards at other people's houses.

Every family has its own private language. Ours was a mixture of Hindustani, Scots and two or three Gaelic words. Kuti, which we sometimes spelt Khuti or Kootie because people thought it was 'cutie' – means bitch, which was her sex, and when we called her to her dinner we cried 'Khana, Khana!' for just as the old Irish spoke to their animals in English, so did the white people in India speak to theirs in Hindustani, a language which my older sisters had at one time spoken more fluently than English. They spoke it with ayahs, soldiers and servants and even with our parents.

We were snobbish about ways of speech, although we had no reason to be so, for ours was neither proper Scots nor proper English. A Cockney accent was disgraceful, an Edinburgh one all right. We laughed at English public schoolboys who said 'witch' for 'which', 'soy' for 'sorry', 'Wales' for 'whales', and our great-uncles and aunts had a similar scorn of the Glasgow accent which was something that my father's sister-in-law Judy suffered from, for Bill had married into a Glasgow family. My father had been sent to Fettes to cure his broad Forfarshire accent, for one day when they were driving in an open carriage out from Brechin, the town where he was born, and he was on the box beside the coachman, they heard him say to the coachman, 'Gi'e us thon whup.'

*

I think everybody says of something ancient, 'It was there before the Flood,' meaning Noah's Flood, but in Nairn amongst old people, not of our family but of the real people of Nairn, it meant before the Great Moray Flood of 1829. They would say, 'This kirk was built, that man died,' so many years before or after the Flood.

> The rivers Findhorn, Nairn and Spey
> Are gleg to rise on Lammas Day
> And delve their banks away.
> In Our Lord's year of '29
> They rose thegither nine times nine.

Lammas Day is a quarter day, when rent is due and Fairs are held all over Scotland, and the Lammas Fludes or Floods are expected on the lower lands of the North East where rivers flow down from the Highlands. Flude is, I think, a more southerly word. We said spate for a swollen river or an exceptionally heavy downpour of rain. Early August is usually a time of heavy rain. The snow which stays all the year round on the mountain peaks has by then been softened by the sun. A downpour loosens it a bit and sweeps all the snow away from the slopes below. One day's downpour is enough to swell the rivers and if the rain goes on for several days the land is flooded. The last strong flood of the river Nairn that I know of was in 1956 when the Jubilee Bridge, a suspension bridge for walkers between the cemetery and the town, was swept away. It was the second Jubilee Bridge to go. The first had been built in 1887, Queen Victoria's Golden Jubilee year, and was swept away in the spate of 1915. The delicate and beautiful bandstand on the Links, which is still there, was also made to celebrate the Golden Jubilee.

Early in August, 1829, a gentleman in Glasgow received a letter from a friend who lived in Nairn:

On Sunday afternoon last I observed an immense black cloud in the SW like a huge mountain poised in the air, and covering a whole hemisphere, wind from

the NE to NNW. Soon afterwards it began to rain . . .
The rain continued with little or no intermission
during Sunday night, the whole of Monday, and until
midday on Tuesday, occasionally thick, close and
drizzly, but more frequently in heavy, pouring
rushes. Wind northerly all the time. Our river rose
very considerably on Monday and was gradually on
the increase; but by Tuesday morning it was an ocean,
with the rapidity of a mill-spout, raising an assemb-
lage of conflicting waves, whose angry, curling tops
bade defiance to description. In short, our small
mountain stream became a mighty sea, extending
from the southern declivity of Nairn to the hilly
boundaries . . .

He describes many ships in distress in the Firth and one
'large schooner or brig' which went down with all hands in
the gale as it was trying to reach the shelter of Nairn
harbour. Watching it founder, men from the Fishertown
bravely tried to launch their boats but the surf and the
breakers which rose ten feet above their heads made that
impossible. They saw no survivors. 'From the things
picked up on the beach on Tuesday morning, she appears
to have been the *Endeavour* of South Shields coal-laden.'

On Tuesday morning the Duke Coach [the *Duke of
Gordon* from Inverness to Aberdeen] passed east as
usual, but at 11 o'clock in the forenoon she returned
with the appalling news that the Findhorn bridge was
totally swept away by the destructive flood . . . There
is in all the plains of Morayshire but havoc and
devastation . . . The Findhorn could no longer be
called a river, and the whole of the rich and beautiful
country was immersed, the wretched inhabitants
were obliged to betake themselves to their house-tops,
to abide their fate . . . These ill-fated farmers and their
families were carried off from their perilous positions
by the Findhorn boats, which came, full sail, over
corn-fields, bridges and dykes, to their relief. The
general course of these boats was across the sands [the
Culbin Sands].

There were two floods that August and in Nairnshire the second, which began on the 27th, was the worse.

The sources of the Nairn are in the Monadhliath Mountains, that high broad range which stretches from the Great Glen to Strathspey, where the Spey forms a cleft between it and the Cairn Gorms. The Nairn is only about thirty miles long and for the first few miles, high up, it does not look like a river at all. Many small streamlets and burns dribble down from the hillsides until they form one stream which, fed by numerous burns, becomes a river which runs from above Strathnairn by Cawdor, Kilravock and Firhall, through the Harbour of Nairn to the sea.

Above Strathnairn, where the river is normally swift but shallow the only large building to be damaged was the Mill of Faillie – a fulling mill for wool which, by the way, is one bit of evidence showing that southern sheep had been established in the county by then. The flood of the first to fourth of August demolished the mill not so much by water as by the stones, tree trunks and gravel that the water carried with it. The heavy, wooden machinery was broken and swept nine miles downstream to Cantray, retrieved, carted back and reassembled in time to be swept away again on 27 August to Kilravock eleven miles downstream from the mill.

Two strong stone bridges on the old military road to Fort George, the Brig o' Dunmaglas and the two-arched bridge across the Achnatruagh burn, a tributary of the Nairn, were destroyed. Near there, just above the ravine of Daviot, the burn of Craggy joins the Nairn. There was another bridge in that place and high up on top of the steep bank about 100 feet above the water stood a small inn, a well-known resting place for travellers in that wild country. The bridge was swept away, the hillside softened, the Inn of Craggy undermined by water. There was a landslide. The inn was only saved by the trees that fell, especially by one great old oak, which turned the course of the flood away from that bank. The mill of Clava, near the Clava Stones, was wrecked by the first flood and demolished on 27 August. The flatter farmland of Holm, between there and Kilravock, was flooded. The horses and cattle were standing three feet deep in water in their stalls when they were rescued, and the rats and moles were swimming about inside every building on the steading. There was in those days a high dry-stone dyke, which made the boundary between Holm and Kilravock, topped with divots instead of coping stones. The water did not quite reach the top. A multitude of rabbits, rats, mice, voles and moles did reach it and the top of the wall for a hundred yards or more was like a crowded narrow causeway over a lake with all these creatures jostling and hurrying towards dry ground.

On the 27th, the day on which Sir Rowland Hill, inventor of the penny post, and Lord Henry Thynne, fishing and shooting guests at Cawdor Castle, left for the south. John Pryse, one of Lord Cawdor's workmen left in the forenoon with a cart 'drawn by a very active mare' to take their baggage to Inverness. On his way home, at about eight o'clock in the evening he stopped to rest himself and his mare at the Inn of Clephanton, about a quarter of a mile north of Kilravock bridge. The landlady warned him not to try to cross the bridge and that even if he did succeed in crossing at it he would get no further, for the water on the level ground south of it would smother mare, cart and man. Pryse was drenched to the skin by the rain, anxious to get home and said that if he found the bridge impassible he would come back. The landlady's ostler offered to go with him across the bridge where, bidding him God's help, he got off the cart and stood to watch. The water was up to his knees. Pryse told him he knew the position of the road although neither of them could see it, but a few minutes later the ostler could not see him; he and his mare and cart were covered with water. He ran back to the inn, crying for help.

The landlord and every man nearby ran down to the bridge and to their relief they heard Pryse shouting for help. They managed in snatches between the roar of wind and water, to hear what he said. He had clung to his cart under water, the mare swimming, until it got stuck on a ledge. With his knife he had cut the mare's traces and freed her from the shafts to swim away. Pryse was standing up to his waist in water on the cart which was rocking underneath him and would soon fall off its perch. They threw ropes but the wind and darkness made it impossible to aim straight. They tried to wade and swim to him with rope ends in their hands, but the current was too strong for them until, about 3 o'clock in the morning, the flood ebbed several feet. He had been seven hours in the water when at last they rescued him and helped him back to the inn.

He seems to have been worried about his mare. The landlady, feeding him with broth, would not allow him to go out and search for her at daylight, but the ostler and some friends went out. They found her, calm and un-harmed, on a hillock, on an island, where 'she had had the wisdom and patience to remain stationary till her master was relieved.'

All the farmlands, with crops half-harvested or waiting for a dry spell in which harvest could begin, were destroyed and many people were drowned or injured. Most of the small farmers and labourers whose little houses were on low ground wandered homeless like the rats and mice. Women with children and babies in arms climbed the hills. James Mackintosh, a farmer whose family had for generations been tenants of the Cawdors on the Haugh of Culbeg was almost drowned for the third time in his life. His house had been flooded, with all crops lost, in 1780 when he was seven years old, and Rose of Kilravock had then entreated his neighbour Lord Cawdor to allow the Mackintoshes to build a new one on the high bank which formed one of the boundaries between the two estates. But the Cawdors of that time were hard landlords, often away in Wales, out of touch with their home tenants, whom they left in the care – if it may be called care – of their factor. Permission was not granted.

James was 73 years old and very deaf in 1829, when early in August his house was flooded at night. He and his family were asleep and did not wake in time to get out safely. They did escape, half wading, half swimming, leaving all their belongings behind, and reached the safety of the high bank on which they sat for two days until the flood subsided. Sir Thomas Dick Lauder who visited the family on the day when they were trying to make their dwelling habitable again, spoke of wreck and desolation: 'the very smell of it was like that of a house newly disinterred, after being buried for a century.'

> They were beginning to recover a little from their panic, when the yet more terrible flood of the evening of the 27th visited their habitation, and filled the rooms to the height of 5 feet, as I ascertained from the stain it had left on the plaster. Being more quickly alarmed, on this occasion, their flight was more precipitate. 'But,' said Mr Mackintosh to me, as we stood on his damp and disconsolate floor, 'I minded me o'something I wad ha'e done ill wanting; and so I wade back again, and crap in at that window there, and after grapin' aboot and gettin' a haud o'what I was seekin', I was gawin' to creep oot again, when I bethought me o'my specks' – 'Specks!' roared I into his ear, 'how could you risk your life for a pair of spectacles?' 'Trouth, Sir,' replied he seriously, 'I could na' ha'e read my Bible without them, and, mair nor that, they were silver specks, and they were specks sent me hame in a praisant frae my son, the Yepiscopal meenister in Canada.' This was unanswerable, and I was glad to learn that the result of his boldness was the salvation of his 'specks,' as well as of the purse or pocketbook, into which I presume to interpret what he called 'the thing he wad ha'e done ill wantin.' Not a particle of corn was spared to him, and even the straw was so completely ruined, that he was compelled to sell off his livestock and to give up the farm. As he told me himself, 'he was three days on the hill looking over this disagreeable affair;' yet I heard no murmur of complaint escape him, and all his talk was of thanks to God for the preservation of himself and his family.

Downstream from Cawdor and Geddes the valley narrows and the river curves like a long S between high banks into the Burgh of Nairn, the left bank being higher than the right. Fir Hall, its steading and large threshing mill, all strongly built of stone, stood on the left bank about 30 feet above the normal water level and 30 feet away from the edge of the river. The flood cut into the base of the bank until the earth above grew soft and Fir Hall was undermined. The whole steep slope gave way and crashed into the water, bringing with it trees, mill and the gable-end walls and roof of a lofty barn. Landslide after landslide succeeded as far as the Washing Green, a two acre stretch of flat grass, which is now used as playing fields, between Church Street and the present Jubilee footbridge. The whole green was destroyed, the part nearest to the river being carried away and the part below Church Street covered with stones, gravel, bits of trees and other debris. It is only a few hundred yards from there to the Constabulary Gardens which are on the level of the High Street high above the river. The gardens, like the Constabulary house, are founded on sandstone rock. The rock split and fell into the water, bringing with it a huge old tree that had been rooted there for over fifty years. The tree and a piece of rock, fourteen foot long and three foot wide, were swept two hundred yards down the river.

It was heavy objects like those, rather than the force of the spate, that wrecked the Nairn bridge on the night of 27 August just before the mail coach from Aberdeen was expected on its way to Inverness.

On 3 August when the river rose nine feet above its ordinary level some of the piers of the three stone arches had been weakened, but that did not interfere with traffic.

The night of the 27th was fearfully dark and two men, walking home to Nairn after visiting friends, held on to the parapet as they groped their way across the bridge. Luckily they were on the north side, the harbour side, or they would certainly have been plunged into the torrent below for, feeling the roadway cracked above the third arch, they suddenly realised that they were on a fragment of the bridge only five feet broad. They crossed in safety and then remembered that it was the hour at which the mail coach was expected. They groped their way back across the bridge and stopped it just in time – a difficult thing to do without signalling with lamps, especially near the bridge where coachmen, impatient for a rest at the end of a stage, usually whipped their horses into a canter over the bridge and up the High Street brae.

The harbour was wrecked, with ships in it. All the land and most of the houses on both sides of the river were ruined and although the valleys of the Nairn, Findhorn, Lossie and Spey appear to have suffered most, the rivers Divie, Don and Dee, Nethy, Dulnan, Aven, Livat, Esk, the burns of Craig and Burkie, the rivers Bogie, Deveron and Isla all caused ruin and calamity.

*

Whatever the compass of a man's knowledge, he should not display it.

If you wish to carry your pocket handkerchief in your breast pocket, crumple it up; do not place a newly ironed one there, sticking up flat like an advertisement.

If you are invited for lunch at one o'clock, leave before three. If your host's dog annoys you, do not strike or kick it near the front door. You may kick it when it bites your ankles below the table, but not so hard as to make it yelp and distress your hostess. After luncheon do not fold your table napkin. Leave it crumpled by your plate unless you are staying the night, in which case fold and roll it neatly. A table napkin ring will be beside your plate.

When you are walking on the pavement with a lady keep to the outside; she may wish to take your arm. Let her hang on your left arm. Keep your sword arm free.

—— Which is my sword arm?

—— The right.

—— But if we cross the street . . . ?

—— You must change over – keep to the kerb side.

—— But my sword arm then . . .

—— She must then hang on your sword arm. But try to avoid that side of the street.

Always raise your hat to a lady even if you cannot remember who she is, and if she stops to speak with you hold it in your left hand until you part. Never shake hands with man or woman without taking off your glove. Never keep your hat on inside any house. If a woman enters a room, stand up and do not sit down again until she sits down.

I did not value or even think about such conventions in my boyhood; I observed them without question; then during my rebellious years renounced them for a time. But I value them now and keep to those few which remain inoffensive to young people who naturally have adopted different rules of conduct. I no longer offer my seat to a woman in a crowded London tube, unless she is carrying a baby or is old and frail. I have been so often repulsed with haughty glances.

But convention and set manners exist even in small, simple communities everywhere in the world, which have not lost ancient tradition, and everywhere they ease social intercourse. For one example the English 'How do you do?' answered by 'How do you do?', which seems ridiculous, is much better than 'How are you?' because no one needs to hear about your latest operation or bout of influenza.

——    Never make personal remarks upon anybody.

Eccentric behaviour, of which there was much at Newton, appeared to be acceptable as something no rules of manners could control. Uncle Jim often went to sleep while guests were having an animated conversation. Uncle Tom always ran his fingers up and down his trouser fly when he came into a room, to make sure, I suppose, that all his flybuttons were done up and while he was sitting in an armchair, talking and listening, he was constantly flicking imaginary crumbs off his waistcoat. Granny sprang her lorgnette and peered at anyone who came into the room, which was distressing to people unfamiliar with Newton society, especially to young guests on their first visit.

I think our great-uncles must have seemed uncouth to English people, for in those days there was much more difference between the two countries than there is now – especially in dress and manners – and our old uncles had not changed their fashion very much since their youth.

Uncle Tom who disliked some of the grouse-shooting guests, not because they were English but because he disliked them, loved making fun of them to us after meals.

He once said that in former days fraternising with the English was punishable by banishment or death. He would like to see those laws re-enacted. Robert could do it if his heart was in the right place.

—— What's wrong with them, then, Uncle Tom?

—— Listen to the way they go 'hawtittie – haw and faw-faw-faw' and look how they fiddle about with their food.

It made me laugh, because at school I had always stared at English boys eating in their funny way. I did not object to it; I admired their patience and skill. For instance, if we had meat with vegetables, they would make a little platform of meat and carefully stack bits of potato, cabbage, even peas, on the back of the fork. The peas often fell off between plate and mouth, and even then they would not scoop them up, but try again to balance them on the back of their fork. They wasted all their gravy at the end of a meal because they were not allowed to mash the potatoes into it or mop it up with bread. Soft food with sauce, like macaroni or cauli-flower cheese, had also to be balanced on the back of the fork. Sometimes I expected them to take their soup from the back of the spoon. But at Dotheboys Hall, when I put salt on my porridge, the English boys passed me mustard and pepper.

Our table manners followed the French conventions, just as many common Scots words are derived from French. For Scotland had always had a closer relationship socially and in political sympathy with France than with England. We used the word ashet for meatplate (*assiette*), *gigot* for mutton, haggis (*hachis*), grosserts (*groseilles*) for goose-berries, *jupe* for a girl's dress – or for some part of it; I forget. There are many more which we heard but only used for fun: a braw man, for a fine man, is *brave*; dour – hard and obstinate – which is used in England in a slightly different sense, is *dur*; fashious for troublesome is *facheux*; to jalouse – to suspect someone or something is *jalouser*; sucker (*sucre*); refort for horse-radish, *raifort*.

At Sandwood croft, the MacDonalds, said goodson, good dochter, or daughter, good-mother, for in-laws – *beau-fils, belle-mère*, etc., and I have read but never heard of a beautiful way of calling a cow to you – Prush, Madame,

*Approche, Madame*. And then we had a kind of shortbread from Edinburgh called Petticoat Tails, which is supposed to be a corruption of *Petits Gateaux*, a kind first made for Mary Queen of Scots by her French chef.

A fashion amongst the gentry of sending their sons to school in England or employing English tutors at home was well-established by the middle of the nineteenth century. Uncle Robert who was born at Newhaven, then a small fishertown near Edinburgh, in 1842, was not of the gentry and went to the Edinburgh Academy where many of the sons of professional people were educated. It was the sons of noblemen and great lairds who were sent to English public schools, a custom which was resented by some and which killed the Scots language within the upper classes of society. An old lady, when asked whether an acquaintance was Scotch or not said,

—— I canna say. Ye a'speak sae genteel now that I dinna ken wha's Scotch.

And when Tytler came home from an English School, although his family were delighted with his appearance, manners and general improvement, his sister burst into tears.

—— Is he not charming? they said.

—— Oh, aye, but he speaks English.

Uncle Robert and his six brothers who were all reared at the Academy were part of the old society. Robert was born only ten years after Sir Walter Scott's death, while Macaulay was MP for Edinburgh, in the very year of the publication of *The Lays of Ancient Rome* and only eight years before the birth of Robert Louis Stevenson (three authors whose work he liked immensely), and although in addition to his knowledge of the Classics, he spoke fluent French, Italian, Spanish and modern Greek and showed exceptional talent in his new profession, he was not well received in London as a young man. 'Provincials' were despised or ridiculed. Scotsmen were often treated with cold politeness or disguised hostility. And then his grave Presbyterian manner may have seemed forbidding. I remember him as having a subtle sense of humour, but it is said that in all his public life, in court or in the Parliament, he never made a joke.

At the English Bar 'He had a slightly rustic air and, with his handsome features, deep set eyes, and good figure, he might have passed as a prosperous Scottish farmer.' He rode every day to his chambers in the Temple from Kensington where he lived on a very old rough looking pony and for part of the way he jogged sedately down Rotten Row among the fashionable riders on their priceless horses.

When I think of his youth in London, I also think of the courtiers and hundreds of servants of King James VI who, when they arrived with him in London, in 1603, were outcasts, not knowing a word of the language, hated or at least resented by the English. The king had not enough money to support them all, or if he had he did not use it for that purpose. Many were homeless and destitute. They saved themselves by establishing a colony in Holborn, a little Scotland cut off from the rest of London. It was there, at a house in Lamb's Conduit, that the famous 'Scots Kist' or 'Scots Box' was placed, a large brass-bound chest into which the more prosperous immigrants put coins for the poor. The Kist has been preserved by the Royal Scottish Corporation which is still active as a charitable society for homeless or poor Scots in London.

Before the Union of Crowns in 1603, Scotsmen were punished for intercommuning with the English. During James V's reign, an enactment was made to prevent any man from passing into England 'without special writings and licence.' And the 'bringing in of Englishmen' to Scotland had been punishable by fine, banishment or death for many years before that.

A border farmer was prosecuted 'Item, for art and part of stouthreif (violent theft) of four score sheep . . . Item, for art and part of the treasonable in-bringing of Sir John Musgrave, an Englishman, and for intercommuning with him at the said time in treasonable manner.'

In 1510, John Neilsome, alias Suppit-out, was convicted of art and part of theft and concealment of three horses etc., etc.:

'*Item*, of his treasonably being and remaining in the Kingdom of England without a licence from the King or Guardian of the Marches. *Item*, intercommuning with the English in theftuous and treasonable manner: *Item*, of treasonable inbringing of sundry Englishmen, at various times within the Kingdom of Scotland . . . his crimes. DRAWN and HANGED.'

So it went on. A more serious case occurred in October 1558, when Christopher Johnstoune with three of his brothers, and their accomplices, brought in Richard and Fergus Grahame, brothers, and 'others of our ancient enemies of England, to the number of five hundred persons . . .'

*

As my eyesight improved, I used my eyes more and more for secret reading, but only of old books in large print of which there were plenty at Newton.

Any visit to the libraries of the ancient castles of the north of Scotland will show that the chieftains, lairds and noblemen, who were always setting fire to each other's houses and stealing horses and cattle, loved music and literature and valued works from every country in Europe.

The great library of the Dukes of Argyll, at Inveraray Castle, is famous – I was once asked to make a catalogue of it, but in the end said no – but small castles such as Brodie, Kilravock and Cawdor, all near Nairn, show the same thing.

The Newton libraries were formed comparatively recently. There were three of them, if you count the billiard room shelves which had an excellent collection of nineteenth century books, – that and a large library upstairs where Mary used to take refuge alone, reading and reading, and Uncle Robert's study where I read like a criminal while he was out.

He had there a great number of legal books amongst which only Pitcairn's *Criminal Trials of Scotland* interested me, for slaughter, as murder is called in it, robbery, and witchcraft. The witchcraft trials were the best for me because they are so sexy, describing physical communion between people and between animals and people. But I also looked through the literary and historical works. There had been a small, invaluable renaissance of those subjects in Scotland during the eighteenth and nineteenth centuries, when clubs were founded for research and printing or reprinting of old documents. The best known were the Abbotsford Club, associated with Walter Scott, the Bannatyne, Maitland and Spalding Clubs. Their publications were financed by subscription and those members who were writers or learned editors gave their work for the love of it. Uncle Robert's father-in-law Cosmo Innes, a great lawyer, historian and antiquarian edited *The book of the Thanes of Cawdor* and *Ane account of the Familie of Innes* for the Spalding Club and contributed many articles to the books of the Maitland and Spalding Clubs, of which he was also a member. I suppose that is why Uncle Robert had so many of these club books on the shelves of his study. The Spalding Club, which met in Aberdeen and was named after the historian John Spalding, published at least a dozen volumes concerned with the North-East, many of which gave detailed histories of Moray and Nairnshire.

Cosmo Innes was a Whig, one time MP at Westminster. Robert, who started as a Liberal Unionist later allied himself with the Conservatives. This may have made him lose some of his popularity in the Fishertown of Nairn. When he stood for election as MP for the Inverness Burghs, my mother went campaigning for him. I cannot think what use she was. She never showed any interest in politics. Probably her hair and the rest of her beauty helped.

What surprises me more is that Robert, devout Presbyterian as he was, had married into the Innes family who not long before had been Catholic Jacobites. Cosmo Innes was formally Protestant and Whig, it is true – he had made the compromise of joining the Episcopalian Church – but in his writings and university lectures he expressed an understanding of and sympathy with Catholicism which made him unpopular in Scotland. He admired and often quoted Guizot. He was sought out by many distinguished French Catholics, including Charles, Compte de Montalembert, a great advocate of Liberal Catholicism, who became a close friend and an admirer of his historical work. Innes's article

in the *North British Review* on 'Scotland before the Reformation', although he attempted in it to show that he saw
both sides of the question, aroused fierce hostility. He was
accused of being a Catholic in disguise.

He had married a sister of Rose of Kilravock and so knew
Nairnshire well. He had been born and reared near
Aberdeen but his ancestral lands were in Moray. One Innes
had been Bishop of Elgin in the fifteenth century, another
was the villain who desecrated the cathedral two hundred
years later in league with Brodie of Brodie. Moray and
Nairnshire were spattered by members of his family, so he
was especially pleased when, in 1840, he was made Sheriff
of Moray, a shrievalty that included Nairn.

A sheriff in Scots law is the chief judge of a district, but by
then the appointment had become an honour usually
requiring very little work. Cosmo Innes had to visit Moray
only twice a year, in spring and autumn. He had a large
family which he took with him for the holidays.

The only rupture in his peaceful tenure of that office
happened in 1847, during the great Irish Famine, when
there were riots in Elgin which so alarmed the local
authorities that they took the unusual step of sending to
Edinburgh for the sheriff of the county. The potato blight,
widespread in Europe, had struck the Highlands causing
hunger and famine which the lairds tried to relieve by
buying meal in such places as the fertile Strathspey. The
merchants of Elgin, delighted by offers of ready cash for
quantities larger than they had ever sold before, put a stop
to retail sales, creating thereby an artificial famine in a
country which had had an exceptionally rich harvest in the
previous autumn. The staple winter diet in Morayshire was
not potatoes, but porridge, oatcakes and bannocks, and for
the better-off bread made of wheaten flour. All was boiled
or baked at home and the meal they could afford to buy was
just enough to feed a family for the week.

It happened too that the men who came to take their food
away were their old enemies, the Highlanders, who for
generations had raided their land. This time they came
protected by the law with Lochiel's money in their hands
and many horses and carts which they had driven all the

way from Lochaber, through Inverness, Nairn and Forres, a journey of nearly a hundred miles.

The people assembled peaceably in an enormous silent crowd which filled the main street, which is as wide as a boulevard, and then went to the lodging place of the Lochaber men hoping to persuade them to go home with a small quantity of meal or none. The Lochaber men locked them out, would not talk. It happened twice. Enraged, they dragged eight carts to the main street, took the wheels off and tossed the carts about. One wheel was later found in the Spey a mile outside the town.

The protest was successful – slightly successful. The Lochaber men perhaps in fear of their lives, perhaps because they had few carts left, agreed to take less meal than they had come for. But the people, by then hungrier and angrier than they had been, gathered to drive them away empty-handed. The police took one prisoner. The mob rescued him and as they did so wounded the police 'to the effusion of blood'.

When Cosmo Innes arrived in Elgin he found matters worse than he had expected. All the fishertowns along the coast were in an uproar. They, too, were desperately short of food and when the news came that the Highlanders had decided to ship the meal instead of taking it through the hostile towns of Forres and Nairn, they made ready for a fight. It was their women who stopped them fighting.

The meal carts were guarded by soldiers, who had been hastily called for, and when the fishermen tried to fight, the fishwives pushed them back, lifted the soldiers off their feet and put them down out of harm's way. 'I was no better than a baby in arms,' said one of them. Soldiers in those days would not fight women. Probably, too, they were in sympathy with the people just as Cosmo Innes was.

He did not read the Riot Act, as other sheriffs would have. He ordered few arrests most of which were of 'the better class of people', and some he had to send for trial in Edinburgh. In Edinburgh when he came home he visited these men in jail and did his best to mitigate their punishment.

A friend of his writing thirty years later, soon after his

death, says that this *émeute* and the action he was forced by law to take against the people of his own family lands remained a disagreeable memory throughout his life. He was a man known in public life as a kind and generous judge and in private life criticised as overindulgent to his numerous children. He was even laughed at for his love of the rare poultry he assembled at Inverleith house. He fed them himself. They flocked around him in the new poultry yard he had built.

His youngest daughter, a hard-worked pet called Mary, but known to us as Biba, was the only child left at home when Uncle Robert met her. Innes's wife and several sons had died. The others had jobs abroad. Biba kept house for him in his old age.

Biba appealed greatly to Mr Robert Bannatyne Finlay, a young barrister-at-law practising in London, who during his vacations in Edinburgh was a frequent visitor to Inverleith House. She loved him but believed she could not be married, could not desert her father. He dreaded her departure, but he had a great liking and respect for Robert and in July 1874, gave his blessing to their betrothal.

At the end of the month he fell ill and on the 25th, two days before he died, he begged that Mary's marriage should not be delayed, 'should anything happen to me.' He was buried on the 5 August and they were married on the 26th.

The Finlays disapproved of this love match because she had a small dowry and no inheritance to be foreseen, but even from the money point of view they were proved wrong, for by the unexpected deaths of brothers and cousins and uncles and aunts, and climbing plants, a vast fortune came to her some years later.

*

Our summer holidays of 1928 are distinct in my memory because that was my last year of living in Nairn, and because after Uncle Robert died in 1929 my parents hired houses for the holidays nearby, in the Seabank Road or Albert Street, and except for occasional visits to Newton we

no longer had the hurly-burly of the old household. I was
fourteen years and six months old that August.

    Somebody died. I don't know who died, but an old lady
reading the letter in the billiard-room laid it on her lap with
trembling hands and said

—— Fitzie's dead.

    Fitzie-Witzie? Fitzjames, Fitzgeorge, Fitzwilliam, Fitz-
herbert, Fitzjohn?

—— But, Euphemia, she was ninety-two. It was to be
expected.

—— Ninety-eight.

—— Then, my dear . . .

—— The funeral's on Thursday. I shall never get there in
time.

—— Where?

—— In the County Westmeath. How I'd hate to make a
sea journey, even after I'm dead! The old lady was almost
weeping.

—— How can they?

—— Family graveyard.

—— Please leave it to me, my dear Euphemia. I shall
escort you. I shall telegraph the Duke and he will delay the
funeral until our arrival. But allow me to find out the hours
of sailing first.

    She was holding a flimsy crochet handkerchief to her
eyes. He pulled the bell-pull and when Johnston came
asked for sherry and whisky and soda and told him to make
enquiries about the Irish boats. I followed Uncle Tom and
others to the conservatory. It was the men's whisky time
and lemonade time for me. We had it outside in the basket
chairs.

—— There is an aeroplane to Dublin from somewhere,
said one of them. They could fly the remains across St
George's Channel.

—— Pythagoras saith that my soul may haply inhabit a
bird.

—— Would they really postpone the funeral?

—— I think so. The relatives will have to stay overnight,
in any event.

—— It is most inadvisable. Anne Duff, the relict of the

Mackintosh of Mackintosh of Dalcross Castle was bank-rupted in the year of Grace 1731 by keeping her Laird's remains in the castle for two months and two days before the burial in the family churchyard of Petty.

Everybody asked why so long and how was she im-poverished by it? It was because no funeral could take place without the presence of all near relatives, and William Mackintosh of Daviot, heir to the chieftainship of the clan, although he had been advised by express of the death, did not turn up at Petty for two months. But the funeral guests began to turn up on 21 October 1731; clansmen, friends and tenants continued to arrive in hundreds during the next few days; cooks and confectioners were summoned from Edinburgh at great expense – and all this host of mourners feasted and rested at the castle until the funeral and interment were solemnized upon the 22 December. On that Wednesday the funeral procession filled the road from Dalcross to Petty Church, a distance of four miles. So great was the multitude of Lady Mackintosh's guests, that the last of them could not leave the castle until the first had reached the graveyard. That funeral ruined the fortunes of the family for several generations.

—— Well, who was it Tom, that was ruined in the eighteen-nineties by a visit from the Prince of Wales?

—— Geddes or Kilravock, I forget. It may have been Culloden. They had to have a new drive made, furniture from Edinburgh and the whole house redone.

We were old enough, in 1928, to have 'luncheon' in the dining-room on days when we could bear to wait till three o'clock, and by then I understood most of the extraordinary goings-on. Uncle Tom would look up some obscure fact of Old Testament genealogy in his *Cruden's Concordance* before lunch and then make a statement, hoping that Uncle Robert would rebuke him for inaccuracy, which usually happened. All the old uncles and aunts would join in the argument until Uncle Tom said to Granny, our hostess at the lower end of the table facing Robert,

—— Allow me, Jessie, to leave the table for a minute. I'll just fetch my Concordance.

He came back with it and proved himself right.

Uncle Robert's wife, Biba, had died in 1911. She, and Granny after her for eighteen years, managed two households, one in Kensington, one at Nairn, until Robert's death in 1929. Great lawyers, like diplomats, have to have a hostess. For Biba, the parties indoors or in the gardens with croquet and charades, had been enormous during the last few years of her father's life at Inverleith House, and were resumed at Newton in the same grandeur during vacations and at 31 Phillimore Gardens during the law terms. It was the fate of widows and unmarried daughters and I suppose some enjoyed the work and the varied, often brilliant company.

But for Granny, Uncle Robert became a difficult master during his old age. As his teeth got fewer and weaker, we heard him silence the company from the head of the table to Granny at its foot by roaring,

—— Jessie! This meat is wholly uneatable.

—— It is from your Edinburgh fleshers, Robert. We have always had it from them.

—— I shall take a slice of cold ham, he would say, looking severely at Gulliver who immediately removed his loaded plate.

It was the custom at Newton as at most big houses in those days for one to read aloud to the company after dinner at night. Uncle Robert used to read to us in the billiard room, but now his eyesight was dimming, from cataract, I think. Uncle Jim, Tom or Ninian or his son Will read.

Robert knew a lot of poetry and literature by heart and sometimes spoke passages, without the book, from Scott, Aytoun, Burns, Dean Ramsay, John Galt. He often quoted funny scraps from law reports written in old Scots. I liked most of it for the strength of character he put into it – the Eastern Lowland and Border Scots which he so naturally assumed. He had an excellent memory and could recite the whole of *Marmion*.

Uncle Jim fell asleep during long pieces like that and would wake up at the change of sound at the end – the quiet, polite words of appreciation – and say

—— Excellent, Robert, excellent!

—— Excellent and soporific, Uncle Robert said.

Most of *Marmion* bored me too, but I liked the bit about Young Lochinvar, which we had learned at Miss Squair's, Young Lochinvar coming out of the West to snatch the bride from a wedding she dreaded.

> So stately his form, and so lovely her face . . .
> One touch to her hand and one word in her ear,
> When they reached the hall door, and the charger stood
>      near,
> So light to the croupe the fair lady he swung,
> So light to the saddle before her he sprung!
> 'She is won! We are gone, over bank, bush and scaur,
> They'll have fleet steeds that follow,' quoth young
>      Lochinvar.

It was his extraordinary memory, which with the help of clerks, enabled Uncle Robert to continue his work at The Hague until the end of his life, when print and manuscript were clouded.

*

I read secretly and as my confidence grew I broke the MacLehose rules more and more on the farm by stooping and lifting, by forking up heavy sheaves on to the carts at leading time; and sometimes at night I prayed guiltily to God, remembering scraps of my guilty reading.

> He is lying in his bed – he is lying seik and sair,
> Let him lie intill his bed two monethis and thrie days mair!

But nothing bad happened.

I could see very much better but I still bumped into things in the dark; and in bright sunlight I sometimes could not distinguish a shadow from the object which cast it – for example the shadow of a single wire across a gap in the dyke. I would see the shadow on the ground before me, step over it and, thinking I had got safely through to the field, fall over the wire; which was, when I think of it now, like the shadows in my mind – shadows of religion, of my sisters when they were not there, of Kolya, of Jeannie and Chrissie when they were not there.

In that last summer I went often to see Mr Rae, Canon
Ballard and Mrs Grimmett, not for lessons, just for talk,
perhaps from sentiment, having an awful feeling that I
might not see them again, perhaps because my mind had
grown so far as to value what they said. And then in those
days there was no division between the town and country.
Shopkeepers and their customers were friends. Fishermen,
dustmen, artisans, farmworkers played golf with the
gentry. Canon Ballard often went to see the MacDonalds at
Sandwood, although they did not belong to his church. Mr
Rae knew all the golf caddies and their parents, and the
connection between the Fishertown and the farms was
close, as I knew well from the Sandwood jobs I gave a hand
in – the milk the fisherpeople bought, the small presents of
butter, eggs and oatmeal which the Farmer asked me to
take to them when times were bad, and the piles of caff-
secks which Joan and I used to take on the milk float drawn
by Flossie to their houses.

Caff-secks are chaff sacks, mattresses as large as a double
bed on which the fisherpeople slept during the herring
fishing which started every year in August and lasted for
several months. Some went to Shetland and Orkney and
the ports of the Moray Firth, but the most exciting voyage,
especially for girls like Mrs Grimmett's niece Jean Bochel,
who went to gut and pack the herring, was to Lowestoft
and Yarmouth.

The fishwives, young and old, made the mattress covers
out of tick which, so far as I remember, was dark blue with
white stripes. These we collected during the milk round,
and at Sandwood we filled them with chaff and Ireen or
Githa or someone sewed the open ends up. It was
memorable and joyful. It was the second of the two
occasions in the year, both sweet smelling and yellow,
when we worked in the great barn, the raftered building
beyond the byre and stables.

At thrashing time, while the traction engine puffed
smoke and steam and the thrashing machine rumbled all
day, I would ride, bareback and sweaty, one of the
carthorses inside the barn round and round as the men
threw the straw underneath me. The horse trod it down,

---

packed it tight. The horse and I rose higher and higher in the barn until I had to bow my head below the rafters. Then, when the barn was full of straw, the horse slid down or scrambled down to the yard with me on its back. It was heavy work for the horse and its sweat stung my bare legs which were covered with pin pricks made by the sharp ends of the straw.

The thrashing machine poured the grain into hundred-weight bags, spilled out the straw from one end, and the chaff from the other. The chaff in a huge heap was kept separate in one corner of the barn.

At caff-seck time we filled the mattress covers from this corner. Joan was often with me, because it was in August, and it often made us laugh in despair because while she held the mouth of the bag open for me to put an armful of chaff in, a sudden gust of wind would blow the chaff away.

I was unusually aware, sometimes happily, often unhappily, of everything I experienced in 1928 because my parents had found a school for me in London where teachers would read aloud to me and where I could do my written work on the typewriter, which, although the prospect pleased me, was also a gloomy sign. It was a sign of the end of a life, of one part of life: this going away to an unknown school in a city that had grown unfamiliar; and probably the fisher boys and girls of about my age, who were leaving Nairn for the first time that August, felt as I did. But they would come back before Christmas and resume the life and friendships with which they had been brought up. I would come back next August, not to my old life and friendships.

Later in August or early in September the fishermen took their boys and family dogs to sea for the herring fishing. Their girls went by passenger ships or trains to the ports where the herring were landed, in Orkney, Shetland, Lowestoft and Yarmouth and fishertowns along the Moray Firth. Their life was harsh. At five every morning a knocker-up came round to their lodging place, banging the windows and crying 'Get up and tie your fingers.' They had to bandage their fingers to protect them from the knife they gutted the herring with and the salt in the barrels into which they packed them. They worked from dawn until it was too dark to work, at night; but this hard life – or so they tell me in retrospect – was enjoyable, filled with singing and laughter among girl friends during the week, and there was a reunion every Sunday when fathers, brothers, uncles and boys came ashore.

And the homecoming to Nairn was a festival, everybody waiting to welcome them, the children sleepless with excitement, for the men always brought back presents with them – toys, dolls, model boats and ornamental crockery for the house. Many of the houses I used to go into had plates, cups and saucers with 'A Present from Yarmouth' embossed on them in gold.

I did not know it then, but the nineteen-twenties were years of despondency in the Fishertown. The export of salted herrings to Germany had been stopped by the war and the large trade with Russia had been stopped by the government for political reasons.

I longed for girls, and sometimes I got up enough courage to speak to the fisher girls of about my age on the links where they were playing or in Park Street outside Mrs Grimmet's house where they skipped to skipping rhymes in the street. But it was like disturbing a flock of starlings. They ran away giggling.

My one beloved girl was Jeannie, but she lived only in my mind. Even her elusive appearances in church had stopped that August and I sat in the midst of my family, Granma, parents, aunts, my Uncle Robin and my sisters, utterly bored. Their presence drowned religious fervour; I could as well have been lazily playing cards with them, my mind elsewhere. The absence of Jeannie and her sister Chrissie disturbed me more than it ever had before. They had often been away on holidays in August but I had known that I would be there when they came back; and now, at the very time when I felt less shy, when I resolved every Saturday night in bed to approach her after church, when I had worked myself up to the peak of daring, the daring wilted because she was not there to test it.

This was one end. Ends are dragon's tails which split into other ends and as they split you do not know that there is an end to the narrow bit you are following.

My sisters and I helped at the leading – the bringing home of the sheaves of oats – a joyful time for everybody on the croft, the end of the farming year.

Joan and I rode big and lively horses that summer belonging to friends of our parents who had stables in Tradespark. One of them usually came with us, anxiously I suppose, in case we or their horses went wild, which on the open carse or low tide sand we did. But they need not have worried. We both rode well by then.

I once told Joan, as we rubbed down the horses after a morning gallop, how one of the things I hated about going back to London was no horses, no more riding.

——— You can, she said. Mother and Father have arranged it, because you can't play football. There's Hampstead Heath and a place called South Mimms where you get to by Green Line bus.

——— Green Line?

——— Aye, green! she said and said more, making fun of me in the Farmer's accent.

Kolya was supposed to be coming to stay at Newton. I was longing to see him, but he did not arrive until after we had left for London. His mother came without him. He had bought an old car, she told me, smiling as though she knew I knew it was the kind of thing he would do. It would take him a week or two from Edinburgh with all those friends on the way.

Ends after ends.

The Farmer left for Canada to see some of his sons and daughters. I went with him to Lamb's Bank to get money for his train and boat fares. He did not count the money in the bank. We went together to the seat near the post office, where once he had reconciled me to Bob, and there we counted it in the wind. Neither of us had ever seen a £50 note before. They were like letters written in beautiful handwriting on large, flimsy sheets of white paper. They blew in the wind and I caught them.

I began, for the first time in my life that I can remember,

to disagree with my father, and this made a split between my mind and heart because inwardly I had my old loving respect for him and his beliefs and outwardly I denied them.

I had become a Scottish Nationalist. I was having lessons in Gaelic in the back room of Mr Stewart's tailor's shop. That did not matter much, although I imagined my father was silently laughing at me for it. I had felt isolated in my enthusiasm for Gaelic from the start because Marian Cameron, Lochiel's daughter, wanted to learn Gaelic with me and her parents dissuaded her, saying that it would distract her from her schoolwork. And now my father showed no interest, made me feel quite alone.

I was also beginning to believe in pacifism, that it is better to submit to an enemy than to fight, which must have seemed to him a denial of his whole career.

It happened, too, that 1928 was the first year in which I began to think about politics. I praised Ramsay MacDonald and the Soviet Union. As soon as I was old enough I would vote Socialist. And more.

My father said little but he felt the little just as I did. But one day, when I was slouching on a chair he said:

—— Sit up straight. You are getting rounded shoulders.

I said nothing in my anger, but when he had gone, I said to my mother:

—— If he thinks I'm a hunchback, I'll be a hunchback.

She tried to make peace between us. When she had gone I began on the typewriter a long gloomy story about Jeannie. I never finished it.

In September we caught the train for London with typewriter, dogs, bags and baggages and bicycles.

*

In January warm your hands and sweep the snow from the lintel.

In February warm your hands and feet and dig the snow from the lintel.

In March yoke your horses and darken the land with the plough.

In April harrow well the seed and lift the last neeps for the cows.

In May loose the cows and feed the bull well.

In June cast a clout.

In July mow the meadow, make the hay.

In August set your hay up in coles, then stack it in the steading and reap your oats if the days are fair and stook them.

In September call the lassies and the loons and lead home your oats, call the piper and the fiddler and the melodeon man and dance and sing in the steading.

In September turn your eyes away from the green and yellow land, the whins and heather, sea and sand, and hear no more the birds. Let the cock crow no more. Let the reek of the train and the city cover you like night.

# Glossary

Most of these words belong to Nairnshire and NE Scotland. Usage varies throughout the country.

Auld Reekie – Old Smoky. Nickname for Edinburgh.

Bailie – magistrate elected by town council.
Bap – soft floury bread roll.
Bawbee – small coin; halfpenny recently.
Bonnet – man's or boy's peaked cloth cap. In Highland dress, the 'Balmoral', round with a bobble on top, and the 'Glengarry', something like a forage cap, both without peaks.
Bothy – hut, often roughly built.
Brae – hill.
Burgh – borough. Burgher – Freeman of borough.
Byre – cowshed.

Camoufletty – frightening commotion.
Carse – flat, low land by sea or river.
Clachan – hamlet.
Cluckit hen – clucking or broody hen.
Clout – cloth, e.g. dishcloth, sometimes used for piece of clothes.
Cole – haycock.
Colliebuction – noisy squabble.
Collieshangie – uproar.
Cookie – a soft bun, usually with a layer of cream or jam.
Couth, couthie – comfortable, loving, pleasant, opposite of uncouth.
Crack – chat, conversation.
Crowdie – white, soft cheese.
Cushie Doo – wood-pigeon.

Dander – stroll, saunter.
Divot – sod of earth with grass on it.
Dominie – schoolmaster
Doo – dove.

Doocot– dovecote.

Doossil – strike, hit, thump.

Dottle-trot – old man's fussy gait, with quick, short steps.

Douce – lovable, pleasant, gentle.

Doune – hill or fort, town, dwelling places built on it.

Dyke – drystone wall, usually low.

Factor – agent, estate manager

Feu – tenure of land or house, originally in return for military service, nowadays on lease.

Fornent – in front of.

Gait – way, direction. The word has several meanings including the English one, 'way of walking'.

Garron – small, stout horse, or large, powerful, thickset pony.

Gleg – quick, keen.

Greet – weep.

Grieve – farm manager or steward.

Haugh – stretch of level land, as in Philiphaugh.

Jimp – slender, graceful, supple.

Kelpie – water demon, usually in form of horse.

Kirk – church.

Knowe – rounded hillock, knoll.

Leading – carting harvested crops from field to farmyard, so-called because one led horse and cart from stook to stook while another pitched the sheaves.

Leith Walk – gloomy mood. Leith Walk is a very long street in Edinburgh. Hence 'a face as long as Leith Walk' and 'a Leith Walk' for a fit of melancholy.

Lintel – threshold, doorstep. (Used in some parts of Scotland for this, and for mantelpiece.)

Loon, loonie – boy.

Manse – dwelling place of church minister.

Mavis – song-thrush.

Merle – blackbird.

Messages – the shopping.

To mind – to remember

The morn – tomorrow.

Moss – bog, wet moorland, as in peatmoss, land for cutting peats.

Muckle – large.

Neeps – 'Swedes', Swedish turnips.

Oxter – armpit, underpart of upper arm.

Poke – bag. In shops, often a piece of paper twisted round contents.
Provost – mayor, head of town or borough council and chief magistrate.

Quean, queanie, in Nairnshire usually quine, or quinie – young girl.

Reek – smoke.
Reive – rob, pillage.
Rig – furrow or strip of ploughed land.

Scaur – steep rock, precipice.
Sheriff – chief judge of a county
Shieling – remote mountain summer pasture, usually with huts for cowherds and dairymaids.
Shoon – shoes.
Sonsie – comely, buxom, good-natured.
Spate – flood.
Spelding – smoked haddock, split flat. Spelt Speldring, east of Nairn.
Steading – out-buildings and yard of farm.
Stouthreif – violent theft.

Tacksman – lessee who can sublet parts of his land. In the old Highlands, often a kinsman of the chief.
Tangie – a *Laminaria* seaweed, brown, with thick rhubarb-like stalk and several long tails like fingers.
Thane – minor noble, inferior to Earl, bound by service to Crown.
Thon – yonder, that over there.
Thrawn – obstinate.
Tocher – dowry, treasure.
Trig – neat, smart, tidy.

Wauking – waking.
Whins – gorse, furze.
Wife, wifie – woman, unmarried or married. As with quinie and loonie, the affectionate diminutive is the usual form.
Wud – mad.

# Note on names

Nairn – probably from Gaelic *Uisge 'nEarn*, the water or river of the Alder, alder trees still abound on its banks. It was once called Inverearne, the Mouth of the Alder River.

But opinions on the origin of the name differ. The medieval Register of Moray records 'the church of Eryn with the chapel of Invernarren', implying that Nairn signifies Éireann, genitive of Éire or Erin, Ireland. Highlanders were known as Irish, because of the language they spoke.

Tigh na Rosan – House of the Roses.

# Sources

Page 5
Three hats in Inverness, Red hand, etc. (well known locally).
For printed version see *Reminiscences of a Clachnacuddin Nona-genarian* (Inverness, Donald MacDonald, 1886).
Pages 7–10: Lloyd George and Ireland
A. J. P. Taylor (ed.), *Lloyd George – Twelve Essays* (Hamish Hamilton, 1971).
Frank Owen, *Tempestuous Journey – Lloyd George, his life and times* (Hutchinson, 1954).
Frances Stevenson, *Lloyd George – A Diary*, ed. A. J. P. Taylor (Hutchinson, 1971).
Lord Longford. *Peace by Ordeal* (Sidgwick & Jackson, 1972).
Page 38
Robert Burns, *Journal of a Tour in the Highlands made in the Year 1787* (Gowan & Gray, London and Glasgow, 1927).
Page 41
Samuel Johnson, *Journey to the Western Isles of Scotland* (Glasgow, 1817).
James Boswell, *Journal of a Tour to the Hebrides with Samuel Johnson* (Chas. Dilly, 1785).
Page 41
Walter Thom, *Journal of a Tour of the North of Scotland* (*New Agricultural & Commercial Magazine*, vol. 1, 1811).
Page 43
William McGonagall, *A Library Omnibus* (Duckworth, 1980).
Page 52
Charles Sellar, *A Glimpse of Old Nairn* (Inverness, Robert Carruthers, Courier Office, 1969).
Page 94
Brodie, *The Diary of Alexander Brodie of Brodie 1652–1680* (Aberdeen, Spalding Club, 1863).
Pages 96–100 References to Culbin sandstorm
George Bain, *The River Findhorn* (Nairnshire Telegraph, Nairn, 1911).
*The Culbin Sands* (Nairnshire Telegraph).

Lachlan Shaw, *The History of the Province of Moray*, vol. II, 3rd edn., ed. J. F. S. Gordon (Adams & Co., London and Thomas D. Morison, Glasgow, 1882).
Page 102
George S. Pryde, *Scotland from 1603 to the present day*, p. 35 (Thomas Nelson & Sons, 1962).
Page 126
Robert Pitcairn, *Trials before the High Court in Scotland* (Edinburgh, 1883).
Pages 150–161
All about Black Ewen based on John Drummond of Balhaldy's *Memoirs of Sir Ewen Cameron of Lochiel* (Abbotsford Club, 1842).
Alexander Mackenzie, *History of the Camerons* (Inverness, A. & W. Mackenzie, 1884).
John Drummond of Balhaldy, op. cit. pp. 73–80.
Pages 205–207
Horseman's Word etc.
George Ewart Evans, Unpublished Interview between George Ewart Evans and Norman Halkett, a member of the Horseman's Word Society until its dissolution; and *Horse Power & Magic* (Faber & Faber, 1976).
Thomas Tusser, *Five Hundred Pointes of Good Husbandrie*, first of many editions, 1557. Perhaps the English Dialect Society's one is best (Truber, 1978).
Page 211
Thomas Campbell, *Lochiel's Warning*.
Page 212
The Battle of Culloden
C. S. Terry, *The Rising of the Forty-five* (David Nutt, 1900). This work includes quotations from numerous eye-witnesses and people who fought in the battle.
J. Bernard Burke, Esq., *Anecdotes of the Aristocracy*, vol. 11 (Henry Colburn, 1849).
Page 216
Irish Piquets
Eleanor Hull, *History of Ireland*, vol. 11 (George G. Harrap, 1931).
Page 216
George S. Pryde, op. cit. p. 64.
Pages 217–218
John Prebble, *Culloden* (Secker & Warburg, 1961).
Charles Fraser Mackintosh, *Antiquarian Notes* (Inverness, A. & W. Mackenzie, 1865).
Peter Anderson, *Guide to Culloden Moor, the Story of the Battle* pp. 147–8 (Stirling, Eneas Mackay, 1920).

George Bain, *History of Nairnshire* (Nairnshire Telegraph, 1928).
Page 255
Alan Breck etc.
George S. Pryde, op. cit. p. 154.
Page 257
John Prebble, *The Highland Clearances* (Penguin Books, 1985).
Alexander Mackenzie, *The Prophecies of the Brahan Seer* (Stirling, Eneas Mackay, 1935).
Page 261
*The Book of the Thanes of Cawdor*, ed. Cosmo Innes (Edinburgh, Spalding Club, 1859).
Pages 264–5
The Duke Coach
*Glasgow Herald*, 14 August, 1829.
Pages 268–271
Sir Thomas Dick Lauder, Bart., *An Account of the Great Floods of August 1829*, 2nd edn. (Edinburgh, Adam Black, 1830).
George Bain, *The River Findhorn* (Nairnshire Telegraph, 1911).
Page 273
Dean Ramsay, *Reminiscences of Scottish Life & Character* (Edinburgh, Robert Grant & Son, 1947).
Pages 275–280
R. F. V. Heuston, *The Lives of the Lord Chancellors 1885–1940* (Oxford, Clarendon Press, 1964).
Anon, *Memoir of Cosmo Innes* (Edinburgh, William Paterson, 1874).
Pages 286–7
Margaret Bochel, *Dear Gremista – The Story of Nairn Fisher Girls at the Gutting* (Edinburgh, National Museum of Antiquities of Scotland, 1979).
Margaret Bochel, *The Fishertown of Nairn* (The Nairn Fisheries Museum, 1983).
Hugh Wilson, *The Society* (Elgin, M&N Print, 1985).

# Select Index of
# Names and Subjects

Abbotsford Club, 277
Aberdeen, 217
Academy of Nairn, 44
Achnacarry, 150, 213, 230
Act of Union (1707), 232, 250
Alton Burn School, 85
Alves, 217
Anne, Queen, 212
'Annexing Act', 254–5
Argyll, Marquis of, see Campbell, Achibald
Athol, Duke of, 212
Auldearn, 140, 163, 172
  famous for witchcraft, 225
  massacre of Covenanters by Montrose at the Battle of, 161
Aviemore, 46

Badenoch, 230
Bailey of Lochloy, Miss, 182
Balblair, encampment of Royalist army in 1746, 220, 221
Ben Aulder, 230
Berwick, 154
Birkenhead, Frederick 1st Earl of, 10
Black Isle, 34, 35, 85, 99, 116, 225, 258
Black and Tans, 8, 254
Black Watch, 253–4, 258
Boece, Hector, 95
Borodale, 213, 214, 230
Boswell, James, on Nairn, 41
Boyne, Battle of the, 216
Brackla Distillery, 195, 197, 198–9
Brahan Seer, prophecies of, 50–1, 256

Brodie of Brodie, Alexander, 94, 96, 160
  desecrates Elgin Cathedral, 101, 102, 181, 278
  diary, 94–5, 100–1
Brodie of Brodie, James, 254
Brodie Castle, 94–5, plundered by Montrose, 160
Burns, Robert, 36, 38–9, 252
Burrel's regiment, destruction of, 227

Caledonian Canal, 51
Camerons of Lochiel,
  Amman, 159
  Dr Archibald, 213, 214, 227
  audience with the Young Pretender, 150, 211–213
  engaged in Battle of Culloden, 222
  Black Ewen, 149–50, 211
  death, 160
  defeats English at Inverlochy, 158–60
  returns to Lochaber as chief, 157
  sides with Royalists, 155–6
  years at Inveraray Castle, 151–3
  Donald, ('The Gentle Lochiel'), 211–13, 250
  advises the Young Pretender to return to France, 214
  devotion to the Young Pretender, 229–30
  engaged in Battle of Culloden, 221, 223, 226, 227
  escapes to France after Culloden, 231

on the run, 228, 229–30
persuaded to join the Rising of
    1745, 214
wounded at Culloden, 227, 229
wounded at Falkirk, 227
John, 213–14
Clan Cameron of Lochiel, 106,
    150–1, 157–9, 190, 227
massacred by Cumberland,
    231–2
Campbells, 151, 218, 219, 224, 255
Campbell, Archibald, Marquis of
    Argyll, 151, 152, 154, 155–7,
    158, 255
Campbell of Cawdor, Sir Hugh,
    262
Castle of Nairn, 91, 136
Caulfield, William, engineer, 39
Cawdor Castle, 180
Chamberlain, Austen, 10
Charles I, 151, 152, 153, 154, 156,
    157
Charles II, 94
Charles Edward Stuart, Prince
    (Bonnie Prince Charlie, the
    Young Pretender), 246
abandons enterprise, 228–9
defeat at Culloden, 151, 218–28
escape to France, 230–1
lands in Scotland, 212–13
on the run, 210, 229–30
persuades Lochiel to join
    Rising, 214
retreat from Derby, 216
victory at Prestonpans, 215, 226
wins Battle of Falkirk, 216, 226
Columba, St, 51
Constabulary Gardens, Nairn, 91,
    135–6, 270
Cope, General
defeat at Prestonpans, 215, 226
Covenanters, 151, 152, 153–6, 201
atrocities, 155
massacred at Auldearn by
    Montrose, 161
Parliament called at St
    Andrews, 155
victory at Battle of
    Philiphaugh, 154, 155

Cromwell, Oliver, 154, 232, 246
Culbin Sands, 39, 53, 91, 99, 220,
    265
church, 91, 97
great sanddrift of 1694, 96–8,
    100
pastures, 95, 96–100
Culbin House, 96, 97, 98
plundered by Montrose, 160
Cullen, 41
Culloden, Battle of, 51, 88–9, 151,
    194, 210–11, 218–28, 246
Culloden House, 216, 232
Cumberland, Prince William
    Duke of, 89, 230
advance on Nairn, 216–17
encampment at Nairn, 220–1
massacres prisoners, 231–2
remembered as The Butcher,
    231–2
victories in Flanders, 219
victory at Culloden, 151, 219–
    28, 229

Dalcross Castle, 282
Dalpottie, Mill of, 96
Daviot Castle, 129
Daviot House, 129
Delnies, carse of, 225
Disarming Acts, 252, 253
Doune of Daviot, 210
*Doutelle* (frigate), 212
Drive of the Big Sheep, 257–8
Drummond, John, of Balhaldy,
    159–60
Drummond, Lord John, 217, 221
Dulsie Bridge, 38–9
Dunbar, Mr, of Thundertown,
    249
Dundas, Henry, 255
Dundas, Robert, 255
Dunkirk, 212

Earnhill Farm, 96
Edinburgh
Academy, 18, 274
falls to Young Pretender, 215
fear and respect of Highlander,
    219
Inverleith House, 280, 283

trial of Elgin rioters, 279
Elcho, Lord, 228, 249
Elgin
  desecration of cathedral, 101-3,
    181, 278
  Museum, 98
  riots of 1847, 278–80
*Elizabeth, The* (ship-of-war), 212
emigration from Nairn, 235, 256
  *Metagama* Bride Ship, 235
*Endeavour* (schooner), 265
English Fred, 52–3
Episcopal Church of Scotland, 30,
  64, 70, 150, 277
Episcopalians, 215

Fairy Hill, 53
Falkirk, Battle of, 216, 219, 226
Faulkner, Robert, 180
Fergus II, 150
Ferguson, William, 254
Fettes College, 199, 240–1, 263
Findhorn, River, 34, 36, 224, 240
  floods, 95–7, 131, 217, 265
Fishertown Museum of Nairn,
  44, 54
floods and sandstorms at Nairn,
  94–101
Forbes, Lord President Duncan,
  216–17, 232
  disgraced by his plea for
    retention of Highland dress,
    251–2
Fort Augustus, 230
Fort George, 253, 258
Fort William, 158
Forres, 41
Foxley, William, excessive sleep,
  149
Fraser, Hon. Simon, 253
Fraser, Simon Lord Lovat, 249,
  253
Fraser of Inchberry, Captain,
  223–4, 227
Fraser Highlanders, 253

Gairloch, 8, 9, 43
gangrels, 51–4

Geddes, 195, 198
  graveyard, 209–10
General Strike (1926), 234–5
George II, 212, 217, 218
George V, 10
Gladstone, William Ewart, 7
Glendalough, Holy City of, 7
golf courses
  Dunbar Links, 92
  Newton Links, 92–3
Gordon, J. F. S., 99–100
Griffith-Boscawen, Sir Arthur, 10
Grigor, Dr John
  brings prosperity to Nairn, 42–
    4
  philanthropy of, 44
  statue of, 44, 162, 163, 193
Gulf Stream, 42–3

Happie Lachie, 52
hardship in Nairn
  18th century, 252–9
  1920s, 234–6, 287
Hawley, General, 226
Hay of Restalrig, John, 222, 223
heritable justice, rights of, 247
herring fishing season, 285–7
*Heureux, L'* (rescue ship), 230
Highland Games, 171, 182
Highland society
  destruction by Cumberland,
    232
  disintegration of, 254
Highlands
  clearances, 259
  education in schools, 102
  government by foreign and
    remote control, 254
  roads in, 37–8, 39
Highlanders
  Black Watch, 253–4, 258
  fear and respect for, 219
  Fraser, 253
  legend of invincibility, 226
  restrictions on dress, 250–1
  recruitment for the Army,
    253–4

holiday town, Nairn transformed into, 42–4
hoofmark men, 248–9
Horologe Stone, 220

Innes, Cosmo, 19, 181, 277–80
death, 280
Elgin Riots, 278–80
made Sheriff of Moray, 278
Innes, Laird of, 160, 181
desecrates Elgin cathedral, 101, 102, 181, 278
Innes, place of, plundered by Montrose, 160
Inveraray Castle, 151–3
great library, 276
Inverleith House, Edinburgh, 280, 283
Inverlochy, 158
Battle of, 158–60
Inverness, 10, 50, 122–3, 218, 223, 224, 228, 229, 231, 257, 258
Burgh of, and the right of the Red Hand, 247–8
punishment of population (1746), 232
seized by Jacobites (1715), 220
*Inverness Courier*, 7–8
Irish Brigade of French Army, 212, 215–16
Irish War of Independence, 8, 254
Irvine, George, 252–3

Jacobites
disposal of estates, 255
Rising of 1715, 37, 220–1
Rising of 1745, 212–30, 246, 249; turning point in Scottish history, 249–50
James VI, 275
on Nairn, 40–1
James Edward, the Old Pretender, 214
Johnson, Dr Samuel, 42
on Nairn, 41
Johnstone, James Chevalier de, 1, 15, 16, 26, 36, 174

memoirs on the Battle of Culloden, 226, 228
Jubilee Bridge, Nairn, 17, 264, 270

Kevin, St, 7
Killiecrankie, Battle of, 226
Kilravock Castle, 180, 221, 222–3
kilts and plaid forbidden, 250–2
Kingsteps, 53
Kinlochmoidart, 213
Kinnairds of Culbin, 95, 96, 160, 180

Lady MacIntosh, 52
Lauder, Sir Thomas Dick, 268–9
Leslie, General, 154
Limerick, Treaty of, 216
Literary Institute of Nairn, 44
Lloyd George, David 1st Earl, 10
achieves Truce in Ireland, 8
discussion with de Valera, 7, 8
holiday in West Highlands, 7–9
partitioning of Ireland, 8
Lloyd George, Mrs, 9
Loch Eil, 158, 159
Loch Linnhe, 158
Lochaber, 150, 152, 157, 158, 230, 255
invasion by General Monk, 158
Lochboisdale, South Uist, 213
Lochiel, see Cameron
Long Tom, 52
Louis XV, 231
Lowland culture, destruction of, 232

MacDonald, Ramsay, 289
MacDonald of Morar, Hugh, 213
Macdonald of Scothouse, 213
MacGillivray of Dunmaglas, 232
McGonagall, William
verse on Nairn, 43–4
Mackenzie, Sir Kenneth, 8, 9
Mackintosh, The, 247
Mackintosh, Anne Duff Lady, 281–2
Mackintosh, James, 268–9
Mackintosh of Daviot, William, 282

Mackintosh of Mackintosh of Dalcross Castle, 282
Macleod, Mr, 228–9
Macpherson of Clunie, 228–9
Macpherson, Cluny, 230
Macpherson of Urie, 230
MacQueen of Pollochaigh and the Magic Candles, 128–32, 157
Marston Moor, Battle of, 246
Mead, Sir Alfred, 10
Melodeon Nell, 52
Merrytown camp of Royalist army, 220, 221
Merrytown Dairy, 208–10
Michie the cabman, 46–9, 51, 67–9, 76, 89, 162, 172, 173, 246
  fishing with, 239–40
Milburn mill, 51
military presence in Nairn, 253–4
Monadhliath Mountains, 266
Monk, General George (later 1st Duke of Albemarle), 157–8
  invasion of Lochaber, 158
Montalembert, Charles Compte de, 277
Montrose, James Graham, Marquess of, 152, 154, 155, 160–1
Moray, 41, 42, 95, 96
  Firth, 218, 225, 265, 286
  floods, 246
  Great Moray Flood of 1829, 264–71
Morgan, Johnnie, 52, 53
Muckle Burn, 96
Murray, Lord George, 215
  at the Battle of Culloden, 221, 222, 223, 227, 228
  organises retreat from Derby, 216

Nairn, River, 129, 180, 198, 210, 217, 221, 223, 224, 228
  floods, 96, 131, 264, 266
*Nairnshire Telegraph*, 234–5
Ness, Loch, 230

Ness, River, 224
Newbiggin, Mrs, 89–90
Newton Farm Show, 171, 182–5

Ogilvy, Lord, 155
O'Toole, St Laurence, 7

Pennant, Thomas, author, 160
Perth, 45, 46, 65–6
Perth, Duke of 221
Petty Kirkyard, 232, 282
Philiphaugh, Battle of, 154, 155
Pitcairn, *Criminal Trials of Scotland*, 276–7
Pitt the Younger, William, 255
pool of Nairn, 189–90
population of Nairn, rapid rise of, 42
punishment of population of Nairn, 1746, 232
Prebble, John, author, 257
Prestonpans, Battle of, 215, 226
*Princesse de Conti, La* (rescue ship), 230
Pryse, John, 267–8
railway from Inverness to Nairn opened, 42
Red Hand, right of, 247–8
Riot of Nairn (1785), 254
roads in the Highlands, 37–9, 39
Roses of Geddes, 198
Roses of Kilravock Castle, 180, 181, 220, 222–3, 231, 268
Ross, Rev. Gilbert, 101, 102–3
Royal Scottish Corporation, 275
Ruthven, 228, 229

St Andrews, 155–6
Scots Royal, French regiment, 215
Scott, Sir Walter, 86, 219, 274, 277
  review of Culloden papers, 251–2
Sellar, Charles, *A Glimpse of Old Nairn*, 52
Shaw, Lachlan, 160
  *History of Moray*, 99–100
Shortt, Mr, 10

Skirving, Adam, 215
Skye, 229
smuggling, 247–8
Society of the Horseman's Word,
    initiation ceremony, 205–7
South Uist, island of, 229
Spalding, John, 102–3, 277
Spalding Club, 277
Spey, river, 217, 266, 279
Spottiswood, Sir Robert, 155–6
Spurgeon the Calvinist, 50
Squair, Miss, School, 30, 31–2
Stevenson, Frances (later
    Countess Lloyd George), 9
Stevenson, Robert Louis, 219, 274
    *Kidnapped*, 230, 255
Stewart, David, 257
Stirling, 154, 217
Strath Rusdale, 258
Strathnairn, 266
Strathspey, 266
Sutherland, Sir Thomas, 212

Terry, Charles, 250
Thom, Walter, 259
    on Nairn, 41–2
Thurso, 206
Tolbooth, Nairn, 220, 242
Tomnahurich cemetery, 50, 51

Urquhart of Cromarty, Thomas,
    185

Valera, Eamon de, 7, 8, 9–10
'Vesting Act' of 1747, 254–5

Wade, General, 37, 39
Walker, Margery (aunt), author
    of *Pioneers of Public Health*,
    73–4
Webster, Dr Alexander, collector
    of census statistics, 42
William of Orange, 216
witchcraft, 224–5
    trials, 276

# Arena

| | | | |
|---|---|---|---|
| ☐ The History Man | | Malcolm Bradbury | £2.95 |
| ☐ Rates of Exchange | | Malcolm Bradbury | £3.50 |
| ☐ The Painted Cage | | Meira Chand | £3.95 |
| ☐ Ten Years in an Open Necked Shirt | | John Cooper Clarke | £3.95 |
| ☐ Boswell | | Stanley Elkin | £4.50 |
| ☐ The Family of Max Desir | | Robert Ferro | £2.95 |
| ☐ Kiss of the Spiderwoman | | Manuel Puig | £2.95 |
| ☐ The Clock Winder | | Anne Tyler | £2.95 |
| ☐ Roots | | Alex Haley | £5.95 |
| ☐ Jeeves and the Feudal Spirit | | P. G. Wodehouse | £2.50 |
| ☐ Cold Dog Soup | | Stephen Dobyns | £3.50 |
| ☐ Season of Anomy | | Wole Soyinka | £3.99 |
| ☐ The Milagro Beanfield War | | John Nichols | £3.99 |
| ☐ Walter | | David Cook | £2.50 |
| ☐ The Wayward Bus | | John Steinbeck | £3.50 |

Prices and other details are liable to change

---

ARROW BOOKS, BOOKSERVICE BY POST, PO BOX 29, DOUGLAS, ISLE OF MAN, BRITISH ISLES

NAME..................................................................................

ADDRESS.............................................................................

..................................................................................

..................................................................................

Please enclose a cheque or postal order made out to Arrow Books Ltd. for the amount due and allow the following for postage and packing.

U.K. CUSTOMERS: Please allow 22p per book to a maximum of £3.00.

B.F.P.O. & EIRE: Please allow 22p per book to a maximum of £3.00

OVERSEAS CUSTOMERS: Please allow 22p per book.

Whilst every effort is made to keep prices low it is sometimes necessary to increase cover prices at short notice. Arrow Books reserve the right to show new retail prices on covers which may differ from those previously advertised in the text or elsewhere.